"In *Faithful Antiracism*, Christina Edmondson and Chad Brennan provide a substantial template for confronting racism that includes a necessary combination of theology (the biblical analysis is fantastic), sociology (the data from their interviews is very insightful), and history (you will learn so much valuable information about both Christian and American history). This book is necessary equipment for the antiracist journey ahead!"

Daniel Hill, pastor and author of *White Awake* and *White Lies*

"*Faithful Antiracism* is the book so many Christians have been waiting to read. Clear, accurate, and informative, it is both an eye opener for the skeptics still unsure about racism and a practical guide for the many already committed to this work. Biblical, historical, and accessible, Christina Edmondson and Chad Brennan's book provides a broad overview of how racism works and what people of faith can do to confront it. Readers will find a rich resource for helping us to see not only that racism exists but also showing how people of faith have sought to address it, and then advising us on what we can all do today. Read, then share!"

Gerardo Martí, professor of sociology at Davidson College and author of *Worship Across the Racial Divide: Religious Music and the Multiracial Congregation*

"What should be uncontroversial—working against the forces of racism (antiracism)—is fraught with contemptuous rhetoric in our current climate. What we need are voices and practitioners who call us out of contempt and into an embrace of what is possible. This is exactly what Christina Edmondson and Chad Brennan have done for us in *Faithful Antiracism*. They lay out a blueprint for change that is grounded in the Scriptures and attuned to contemporary research on racial views within the church in the United States. This is your book if you are among those who want to know how Christians can actively press against racism and promote justice."

Irwyn L. Ince Jr., author of *The Beautiful Community: Unity, Diversity, and the Church at Its Best*

"Edmondson and Brennan weave together data and statistics, church and cultural histories, Scripture and personal narrative, inviting readers into a spiritual journey of repentance and conversion—both personal and communal. *Faithful Antiracism* is a timely reminder that seeking justice ought never be a trend for the church to follow, for it is core to the church."

Kathy Khang, speaker and author of *Raise Your Voice*

"What. A. Book. This is one of those books that moves you in your head and in your heart. The authors resist the temptation of rehearsing old clichés and paralyzing polemics. It is a well-researched work of art, firmly grounded in Christian faith and Scripture and weaves together ideas and practices as few books are able to. *Faithful Antiracism* doesn't leave you stuck in shame and guilt, not knowing how to move forward, but casts a vision for how we can move forward together. This book is a gift to the world."

Shane Claiborne, author, activist, and cofounder of Red Letter Christians

"Brilliantly researched, superbly written, brazenly honest, and inspiringly transparent, *Faithful Antiracism* answers the questions left from reading other texts on the subject. With grace, courage, and wisdom, Edmondson and Brennan offer a dialogue-inducing, interactive guide with practical steps grounded in Scripture that will stimulate measurable change. This is the book we have all been waiting for!"

Emmett Price III, president and CEO, Black Christian Experience Resource Center (BCERC)

"*Faithful Antiracism* will help you discern how you can advance racial justice in word and deed, with care for the orientation of your heart as well as for your actions and activism. Edmondson and Brennan will help you oppose racism without making it all about you. I can see many churches and communities benefiting from this thoughtful work, and I'm grateful for the hearts and minds the authors bring to the vital endeavor of promoting racial justice."

Michael Wear, founder of Public Square Strategies and author of *Reclaiming Hope*

"This book is written by experts who take the Bible, history, research, and data seriously. *Faithful Antiracism* seeks to change behavior. As an educator and Christian leader, I want to be my best. This book challenged, taught, and inspired me to be, and more importantly to do, my best. Being antiracist is a gospel goal. Engage this material individually or in a group and grow so that you will be a kingdom actor to end racism."

Shirley Hoogstra, president of the Council for Christian Colleges and Universities

"This book prophetically illustrates how and where Scripture calls the body of Christ to pursue antiracism. It goes beyond theory and lays the foundation for practical application. This book will equip believers to live out a holistic gospel."

Dominique DuBois Gilliard, author of *Subversive Witness: Scripture's Call to Leverage Privilege* and *Rethinking Incarceration: Advocating for Justice That Restores*

"In *Faithful Antiracism*, Edmondson and Brennan provide a comprehensive blueprint for understanding and addressing racial injustice. Their fresh research is accessible; their recommendations are practical. Edmondson and Brennan have produced a guide for Christian individuals, congregations, organizations, and universities who sincerely commit to replace systems of racism with biblically envisioned community. They invite and demand that we be faithful and become antiracist!"

Curtiss Paul DeYoung, CEO of the Minnesota Council of Churches

CHRISTINA BARLAND EDMONDSON
& CHAD BRENNAN

FOREWORD BY KORIE LITTLE EDWARDS AND MICHAEL O. EMERSON

FAITHFUL

ANTI-

RACISM

MOVING PAST
TALK TO
SYSTEMIC CHANGE

WITHDRAWN

An imprint of InterVarsity Press
Downers Grove, Illinois

InterVarsity Press
P.O. Box 1400, Downers Grove, IL 60515-1426
ivpress.com
email@ivpress.com

InterVarsity Press® is the book-publishing division of InterVarsity Christian Fellowship/USA®, a movement of students and faculty active on campus at hundreds of universities, colleges, and schools of nursing in the United States of America, and a member movement of the International Fellowship of Evangelical Students. For information about local and regional activities, visit intervarsity.org.

While any stories in this book are true, some names and identifying information may have been changed to protect the privacy of individuals.

The publisher cannot verify the accuracy or functionality of website URLs used in this book beyond the date of publication.

Figures used courtesy of the authors.

Cover design and image composite: David Fassett
Interior design: Daniel van Loon
Images: rolled black ink: © IntergalacticDesignStudio / E+ / Getty Images
    texture: © kundoy / Moment / Getty Images

ISBN 978-0-8308-4723-5 (print)
ISBN 978-0-8308-4724-2 (digital)

Library of Congress Cataloging-in-Publication Data
Names: Brennan, Chad, 1972- author. | Edmondson, Christina, 1979- author.
Title: Faithful antiracism : moving past talk to systemic change / Chad Brennan and Christina Edmondson.
Description: Downers Grove, IL : InterVarsity Press, [2021] | Includes bibliographical references.
Identifiers: LCCN 2021041934 (print) | LCCN 2021041935 (ebook) | ISBN 9780830847235 (print) |
    ISBN 9780830847242 (digital)
Subjects: LCSH: Racism--Religious aspects--Christianity. | Race relations—Religious aspects—Christianity. |
    Racism—United States. | Race relations—United States.
Classification: LCC BT734.2 .B55 2021 (print) | LCC BT734.2 (ebook) | DDC 277.308/3089—dc23
LC record available at https://lccn.loc.gov/2021041934
LC ebook record available at https://lccn.loc.gov/2021041935

P 25 24 23 22 21 20 19 18 17 16 15 14 13 12 11 10 9 8 7 6 5 4 3 2 1
Y 43 42 41 40 39 38 37 36 35 34 33 32 31 30 29 28 27 26 25 24 23 22

Christina's Dedication

This one is for Mika.

Chad's Dedications

I dedicate this book to Laurie, Aliya, Anya, and Milena.

CONTENTS

Foreword by Korie Little Edwards and Michael O. Emerson . . . .   *ix*

Introduction *1*

1 Faithful Antiracists Have Wisdom *11*

2 Faithful Antiracists Apply the Bible *35*

3 Faithful Antiracists Stand for Justice *53*

4 Faithful Antiracists Understand Our Past *68*

5 Faithful Antiracists Understand Our Present *86*

6 Faithful Antiracists Understand Racial Trauma *107*

7 Faithful Antiracists Do Not Rely on Magic *124*

8 Faithful Antiracists Follow the Example of the Early Christians .   *144*

9 Faithful Antiracists Seek Out Help and Help Others *165*

10 Faithful Antiracists Effectively Measure Progress *180*

11 Faithful Antiracists Help to Change Our Society *192*

Epilogue *208*

Acknowledgments *212*

Appendix A: Key Terms *216*

Appendix B: Interviewees and Interview Themes *219*

Notes *223*

FOREWORD

DR. CHRISTINA EDMONDSON AND CHAD BRENNAN outline in a clear and accessible manner how we can be faithful antiracists. Relying on rigorous research, they show us where we have gone astray and then, with grace, they encourage us to embrace with honest and humble hearts the only remedy needed to heal our world from white supremacy: the gospel of Jesus Christ. Indeed, we need to face the emotional, mental, physical, and spiritual damage that white supremacy has done and continues to do to the souls and bodies of people, particularly those of people of color. They call us to both acknowledge and feel the pain of living under the trauma and oppression of a white supremacist world. More importantly, the authors lead us to repentance. It is repentance from white supremacy that is required for our own hearts and society to heal. The authors' encouragement to actively seek wisdom, truth, and justice is refreshing. Their approach is a much-needed addition as we engage the work of antiracism in our personal lives, the church, and broader society.

What I especially appreciate about this book is the stories the authors share about their own journeys. Womanist theologies have for some time encouraged us to acknowledge, with vulnerability and humility, our own positionality and standpoints. Edmondson and Brennan do so here. And in so doing, they model for us how we must begin to do this work: by being open about and interrogating how our own paths and perspectives have been affected by white supremacy.

Faithful Antiracism is for any person or group that wants to understand and implement a biblical approach to undoing systems of white supremacy in their personal lives and this world. It is a critically important contribution to the biblical and sociological works on race and Christianity in the United States.

Korie Little Edwards

■ ■ ■

THE TRUTHS, NUGGETS, BIBLICAL WISDOM, AND GRACE found in this volume are worth their weight in gold and silver. Through years of experience and research, Dr. Christina Edmondson and Chad Brennan walk us through what can often seem like the minefields of working against racism in our society and creating righteousness in our churches and beyond.

I cannot help but be impressed by the way they have written this work, with each author contributing substantial insights, and packaging it into manageable and practical chapters. As I told them when I first read a draft of the work, I wish for every church in the nation to work through this book. It is perfect for a small group curriculum or for wider church discussions.

This book is not written so you can expand your knowledge (though it most certainly does do that). It is written for us to collectively wrestle with how to apply its lessons. And it provides a crystal-clear path for every step along the way. If we put into practice the lessons it offers, we truly would be Christians walking the very direction Christ set out for us. And that direction is this: though we are separate creeks wanting to go our own ways, we are called to conjoin into one mighty river of justice and unity as we flow to our singular destination of the ocean of God and heaven.

But we can never realize our call in a society and church divided. As long as injustice and unfairness continue, we will have division. Our Holy Scriptures teach us this exactly.

That is why *Faithful Antiracism* is an essential book. It is a Christian guide for our troubled waters. It shows us step by step how to work toward systematic change. May it be a blessing to us all.

Michael O. Emerson

INTRODUCTION

WHEN IT COMES TO RACIAL DYNAMICS in the United States, it is easy to get overwhelmed by the magnitude of the complexities and challenges. The protests that took place across the United States in the summer of 2020 were an example of the enormous pain and concern that continues to be felt by millions of Americans. For hundreds of years, individuals have worked to end racism and racial injustice in the United States, yet it still remains a powerful and persistent force. There is so much that needs to be acknowledged, understood, and dismantled that it can feel like an impossible mountain to climb.

The challenges are real, but so are the possibilities. As we begin this book, we hope and pray you will also have a sense of the magnitude of the possibilities; imagine how different our lives could be if our society was rid of the disease of racial injustice. No more dealing with the spiritual and psychological burden of receiving advantages or disadvantages simply because we are categorized by society in one way or another. No more strained and divided cross-racial relationships. No more passing down a legacy of racial dysfunction to our children. Imagine if Christians were living out God's plan for us to love our neighbors as ourselves (Matthew 22:37-39) and to do what is right and just (Genesis 18:19). Imagine how different our Christian organizations could be if we were living out Jesus' prayer that we would be one as he and the Father are one (John 17:20-21). Imagine how different our society could be if our cultural and ethnic differences were a source of strength and joy rather than a source of division, conflict, and injustice. Imagine if we could work together across racial, ethnic, and cultural lines to address the major challenges we and our children will face in the coming centuries.

The journey toward the above realities is not easy, but it is well worth it. Even if we don't arrive at the top of the mountain within our lifetimes, every step we take toward the summit is a step away from evil, pain, confusion, and conflict, and toward Christ's peace, healing, truth, and love. We are excited to journey with you.

In the following pages, we wrestle with these questions:

- What are some key concepts we need to understand in order to have a biblical, effective approach to addressing racism? (chapter one)

- What are some principles in the Bible that apply to racial injustice? (chapter two)

- What can we learn from Christians who have attempted to stand for justice in the past? (chapter three)

- What do we need to understand about past and present racial realities? (chapters four and five)

- What do we need to understand about racial trauma? (chapter six)

- What are common, ineffective ways that Christians work toward racial progress? (chapter seven)

- What can we learn from the example of the early church? (chapter eight)

- How can we seek out help and help others? (chapter nine)

- How can we effectively measure progress? (chapter ten)

- How can we help change society? (chapter eleven)

Before we jump into the above content, we want to define some key terms and share a little about our backgrounds and the research that laid the foundation for this book.

WHAT WE MEAN BY *FAITHFUL ANTIRACISM*

We are using two senses of the term *faithful*. First, faithful describes someone who is trustworthy and loyal: *faithful antiracists* are steadfastly committed to working toward antiracism. Second, *faithful antiracists* are full of faith or faith-full. We believe it is essential to rely on God's power and leading in order to make progress. As Jesus said, "I am the vine; you are the branches. If you remain in me and I in you, you will bear much fruit; apart from me you can do nothing" (John 15:5).

By *racism* we mean race-based discrimination and social hierarchies where individuals receive advantages or disadvantages because of perceived racial differences. If you find that sentence confusing, hang in there. We will explain what we mean by these concepts. By *antiracism* we mean working against the forces that sustain racism. We use *racism* and *racial injustice* interchangeably throughout this book. For brief definitions of other key terms we use, please see appendix A.

MY STORY (CHRISTINA)[1]

The mural was huge and he was the focal point. There we saw mahogany brown skin contrasted with deep red blood coming from his brow under the crown of thorns. The Jesus figure had hair like mine as a child—full, thick, dark, and wavy. At the foot of the cross were people that looked like my neighbors in Baltimore. Men, women, and children painted in contemporary attire but at the foot of historic Golgotha. Some were crying, some covering their faces in shame, and others reaching out to the figure on the cross. There it was, raised up in the church chapel, a twenty-foot picture of the near, accessible, and relevant Jesus.

I grew up well acquainted with "Black folks' Jesus." A Jesus that was an "ever present help in times of trouble." A Jesus that "don't like ugly." A Jesus that made you sing songs like "I am going to treat everybody right" and a Jesus that had "paid it all." I didn't consciously meet "White Jesus" until my early twenties. Subconsciously until that point, I believed there were not many White Christians in America. This is likely because I was not shielded from racism as a child and had assumed that White Christian Americans couldn't be connected to the only Jesus I knew while clearly hating Black folks.

As I grew in sociological adeptness, and hopefully in spiritual discernment as well, I saw many "Jesuses," at times within the same congregations when worshiping among various traditions and ethnicities. White Jesus over time became more unveiled. He required little repentance but lots of solidarity and allegiance to partisan right-wing political power. White Jesus placed White male approval, theological framing, and standards at center. White Jesus might have been open to Black faces but rarely Black voices and certainly never Black pain or power. Unlike the mural described above, White Jesus was stuck in a time warp and instead of making all things new and coming to us here and now, he was committed to returning to a mythical land known as the "city on a hill America."

How I ended up in the past several years in predominantly White religious spaces, a testimony to the humor and providence of God, is perhaps a bit different from some other people of color's entry points. I'm from a Black city, was baptized by a Black pastor mentored by Dr. Martin Luther King Jr., and have attended and taught at Historically Black Colleges. I never attended predominately White K–12 schools for more than a year, nor colleges or churches growing up. I have one memory of sitting at a service in a large, affluent, White church in Maryland—I feel certain it was my family's only visit there. I never had a fall out with the Black church; she is the imperfect yet endearing mother that birthed me, nursed me, and loved me, and her voice still overlaps mine. I don't find White theology "more robust" or "sound." Frankly, that sentiment triggers a sense of sadness and annoyance in me, like when I hear internalized racist statements about "good hair, bad hair." With my college sweetheart, now my husband and a pastor, we saw ourselves nearly twenty years ago as one day getting married and serving in the leadership of a Black church while he pursued the atmospheric sciences and I the social sciences.

With the exception of my engagement in psychology and the social sciences, our life looks very different from our initial hopes and assumptions. Yet I firmly believe that the biblical gospel is catholic, or global, and if true endures within all our cultures and people groups. I am grateful for the Spirit-wrought global contributions to the practices and hermeneutics of the church. At the same time, I recognize that due to the sins of colonization the "Christian industrial complex" deifies Eurocentrism and protects White patriarchal supremacy. It is "Black folks' Jesus" that has kept me from hopeless deconstructing or physical departure from the local church because I know Christ can hit a "straight lick with a crooked stick."

Like Jonah, I'd have little desire apart from the work of the Spirit to see the group associated with the dehumanization and suppression of my kinfolk, Black folks, receive grace. If there was a way to confront racism without dealing with resistant White people, I'd gratefully take that path. Christian antiracists work with actual racists—those who know they are racist and those who don't. I am under no delusions; racism cannot simply be cuddled and wooed through Negro spirituals into loving Black people or releasing its idolatrous grip on White people. Racism must be resisted and the captives set free. This includes the captives that don't know they are imprisoned by false gospels and cultural idolatry.

I show up to do this work, and it is taxing work, because I am compelled by the Scriptures and empowered by the Spirit, and I desperately want something better for my kids and millions of kids like them. I know "Black folks' Jesus," and more fully the catholic Jesus, is returning for the church and will place racism in hell. For now, the songs of my youth still ring out as a call to action:

> What if God is unhappy with our praise?
> What if He is not pleased with the words we say?
> What if he takes away his love and his Spirit from above?
> What if God is unhappy with our praise?[2]

While I am fully confident in God's sovereign power to hold the invisible church as his own, the Scripture is clear that we must get to work (Philippians 2:12-18). As James the Just reminds us, "Faith without works is dead." I am working in light of the unity Christ died for and resting in the peace Christ has given. In the overlapping voice of my mother church, we work, we rest, and we "run on to see what the end will be."

MY STORY (CHAD)

Like Christina, the journey the Lord has taken me on to coauthor this book is a testimony to the humor and providence of God. I was blessed to be raised in a loving, Christian family. We lived in a predominantly White, blue-collar community in the suburbs of Dayton, Ohio. I would describe my views toward racial dynamics until my early twenties as a combination of indifference ("I'm more concerned about other things"), cynicism ("People make it into a bigger deal than it really is"), colorblindness ("I treat everyone the same"), and offense-avoidance ("I try my best to not do or say anything that is offensive").

A major shift in my thinking began to take place in 1994 when I was a junior at the Ohio State University. I went on a spring break trip to work on homes in Canton, Mississippi. As a part of our trip, local leaders shared about the racism and structural injustice they experienced in their community. At that stage, I was unwilling or unable to fully take in the reality of what they shared, but it was a beginning step toward having my eyes opened.

After graduating from OSU with a civil engineering degree, I joined the staff of Cru, a campus ministry. I spent a one-year stint with Cru in the Middle East from 1996 to 1997. Living in an environment where my very White skin[3] caused me to stick out every day and where I was in the religious minority,[4] helped me begin to understand what it felt like to be "the other." It also helped me to understand that I have a White American cultural identity that includes a unique set of values, perspectives, and practices. Being White did not mean that I was culture-less or "neutral."

After returning to the United States, my wife and I spent five years serving with Cru in Queens, New York, one of the most racially diverse neighborhoods in the United States. Our time in Queens began to open my eyes to the concepts explored in this book. Over time, I became increasingly motivated to help work toward cross-racial partnership and unity among Christians. But I mistakenly thought the solution was simply gathering people of different races together for worship, prayer, and dialogue. I partnered with local Christian leaders to organize a number of cross-racial unity gatherings. Those events were fun, encouraging, and productive, but they didn't address the underlying dynamics that kept us divided or the racial injustice that the people of color who attended were experiencing on a regular basis.

In 2003, my wife and I returned to Ohio and continued to serve with Cru along with raising our growing family. During that time, my pastor handed me a copy of the book *Divided by Faith*[5] and said simply, "I think you will like this book." I did! The book's research-based insights gave me new tools to understand the systems and ideologies that keep Christians divided by race. Years later, the book's coauthor, Michael Emerson, would become a close friend, mentor, and co-researcher.

In 2005, we left Cru and started an organization called Renew Partnerships, which focuses on helping Christians have a biblical and effective approach to racial dynamics. Since that time, I have had the opportunity to work with thousands of Christians across the country on a variety of projects including research, training, leadership coaching, and measuring the racial climate in many Christian organizations. I share about those experiences throughout this book.

As I reflect on my journey, I realize that many of the approaches I have used in the past to try to promote racial partnership and unity were misguided, inadequate, and sadly in some cases detrimental. Over time, with the help of Scripture, friendships, failure, experience, research, and the mentoring of leaders and experts, my efforts have shifted to the approaches we will cover in this book. Over the last thirty years, I've learned enough to know that there is still a lot more that I need to learn! All too often, I'm reminded of how much I need to grow in both my knowledge and my practice. As you read, know that I am on the journey with you.

About This Book

As you may be aware, there are many excellent books focused on antiracism from biblical, historical, relational, and sociological perspectives. We are thankful for those books and encourage you to utilize the resources we cite for more details. This book is focused on helping readers to apply the teachings of the Bible and take practical steps for measurable change. We are not primarily concerned with what we must *say* or *know*—though incredibly important—but what we must *do* and *stop doing* in order to see change.

This book moves fast. Because our focus is measurable change, we only touch on essential concepts like the definition of terms, the history of racial injustice in the United States, and systemic racism versus individual prejudice. Here are a few additional ways this book is unique:

1. *It is rooted in Scripture.* We believe that, "All Scripture is God-breathed and is useful for teaching, rebuking, correcting and training in righteousness" (2 Timothy 3:16). The Bible is our primary source for the principles and action steps we cover.

2. *It is based on extensive, national research.* See below.

3. *It is based on the input of leading experts.* Many experts in the United States provided us with helpful input as we worked on this

book. Drs. Glenn Bracey and Michael Emerson were especially generous with their time and insights. In appendix B, we list many of the individuals we interviewed while working on the content and explain how you can watch excerpts of our interviews with them.

4. *It is designed to prompt dialogue.* We hope it will be used as a part of small groups and training programs. To help in that regard, we include discussion questions at the end of each chapter.

5. *It incorporates research-based resources that can help you with your efforts.* We will describe the resources and how they can help in chapters nine and ten.

About the Data We Share in This Book

The data we share in this book comes primarily from the following sources:

1. Race, Religion, and Justice Project (2019–2020): the RRJP was a two-year, national research project that Chad directed. It was a collaboration between the Barna Group; the Racial Justice and Unity Center (a ministry of Renew Partnerships); lead researchers Drs. Glenn Bracey and Michael Emerson; and Lilly Endowment. The RRJP is one of the largest studies of racial dynamics in US Christianity that has been conducted. It consisted of interviews with 115 leaders and experts in ten cities, a nationally representative survey of 3,260 individuals (the margin of error for the RRJP Survey was plus or minus 1.9 points at a 95 percent confidence interval), focus groups with 119 congregants in seven cities, and ethnographic studies of churches in four cities. A collaboration team of over 200 experts and leaders helped with the project. For details visit rrjp.org.

2. Renew Partnerships Campus Climate Survey (2016–2020): the RPCCS was conducted at eighteen Christian colleges and universities between 2016 and 2020. It is one of the largest studies of racial dynamics in Christian colleges, with 13,580 responses collected. For details visit rjuc.org/campus-survey.

3. Barna Group research: this book also includes data from several studies conducted by our research partner, the Barna Group (barna.com).

RECOMMENDED PRAYER

At the end of each chapter we include a recommended prayer to invite God's presence as you read this book and seek to apply it in your life. Here is a recommended prayer from the book *The Inward Journey* by Howard Thurman.

Lord, make me an instrument of Thy Peace. Teach me how to order my days that with sure touch I may say the right word at the right time and in the right way—lest I betray the spirit of peace. Let me not be deceived by my own insecurity and weakness which would make me hurt another as I try desperately to help myself. Keep watch with me, O my Father, over the days of my life, that with abiding enthusiasm I may be in such possession of myself that each day I may offer to Thee the full, unhampered use of me in all my parts as "an instrument of Thy Peace." Amen.[6]

CHAPTER ONE

FAITHFUL ANTIRACISTS HAVE WISDOM

THE ART OF BEING A FAITHFUL ANTIRACIST (CHRISTINA)

A few years ago, after the mass shooting at Mother Emanuel AME Church in Charleston, South Carolina, I taught a group of grief-stricken and frustrated churchgoers and clergy. During the teaching, to the side of the stage, was a local artist hired to paint in real time an image of the speakers and the heart of their message. Throughout my talk, she created a beautiful painting. There were times as the image was being developed it only looked like flashes of color with no rhyme or reason. However, by the end of my teaching it became clear the artist had a plan and skills to accomplish it. As I exited the stage, there it was. A large painting with my likeness and an image of growth and restoration. The artist's observations, skill, patience, and time-management were on full display. The artist demonstrated wisdom and skill so apparent that it felt like magic. How did she pull this off?

It is fascinating to watch a skilled artist at work. A carpenter building a chair. A fashion designer shaping a dress. A chef meticulously crafting a meal. Step by step, they apply their knowledge, skill, experience, and creativity. Eventually, something functional, stunning, or delicious appears. To those like myself, without such skills, the creation is even more intriguing and beautiful.

Being a faithful antiracist is an art, not a formulaic process. Like painting a picture, building a chair, shaping a dress, or crafting a meal, it requires knowledge, skill, experience, and creativity. Most importantly, it requires the leading of the Holy Spirit. No amount of knowledge or experience can prepare us for every question and situation that will come up. We need a master artist who can guide our hands and help us to create something beautiful.

THE BIBLE'S TEACHINGS ON WISDOM

The Bible's description of wisdom includes much more than simply knowing facts. It is a combination of humility, creativity, skill, expertise, and competence. For example, in Exodus we see that God gave Bezalel "wisdom" as a master artist so that he could help decorate the tabernacle: "And [God] has filled [Bezalel] with the Spirit of God, with wisdom, with understanding, with knowledge and with all kinds of skills" (Exodus 35:31).

The same Hebrew word that is translated "wisdom" (*chokmah*) in Exodus 35:31 is also used in Psalm 107:27 as a description for sailors who are unable to navigate through a challenging storm. In the NIV, the verse is translated, "they were at their wits' end." More literally, "they were at their wisdom's end." In other words, their experience, skill, and ingenuity were not enough to save them from an overwhelming circumstance. For a helpful visual overview of the Bible's teachings on wisdom, we recommend the five-minute video *The Book of Proverbs* by the BibleProject.[1]

The Bible calls us to live with wisdom—effectively applying our knowledge and skills to everyday life in ways that align with God's will and that benefit our own lives, our neighbors, and society. This is true in all areas of our lives, including our approach to racial dynamics. Wisdom isn't something we muster up in our own strength or by academic study alone. Wisdom is given as a gift and even more specifically as an answer to prayer. As James explains, "If any of you lacks wisdom, you should ask God, who gives generously to all without finding fault, and it will be given to you" (James 1:5).

The Bible also emphasizes we must have a healthy "fear" of God in order to grow in wisdom. As Solomon explains, "The fear of the LORD is the beginning of wisdom, and knowledge of the Holy One is understanding" (Proverbs 9:10). *Fear* in this sense refers to honoring and submitting to God's will and taking on a posture of humility and teachability. It is acknowledging that God is the source of all wisdom, not ourselves.

We hope and pray this book will help you grow in your *wisdom in regard to racial dynamics*—that is, your ability to apply your creativity, skills, and knowledge to the complexities of racial dynamics. That requires more than just learning facts and principles. It requires you to ask God for wisdom in a posture of humility and teachability. It also requires you to reflect on the unique mix of experiences and abilities God has given you. How have you been uniquely equipped to be a faithful antiracist?

A Difficult Reality to Accept (Chad)

In the following sections, we will look at research data showing that Christians in some racial groups generally have less accurate racial views than non-Christians within their racial group. When I first began to study racial dynamics in the United States, that was a difficult reality for me to accept. I have been a Christian for as long as I can remember, and I have been surrounded by loving, committed Christians throughout my life. I grew up viewing Christians as people who stand for what is right, love their neighbors, turn the other cheek, and walk the extra mile. But the more I learned about the relationship between Christianity and racial injustice in our country, the more I was disturbed by what I saw.

Studying racial dynamics in US Christianity can challenge our view of our Christian heritage, our respected mentors, our organizations, and ourselves. In the past, I have wanted to dismiss the realities we share in this book as inaccurate, exaggerated, politically motivated, or unfair. If you feel that way, I encourage you to take the time to explore with an open mind the data and historical examples we share, and I believe you will discover what I discovered. There is a tremendous amount of evidence that the views and actions of many Christians, both in the past and present, are very far from what Christ taught and modeled.

Oftentimes, I have wanted to close my eyes and wish it all away or go back to the days when I wasn't able to see what I can see now, but I am thankful that is not possible. I now realize that my desire to "unsee" racial injustice is an expression of my privilege.[2] As Christians we do not need to be afraid of the truth, even when it hurts. As Jesus said, "If you hold to my teaching, you are really my disciples. Then you will know the truth, and the truth will set you free" (John 8:31-32). The truth gives us freedom. Lies, denial, and willful ignorance keep us trapped in bondage.

Throughout this book, some readers may feel we are being overly critical of US Christianity. James Baldwin famously said, "I love America . . . and, exactly for this reason, I insist on the right to criticize her perpetually."[3] Similarly, it is our love for the church that compels us to point out the weaknesses that keep it from being the source of light, hope, truth, and love that God desires for it to be. Our criticism is an act of love. We point out these areas of concern for the benefit of the church, individual Christians, and our society.

About the Graphs We Share

In the remainder of this book, we share graphs displaying how different groups responded in our research. The following are some questions we anticipate may be on your mind.

Why don't you include the views of multiracial or Indigenous Americans? The data we share in this book primarily focuses White Americans, Hispanic/Latino Americans, Black Americans, and Asian Americans because they are the four largest racial groups in the United States.[4] As of 2020, the population of the United States was approximately 60% White, 17% Hispanic/Latino, 13% Black, and 6% Asian.[5] The data we have collected to date has not included a large enough sample of multiracial Americans (3% of the United States), Indigenous Americans (1% of the United States), or other racial groups for us to make accurate statements about dynamics within those groups. In the coming years, we hope the assessment tools we share in chapter ten, as well as other research, will allow us to capture data for additional groups. Also, the size constraints of this book make it difficult for us to go into detail about the dynamics outside of the four largest racial groups. We need to leave that important topic to other books. For an exploration of Indigenous American Christian views on racial dynamics in the United States, we recommend the book *Rescuing the Gospel from the Cowboys: Native American Expression of the Jesus Way* by Richard Twiss.[6]

Why don't you compare the views of different types of Christians? Many books that are focused on racial dynamics in US Christianity compare the views of various Christian groups such as evangelicals, mainline Protestants, and Catholics.[7] In this book we take a simplified approach and primarily focus on the differences in views between Christians and non-Christians and the differences between Christians in different racial groups.[8] It is important to realize there are significant differences in the dynamics in various Christian groups, but there are also many similarities. This is especially true when we look at Christians in the same racial group. For example, the views of White Christians are often very similar regardless if they are evangelical, mainline Protestant, or Catholic. With the data we share, we prioritize simplicity so we can get to the primary focus of the book, which is practical action steps.

SOME FINDINGS FROM OUR RESEARCH

Christians often have less accurate racial views. Figure 1.1 displays responses to the question, "Do you agree or disagree with the statement, 'Historically, the United States has been oppressive to minorities'?" The options were: *strongly agree, somewhat agree, neutral, somewhat disagree, strongly disagree.* Notice that White, Hispanic/Latino, and Asian Christians were less likely than non-Christians in their racial group to agree. Black Christians, on the other hand, were more likely than non-Christians in their racial group to agree.

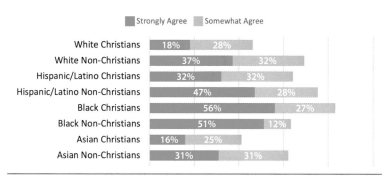

Figure 1.1. Respondents who agreed that historically the United States has been oppressive to minorities (Barna Group, Race Today, June/July 2020, n=1464)

The most accurate response to the question above is *strongly agree*. Tragically, the history of the United States is filled with examples of minority groups being oppressed. The following are a few examples; we share additional examples throughout the book.

- Between 1492 and 1880, between 2 and 5.5 million Indigenous Americans were enslaved in the Americas.[9] In the eighteenth and nineteenth centuries, the US government authorized over 1,500 wars, attacks, and raids on Indigenous Americans.[10]

- Between 1525 and 1866, approximately 12.5 million Africans were shipped to the Americas. Of the 10.7 million who survived the journey, approximately 388,000 were shipped directly to North America.[11] Historians estimate "as many as 6 million people lived and died in the American slave industry before 4 million people were declared free by 1865."[12]

- During the nineteenth and twentieth centuries, historians estimate thousands of Hispanic/Latino Americans were killed due to acts of racial violence.[13]

Figure 1.2 displays responses to the question, "In general, in our country these days, would you say that [Black people are treated less fairly than White people or White people are treated less fairly than Black people], or both are treated about equally in each of the following situations?" (The two phrases in the brackets were randomly rotated during the survey.) Notice that White Christians and Asian Christians were less likely than non-Christians in their racial group to indicate that Black people are generally treated less fairly in regard to hiring, pay, and promotions. Black Christians, on the other hand, were more likely than non-Christians in their racial group to

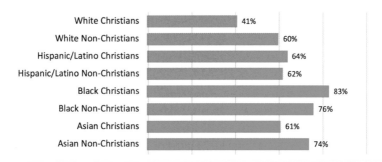

Figure 1.2. Respondents who indicated that Black people are generally treated less fairly than White people in regard to hiring, pay, and promotions (RRJP Survey, July/Aug 2019, n=2797)

indicate that Black people are generally treated less fairly. The responses by Hispanic/Latino Christians and Hispanic/Latino non-Christians were nearly the same.[14]

The most accurate response to the question above is, Black people are generally treated less fairly than White people in regard to hiring, pay, and promotions. Studies focused on employment practices consistently determine this to be the case. For example, a recent analysis of twenty-four field experiments, which included data from more than 54,000 applications across more than 25,000 positions, determined, "At the initial point of entry—hiring decisions—Blacks remain substantially disadvantaged relative to equally qualified Whites, and we see little indication of progress over time."[15]

Christians are often less motivated to address racial injustice. In figure 1.3, you can see the respondents who selected "very motivated" for the question, "How motivated are you to address racial injustice in our society?" Notice that White, Hispanic/Latino, and Asian Christians were less likely than non-Christians in their racial group to be very motivated to address racial injustice in our society. Black Christians, on the other hand, were more likely to be very motivated to address racial injustice in our society than non-Christians in their racial group.

Understanding the above trends should not lead us to false assumptions. It is important to keep in mind that being a White, Hispanic/Latino, or Asian Christian does not always correlate with having inaccurate

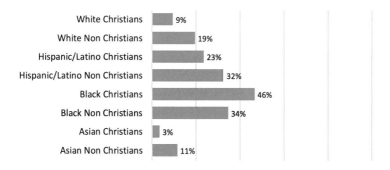

Figure 1.3. Respondents who indicated they were very motivated to address racial injustice in our society (Barna Group, Race Today, June/July 2020, n=1464)

views and being a Black Christian does not always correlate with having accurate views. For example, notice that almost half (46%) of White Christians agreed that historically the United States has been oppressive to minorities. And, that one in six (17%) of Black Christians did not agree that historically the United States has been oppressive to minorities.

COMMON QUESTIONS

The following are some common questions that come up when we share about the differences in views described above.

Are Black Christians' views different from the other groups because they are deceived? Some readers may believe the differences in racial perspectives are caused by Black Christians being deceived because of their personal experiences, social circles, or political affiliations. But this explanation denies the extensive data that exists on racial dynamics in our country. The views of Black Christians tend to line up more closely with the racial realities consistently measured by national research. For a more in-depth exploration of reasons why Black Christians typically have more accurate racial views, we recommend the book *Blacks and Whites in Christian America* by Michael Emerson and Jason Shelton.[16]

Are some Christians simply uninformed about racial issues? Some readers may wonder if Christians have less accurate racial views because they have never been provided accurate information. It is important to keep in mind the survey respondents were at least eighteen years old (the average age was forty-six). It is unlikely that the respondents had never been told or been given access to accurate information about past and present racial injustice in the United States. Accurate information was likely available to them through personal experiences, their education, training programs, the internet, movies, documentaries, museums, and more.

If people have less accurate racial views because they have not received enough education, we would expect there to be a strong correlation between having more accurate views and the level of education attained. But we find that Christians in the same racial group typically have similar views, regardless of their level of education. Notice in figure 1.4 that White Christians had similar responses to the question, regardless of their level of education.

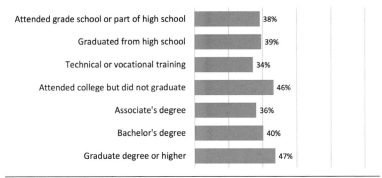

Figure 1.4. Respondents by level of education who indicated that Black people are generally treated less fairly than White people in regard to hiring, pay, and promotions (RRJP Survey, July/Aug 2019, n=2797, White Christians only)

With our work and research we find there are more complex reasons why people have inaccurate racial views than simply being uninformed. Providing education on racial realities can be helpful, but there are other barriers that prevent people from accepting the information as accurate. We look at some of these barriers throughout this book.

Are the Christians you studied only Christians by name? Some readers may wonder if the Christians we studied describe themselves as Christians but their faith has little impact on their life and they rarely read the Bible or go to church. Perhaps that can explain why the Christians we studied have less accurate racial views. Unfortunately, we find that White, Hispanic/Latino, and Asian Christians who are more active in their faith tend to have less accurate racial views than Christians who are not active in their faith. The following are two examples.

Practicing Christians.[17] Notice in figure 1.5 the difference between White and Asian Christians who are "practicing" and White and Asian Christians who are "not practicing." The practicing Christians were less likely than non-practicing Christians in their racial group to indicate that Black people are generally treated less fairly than White people in regard to hiring, pay, and promotions.

Evangelical Christians.[18] Note in figure 1.6 that White, Hispanic/Latino, and Asian evangelical Christians were much less likely than non-evangelical Christians in their racial group to indicate that Black people

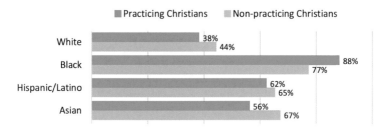

Figure 1.5. Respondents by practicing and non-practicing Christians who indicated that Black people are generally treated less fairly than White people in regard to hiring, pay, and promotions (RRJP Survey, July/Aug 2019, n=2797)

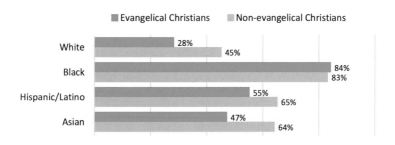

Figure 1.6. Respondents by evangelical and non-evangelical Christians who indicated that Black people are generally treated less fairly than White people in regard to hiring, pay, and promotions (RRJP Survey, July/Aug 2019, n=2797)

are generally treated less fairly than White people in regard to hiring, pay, and promotions.

ACCURATE EXPLANATIONS FOR THE ABOVE TRENDS

The following is an introductory summary of some of the more likely explanations why a high percentage of Christians in some racial groups have inaccurate racial views and a lack of motivation to address racial injustice.

The historic legacy of racism. European Christian colonists who first settled on this continent believed they were "a chosen people, endowed by the Creator with certain inalienable rights, and able to bring civilization and Christianity to a savage 'New World.'"[19] As we will see in chapter four, racism was woven into the economic, political, and religious systems of our country from its earliest stages. That tragic legacy continues to powerfully affect views and dynamics in the United States today.

Motivated reasoning. Social scientists find that people are more inclined to accept new information that supports their existing assumptions and desires. This is called *motivated reasoning*. Individuals are especially prone to motivated reasoning "when their self-worth, their future, or their understanding and valuation of the world are at stake."[20] It is "a way to avoid or lessen cognitive dissonance, the mental discomfort people experience when confronted by contradictory information, especially on matters that directly relate to their comfort, happiness, and mental health."[21] In our research, we see a consistent pattern of Christians rejecting new information because receiving the information would challenge their existing views, disrupt their sense of identity, or produce a sense of responsibility to change their actions. It is much easier to dismiss the challenging information. Simply put, it is harder to learn something new, even if proven true, that doesn't align with our biases or convictions.

Cultural toolkit. As part of his research in the late 1990s, Michael Emerson identified a cultural toolkit that many Christians use to understand racial dynamics. The toolkit includes the following emphases:

- *Accountable freewill individualism:* Many Christians believe "individuals exist independent of structures and institutions, have freewill, and are individually accountable for their own actions."[22]

- *Relationalism:* Many Christians place a strong emphasis on the role that interpersonal relationships play in racial dynamics.

- *Antistructuralism:* Many Christians believe it is wrongheaded to blame systems and structures for problems or inequalities in society; the root of all problems is individuals who are making bad decisions.

Our research from 2019 to 2020 confirmed that the cultural toolkit Emerson observed twenty years ago continues to describe the views of a large percentage of Christians today. Many Christians use the toolkit to evaluate whether information they receive about racial dynamics in the United States is true or false. If the information does not align with their toolkit, then they reject the information as fake, misguided, or counterproductive. What Emerson and Smith wrote in 2001 is still true today: "Suggesting social causes of the race problem challenges the cultural elements with which they construct their lives. . . . This is why anyone, any group, or any program that challenges their accountable freewill individualist perspective comes itself to be seen as a cause of the race problem."[23]

Social circles. The above barriers to racial wisdom are compounded by the fact that the social circles of Christians are typically composed almost exclusively of people who share their race and religion. For example, a 2013 study by the Public Religion Research Institute found that "among White Americans, 91 percent of people comprising their social networks were also White."[24]

Influences. It is easy for us to be powerfully influenced by the organizations we are a part of and the media outlets we rely on for information. Unfortunately, many of the organizations and media outlets Christians rely on for information about racial dynamics provide inaccurate and misleading information. We will explore that reality in chapter five.

Racial Hierarchy in the United States

In order to be effective faithful antiracists, it is essential to understand the racial hierarchy in our country. In societies with social hierarchies, some groups have greater power, wealth, and influence than other groups. Social hierarchies can be based on many things such as age, gender, language, family status, citizenship, or physical abilities. In the United States there is a powerful, race-based social hierarchy—we use the term *racial hierarchy* for brevity.

Some of the clearest indicators of the racial hierarchy in the United States are the differences in average income, wealth, poverty, and incarceration rates. Those differences are referred to as *racial disparities*. Figure 1.7 summarizes a few examples.[25]

Notice in the graphs that White and Asian Americans have the highest levels in the desirable categories (*income, wealth*) and the lowest levels in the undesirable categories (*poverty, incarceration*). Some readers may wonder, *Does this data indicate that Asian Americans are at the top of the racial hierarchy because they have the highest average income and wealth?* In order to understand who is at the top of the racial hierarchy, we must also consider who holds the economic and political power in society. Figure 1.8 shows the race of millionaires in the United States,[26] the race of political officeholders,[27] and the race of the board of directors of Fortune 500 companies.[28]

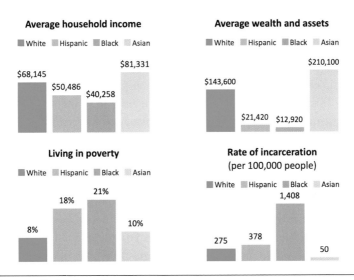

Figure 1.7. Racial disparities

As you can see in figure 1.8, the economic and political power of White Americans exceeds their numbers in society. If we take economic and political power and other social indicators into consideration, it is clear that White Americans are at the top of the racial hierarchy, Black Americans are at the bottom, and other racial groups fall somewhere between the two.

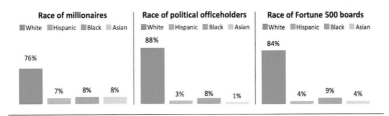

Figure 1.8. Additional racial disparities

Why do racial disparities exist? It is essential to have an accurate answer to this question in order to be an effective faithful antiracist. If we do not understand the problem, it is unlikely we will find an effective solution. For example, imagine a farmer whose crops are infected with a rare insect. As long as she is unaware of what is destroying her crops, it will be impossible for her to effectively address the issue.

Explanations for racial disparities fall into two types of theories:

1. *Structural theories.* People in some racial groups are given advantages or disadvantages through social systems, e.g., economic systems, political systems, educational systems, and criminal justice systems. This is sometimes referred to as *structural racism.* For example, a structural theory would be, "Black Americans have the lowest average household income because they face disadvantages in regard to hiring, pay, and promotions."

2. *Nonstructural theories.* People in some racial groups make better decisions, have a better work ethic, have more intelligence, value education more, are more skilled, have higher morals, have better cultural values and practices, and so on. For example, a nonstructural theory would be, "Black Americans have the lowest average household income because they do not value education as much as other racial groups."

Nonstructural theories are rarely, if ever, supported by data. They are typically based on inaccurate views. A few common examples are

- "___ *work harder than* ___." Many people assume that people in some racial groups work harder than people in other racial groups. These theories are typically based on superiority mindsets and negative racial stereotypes.[29] In every racial group, there are people with high/ low work ethics, high/low intelligence, high/low skills. However, *entire racial groups* do not have high/low work ethics, high/low intelligence, or high/low skills.

- "___ *have better morals than* ___." These theories are similar to those above, but are more focused on the general culture or morals of racial groups rather than specific actions. These theories are also typically based on superiority mindsets and negative racial stereotypes. This is sometimes referred to as *cultural racism.*

- "*Data proves that* ___." Unconscious (or implicit) racial prejudice often drives misinterpretations of data. For example, someone may say, "Only 26% of Black Americans earn college degrees, but the national average is 36%. That is one of the reasons why income rates for Black Americans are low. They do not value education as much as other racial groups." The statistic is correct,[30] but the interpretation is false. According to a 2016 Pew Study, "79% of Black parents with children under 18 say it is either extremely or very important that their children earn a college degree. By comparison, about two-thirds (67%) of White parents say the same."[31] Lower college-degree attainment by Black Americans is not caused by not valuing education. It is a product of structural disadvantages like K–12 education disparities.[32]

■ *"I know someone who is ___ who___."* Individuals often base their views about racial groups on statements or actions by a small group of individuals they have interacted with. For example, someone may say, "All of the Hispanic/Latino people I know think talking about race is detrimental." We cannot reach accurate conclusions about the views and actions of entire racial groups (millions of people) based on our experiences with only a few individuals. It is very easy to fall into the trap of picking out examples that support our theories and ignoring examples that contradict them.

On the other hand, there is an enormous amount of data that supports structural theories. We shared some examples earlier in this chapter. For additional examples, we recommend the five-minute video *Systemic Racism Explained*[33] and the seventeen-minute video *Race in America.*[34]

It is essential to recognize that structural advantages and disadvantages did not appear out of thin air. Structural injustice is not an impersonal "force" of society that operates without the involvement of people. Millions of individuals have played a role in creating and sustaining the racial hierarchy in the United States for over four hundred years. Racial injustice is built and sustained by people, and it must be dismantled by people.

Is *"taking personal responsibility"* the solution to racial disparities? With our research, we often hear comments like the following:

[Race/ethnicity] is used as a crutch for people to be rude and lazy. Everyone is equal in our society but minorities use [race/ethnicity] to blame for their failures. . . . The only race issue is babying those who use it as an excuse. (White, female, under 20)[35]

Many people argue that racial disparities would be eliminated if people of color took personal responsibility for their actions and stopped "blaming the system." However, there is a great deal of evidence that racial disparities are *not* caused by individuals not taking personal responsibility. For a detailed explanation why that is the case along with related statistics, we recommend the paper, "What We Get Wrong About Closing the Racial Wealth Gap."[36]

However, it is true that our decisions and morals have a powerful impact on our life experiences, regardless of our race. To understand the relationship between structural racism and personal decisions, let's consider a fictional scenario that is based on likely dynamics.

> Brian is White. He is entrepreneurial, hardworking, and has exceptional people skills. After graduating from college, he started a restaurant that quickly grew into a successful business. He currently owns three restaurants and earns $320,000 per year.

> Greg is Black. He is entrepreneurial, hardworking, and has exceptional people skills. After graduating from college, he started a restaurant that quickly grew into a successful business. He currently owns three restaurants and earns $140,000 per year.

Some people might assume that the difference in income between Brian and Greg is a result of Brian working harder or being a better business owner. But to understand the difference in their income, we must factor in racial dynamics. For a helpful summary of common differences between White and Black small-business ownership, we recommend the paper, "Small Business Owner Race, Liquidity, and Survival."[37] Here are a few common examples of the many ways that their race could influence Brian's and Greg's income:

> Brian benefited from generational wealth that was passed down to him through his parents.[38] Therefore, he did not need loans to pay for his college education.[39] He purchased a $300,000 home in a predominantly White neighborhood that quickly increased in value due to housing segregation.[40] He used the wealth in his home to help fund the expansion of his business. When Brian decided to open additional restaurants, he was able to quickly attain a loan at competitive interest rates. In addition, Brian's restaurants are located in predominantly White neighborhoods, which have high levels of household wealth. Therefore, he is able to charge higher prices.[41]

As a result of historic racism, Greg's family was not able to provide him with generational wealth or pay for his college education. He purchased a $300,000 home in a predominantly Black neighborhood that slowly declined in value due to housing segregation.[42] Therefore, he was not able to use the equity in his home to help fund the expansion of his business. When Greg decided to open additional restaurants, he struggled to get a loan because of his college debt and racial bias toward Black business owners. He was forced to acquire loans at high interest rates.[43] In addition, Greg's restaurants are located in predominantly Black neighborhoods, which have low levels of household wealth.

In the example above, both Brian and Greg had positive personal attributes (entrepreneurial, work ethic, and skills) that helped them to be financially successful, but Brian was *more* financially successful because of structural racism. In other words, Greg's "upside" for his positive personal attributes was lower than Brian's.

If Brian and Greg both had negative personal attributes (lazy, poor people skills, dishonest, drug addiction, etc.) it is less likely that Brian would face long-term unemployment[44] or be convicted of drug possession.[45] In other words, Greg's "downside" for negative personal attributes is lower than Brian's.

If we ignore or diminish the reality of structural racism, it hurts rather than helps our efforts to promote good decision-making, a strong work ethic, and good morals. It makes us more prone to misinterpret why people are succeeding or struggling and therefore less likely to encourage them in effective ways. A better path forward is acknowledging the powerful impact of structural dynamics as well as acknowledging the powerful role of decisions, abilities, and morals in determining our life experiences.

Additional Barriers to Structural Understandings

Many people reject the concept of structural racism because they believe the United States is a *meritocracy* or a "society in which people are chosen and moved into positions of success, power, and influence on the basis of their demonstrated abilities and merit."[46] Here is an example comment.

I have worked hard to get where I'm at in my life right now and my race had nothing to do with it. It was my hard work and dedication that got me where I am now. (White, female, 20s)[47]

The reality is that America is not a meritocracy. There are many factors, such as race, that powerfully influence a person's ability to achieve success, power, and influence. Many people reject that reality because it challenges their view of themselves, their family's history, their financial success, and more.

Another common reason people reject the concept of structural racism is because they believe everyone experiences prejudice and challenges, and therefore it is unfair to focus on some people's experiences and not others. For example, a White person might say, "I grew up in a school that was majority Hispanic. I was constantly picked on because I was White. What about the prejudice and challenges I have faced?"

Unfortunately, almost everyone experiences prejudice and challenges throughout their life. Being picked on for being White in school is painful, and we should do everything we can to prevent that from happening. But it is important to recognize the difference between being picked on in school and experiencing a lifetime of systemic disadvantages in terms of employment, housing, education, and criminal justice. In this book, we focus on addressing structural racism because of the uniquely powerful ways that it hurts individuals, Christian organizations, and our society. We believe Christ's love and example should motivate us to especially focus on helping those who are experiencing the most intense levels of hardship and oppression (Matthew 25:31-46).

EXPLANATIONS FOR RACIAL DISPARITIES

So far in this chapter, we have explained why we believe it is essential to have a structural understanding of racial dynamics in order to be effective faithful antiracists. But what percentage of Christians have a structural understanding? Let's look at some recent data. In our RRJP survey, we asked respondents why Black people have lower quality jobs, housing, and income than White people. Figure 1.9 shows some of the most common responses by Christians.

The first and second responses are examples of structuralist responses. The third and fourth responses are examples of non-structuralist responses. The fifth response is an example of denying that racial disparities exist.

Based on their responses to a variety of questions, we grouped Christians into the following five profiles. Individuals in the "lean structuralists"

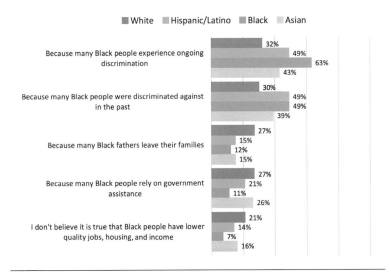

Figure 1.9. Responses by Christians why Black people have lower quality jobs, housing, and income than White people (RRJP Survey, July/Aug 2019, n=2797)

profile gave more structural responses than nonstructural. Individuals in the "lean non-structuralists" gave more non-structuralists responses than structuralists. We categorized individuals who denied that racial disparities exist as "disbelievers."

As seen in figure 1.10, there was a large percentage of Christians in all racial groups who provided nonstructural explanations or denied the existence of racial disparities. That is a major barrier to Christians helping to address racial injustice. If we do not understand the problem, it is much more likely that we will continue to perpetuate it rather than helping to address it.

ANTI-BLACK AND ANTI-INDIGENOUS RACISM

It is also important to recognize that racism in the United States has not impacted all people of color in the same way. Some assume that all people of color face the same types of structural disadvantages, and therefore make inaccurate assumptions about why Black people are at the bottom of the racial hierarchy. For example, they may believe "Black people and Asian people both face challenges due to racism, but Asian people have higher incomes and wealth. Therefore that shows that Asian people generally have a stronger work

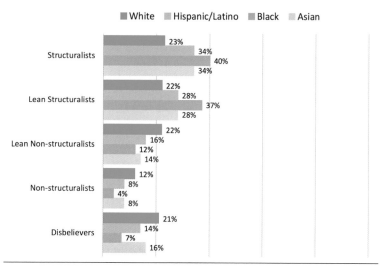

Figure 1.10. Structuralists, lean structuralists, lean non-structuralists, non-structuralists, and disbelievers (Christians only) (RRJP Survey, July/Aug 2019, n=2797)

ethic." This type of belief is based on the inaccurate assumption that Black and Asian individuals face the same types and intensities of challenges.

As we will see in chapters four and five, Black and Indigenous people have faced especially intense racial prejudice and structural disadvantages throughout our country's history. This is referred to as anti-Black and anti-Indigenous racism. We recommend watching the documentaries *Many Rivers to Cross*[48] and *We Shall Remain*[49] to learn about the history of anti-Black and anti-Indigenous racism in the United States. Some people choose to use the acronym BIPOC (Black, Indigenous, and People of Color) rather than "people of color" in order to make a distinction between the unique challenges faced by Black and Indigenous people and other people of color. Regardless of the terminology, it is important to acknowledge that people in different racial groups often experience different types and intensities of racism.

SHOULD OTHER MORAL ISSUES TAKE PRECEDENCE OVER RACIAL INJUSTICE?

We often hear comments like, "I agree that racial injustice is a problem, but I think other moral issues are a higher priority." Here a few example comments from our surveys.

[Racial dynamics] ought to be addressed, but the church has other top priorities. (White, female, 50s)

I think there are other issues to be talked about. We all know race is an issue but there is more going on in the world—abuse, drugs, war, mental illness, trauma. . . . The church needs to talk about other things. (White, female, 20s)[50]

Should racial justice be a higher or a lower priority than other issues like "abuse, drugs, war, mental illness, trauma"? The following are some important things to keep in mind as we seek to answer that question.

They are not independent. It is difficult to find a moral issue in the United States that is not affected by racism and the racial hierarchy. Passionate about lowering poverty? A person's race is the most powerful predictor of whether a person will live in poverty.[51] Passionate about education? A person's race has a powerful impact on the level of education they receive.[52] It is nearly impossible to make progress on any social issue without also understanding and addressing racial dynamics.

We should emphasize moral issues that are emphasized in Scripture. As Christians, we must allow the Bible to shape our prioritization of moral issues. We hinder our effectiveness and witness when we make the minor major and the major minor. We will look at that more in chapter two.

Our priorities should not be determined by our self-interests. If we are not personally suffering from injustice (or we are benefiting from it) it is easy to think, *That issue is not urgent.* As Christians, we are called to love our neighbor as ourselves (Leviticus 19:18; Mark 12:31), feel their pain, and prioritize what is important for them (1 Corinthians 12:26) even if it requires us to make sacrifices (Philippians 2:3).

THE GIFTS OF LAMENT, CONFESSION, AND REPENTANCE

In this chapter, we have explored some difficult truths. As we learn about difficult truths, it's easy for us to be defensive, deny their reality, or tune out the message. Our hope and prayer is that we will choose more beneficial responses such as lament, confession, and repentance. These are gifts that God has given us for dealing with the brokenness in our lives and society.

1. *Lament*: Expressing our grief and sorrow over the sin and brokenness in our lives and society

2. *Confession*: Acknowledging the sin in our lives and society

3. *Repentance*: Turning from the sin in our lives and society

Most Christians are familiar with the concept of personal confession for personal sins. But many Christians are not familiar with the idea of individual and communal confession for group sins (family, tribe, nation). The Bible encourages both individual and communal expressions of lament, confession, and repentance for both individual and group sins. As Soong-Chan Rah writes:

> Personal and corporate confession is exemplified in Lamentations but also in the corporate laments found in the Psalms, 2 Chronicles 7:14, in the example of Nehemiah, Jeremiah 18:8, in the Gospel of John's use of cosmos, and 1 John 1:9.
>
> Lamentations, therefore, does not limit the understanding of human brokenness exclusively to the realm of corporate responsibility or individual responsibility. Both corporate and personal expressions are necessary. Communal laments are offered on behalf of the entire community, but never lack a personal expression (see Jeremiah's individual confession on behalf of all of the people of God). In the same way, the expressions of individual lament are not spoken in isolation and do not operate separate from each other.[53]

When we are faced with difficult truths about our lives, groups, or society, we must avoid destructive responses such as shame and denial. In order to make progress, we must be willing to acknowledge our individual and group sins and take the restorative path of lament, confession, and repentance. Our grief can lead to growth and new life rather than death: "Godly sorrow brings repentance that leads to salvation and leaves no regret, but worldly sorrow brings death" (2 Corinthians 7:10).

DISCUSSION/REFLECTION QUESTIONS

1. Do you think you have *wisdom* (creativity, skill, expertise, and competence) in regard to racial dynamics?

2. We shared some reasons why Christians often have less accurate racial views and less motivation to address racial injustice than non-Christians. Do those reasons influence your understanding and motivation? If so, how?

3. Before reading this chapter, did you believe that racial disparities existed in the United States? If so, what did you believe caused them to exist?

4. We looked at the four common reasons people give for racial disparities (see below). Do you believe they provide an accurate explanation? Did this chapter affect your thinking? If so, how?

   a. "___ *work harder than* ___."

   b. "___ *have better morals than* ___."

   c. "*Data proves that* ___."

   d. "*I know someone who is* ___ *who* ___."

5. Should racial justice be a high priority for Christians? Why or why not?

6. How can lament, confession, and repentance help us to grow as faithful antiracists?

7. How do you plan to apply the content in this chapter?

Recommended Prayer

Thank you for the unique way you have created me and the unique experiences you have given me. Please help me to understand how I can apply the creativity, skill, and expertise that you have given me to work toward racial justice. If there are areas where I do not have an accurate understanding, please help me to have clarity.

I confess the actions that I have done that are contrary to your will in regard to racial justice.

(Take time for reflection.)

I confess the actions that the groups that I am a part of have done that are contrary to your will in regard to racial justice.

(Take time for reflection.)

I confess the actions of our nation that are contrary to your will in regard to racial justice.

(Take time for reflection.)

Help me to do my part to prevent similar actions from continuing into the future. Thank you for your unending grace and love and the freedom and forgiveness for individual and corporate sin that we can experience through Christ.

CHAPTER TWO

FAITHFUL ANTIRACISTS APPLY THE BIBLE

IN A MUSEUM IN THE United Kingdom you can view one of the saddest historical relics in the world. It is a copy of the Bible that excludes the majority of the Old Testament and about half of the New Testament. Why? It was published to be distributed to people who were enslaved in the British West Indies. Therefore any passages that might encourage the people who were enslaved to pursue freedom were removed.

If the "Slave Bible" was created by slave owners it would be tragic and evil, but the reality is even more disturbing. The "Slave Bible" was created by *Christian missionaries.*

> The abridged work was first printed in London in 1807, on behalf of the Society for the Conversion of Negro Slaves. The missionaries associated with this movement sought to teach enslaved Africans to read, with the ultimate goal of introducing them to Christianity. But they had to be careful not to run afoul of farmers who were wary about the revolutionary implications of educating their enslaved workforce.[1]

The missionaries were attempting to evangelize people who were enslaved who were living under terrible conditions.

> Weakened by the Middle Passage across the Atlantic, and then forced to work incredibly hard in the tropical sun, often with insufficient food, clothing and shelter, enslaved people died in great numbers, often within a short period of their arrival in the Caribbean. Tropical

diseases including malaria, yellow fever and smallpox all killed many more. . . . Some mothers who were weakened by arduous work, pregnancy and childbirth, and insufficient food died during or after childbirth. This all made it difficult for enslaved people to form stable and long-lasting families, as parents and children were constantly dying. At the same time, masters and owners regularly sold slaves to other white people, in the process separating husbands from wives, and parents from children.[2]

The Society for the Conversion of Negro Slaves wanted to convert the enslaved people to Christianity without challenging the existing unjust economic and political systems that were crushing their lives and tearing apart their families. Missionaries "adjusted" the Bible's message to accommodate the threats and pressure they received from economic and political systems. In other words, rather than fighting against injustice, they helped to sustain it using the name of Christ.

It is easy for us to shake our heads at the Society for the Conversion of Negro Slaves and wonder how they could have been so misguided. We may not be willing to cut sections out of our Bibles, but it is helpful for us to reflect on whether we are willing to ignore or neglect teachings in the Bible that oppose injustice for fear that we will experience alienation or persecution.

Applying the Bible's Teachings on the Gospel

Unfortunately, unbiblical and incomplete views of the gospel hinder the ability of many Christians to effectively apply all of the Bible's teachings in regard to racial injustice in our society. Contrary to popular belief, the Bible does not teach that our relational dynamics with one another are separate from the gospel, a distraction from the gospel, or a much lower priority than the gospel.

In Ephesians 2, the apostle Paul provides one of the clearest descriptions of the gospel in the Bible. In the first half of the chapter (verses 1-10), he describes the new *vertical* relationship that Christians have *with God* through Christ.

As for you, you were dead in your transgressions and sins. . . . But because of his great love for us, God, who is rich in mercy, made us alive with Christ even when we were dead in transgressions—it is by grace you have been saved. And God raised us up with Christ and seated us with him in the heavenly realms in Christ Jesus, in order that in the coming ages he might show the incomparable riches of his grace, expressed in his kindness to us in Christ Jesus. For it is by grace you have been saved, through faith—and this is not from yourselves, it is the gift of God. (Ephesians 2:1, 4-8)

In the second half of the chapter (verses 11-22), Paul describes the new *horizontal* relationship that Christians have *with one another* through Christ. He focuses on the "dividing wall of hostility" between Jews and Gentiles ("Gentiles" is a translation of *ethnos* in the Greek; it is a term for all non-Jews) because it was one of the primary sources of horizontal division and conflict in the early church.

[You Gentiles] . . . remember that at that time you were separate from Christ, excluded from citizenship in Israel and foreigners to the covenants of the promise, without hope and without God in the world. But now in Christ Jesus you who once were far away have been brought near by the blood of Christ. For he himself is our peace, who has made the two groups one and has destroyed the barrier, the dividing wall of hostility, by setting aside in his flesh the law with its commands and regulations. His purpose was to create in himself one new humanity out of the two, thus making peace, and in one body to reconcile both of them to God through the cross, by which he put to death their hostility. . . . Consequently, you are no longer foreigners and strangers, but fellow citizens with God's people and also members of his household, built on the foundation of the apostles and prophets, with Christ Jesus himself as the chief cornerstone. (Ephesians 2:12-20)

Paul explains that God's plan is to save our broken, fallen world by reconciling us with God (*vertical arrows* in figure 2.1) and one another (*horizontal arrows* in figure 2.1) through Christ. If we read Paul's words carefully, it is obvious that our relationship with God is interconnected with our relationships with one another.

From Genesis to Revelation, the Bible emphasizes God's passion for creating healthy, intimate relationships between God and humanity (vertical) and within humanity (horizontal). The following are just a few of hundreds of examples that could be given. Phrases that emphasize the vertical are shaded with this color and phrases that emphasize the horizontal are shaded with this color.

He has shown you, O mortal, what is good. And what does the LORD require of you? To act justly and to love mercy and to walk humbly with your God. (Micah 6:8)

Hearing that Jesus had silenced the Sadducees, the Pharisees got together. One of them, an expert in the law, tested him with this question: "Teacher, which is the greatest commandment in the Law?" Jesus replied: "'Love the Lord your God with all your heart and with all your soul and with all your mind.' This is the first and greatest commandment. And the second is like it: 'Love your neighbor as yourself.' All the Law and the Prophets hang on these two commandments." (Matthew 22:34-40)

My prayer is not for them alone. I pray also for those who will believe in me through their message, that all of them may be one, Father, just as you are in me and I am in you. May they also be in us so that

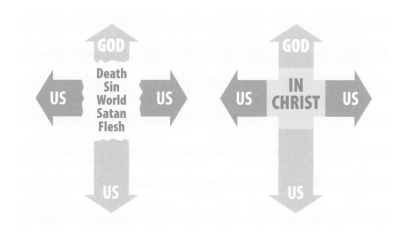

Figure 2.1. Our relationship with God is connected to our relationships with one another

the world may believe that you have sent me. I have given them the glory that you gave me, that they may be one as we are one—I in them and you in me—so that they may be brought to complete unity. Then the world will know that you sent me and have loved them even as you have loved me. (John 17:20-23)

Despite the Bible's consistent emphasis on both the vertical and horizontal facets of the gospel, many Christians believe that focusing on the horizontal is not nearly as important as the vertical. The horizontal aspects of the gospel include racial dynamics. In the comments below, notice that respondents believe that focusing on racial dynamics is separate from the gospel, a distraction from the gospel, and/or a much lower priority than an individual's relationship with God.

> I believe that Christians and their organizations should confront and actively prevent themselves from contributing to racism, but I also believe the gospel is a higher priority. (White, female, 20s)

> Sometimes I feel that (our organization) focuses too strongly on the importance of race/ethnicity. . . . Our goal is to become more like Christ and help the students in this goal. The gospel is what matters most. . . . Racial reconciliation should be just a result of our pursuit of Christ. Yes, it should be intentional, but we should not sacrifice the gospel in our pursuit of it. (White, male, 20s)

> I'm a minority, but even I realize that while it's important to be mindful of racial injustice and diversity, we also can't let it paralyze us from pressing on for what Christ has called us. . . . Let's not bring so much attention to this that we forget what matters most: the pointing of people to Christ and the gospel.[3] (White/Asian, male, 30s)

Jesus and the authors of the New Testament placed a major emphasis on what the gospel is and its implications for our lives with God and one another. Without a common understanding of the gospel, we lose hope, joy, focus, and solidarity. Therefore, one of the most practical and effective ways we can work toward racial justice is by helping our fellow Christians to have a more comprehensive understanding of the Bible's teachings on the gospel.

REGARDING THE UNITED STATES AND THE PEOPLE OF ISRAEL (CHRISTINA)

In the following sections we will consider if and how to apply the laws God gave to the ancient people of Israel in the United States today. We feel it is important to raise a distinction between the people of ancient Israel and American Christians.

Many Christians in America believe the United States to be a Christian nation. This idea is rooted in both the realities and mythologies of the nation's founding. The reality is that groups of European Christians came to what is now the United States and over time sought freedom from religious and British colonial rule, for example. Deists and Christians used language from Scripture to shape culture, laws, and practices. The idea of American exceptionalism is a part of the nation's mythology that includes the minimization of genocide and slavery. Here we can find the roots of what we know today as Christian nationalism.

It is also true that a number of abolitionists were themselves ministers of the gospel and risked life and status to denounce the systems of oppression that built the wealth of the United States. How one group of Christians could believe that the Bible gives them the right to own other people or take their land and the other believe that they have the duty to set people free can be found in varying hermeneutical traditions represented in America.

This gives us great humility when we consider how Christians can misapply Scripture to meet their social and personal purposes. The United States is not God's chosen nation. As a matter of fact, when the Scripture refers to the gospel going to the "ends of the earth" (Acts 1:8), that includes readers in the United States today. It is important to keep this in mind as we move into a portion of this book that will attempt to glean biblical wisdom to apply to our lives as believers in a pluralistic America.

PEOPLE OF RIGHTEOUSNESS AND JUSTICE

One of the strongest themes that runs through the Bible is called *mishpat* in Hebrew (Old Testament) and *dikaiosyne* in Greek (New Testament). *Mishpat* and *dikaiosyne* are typically translated into English as "justice." For a brief overview of the Bible's teachings on justice, we recommend the six-minute video "Justice" by the BibleProject.[4]

Mishpat first appears in the Bible in the context of God describing his plans for Abraham and his descendants. God explains:

> For I have chosen him, so that he will direct his children and his household after him to keep the way of the Lord by doing what is right and just, so that the Lord will bring about for Abraham what he has promised him. (Genesis 18:19)

In the verse immediately after, Genesis 18:20, the Bible describes God's plans to destroy the cities of Sodom and Gomorrah because, "The outcry against Sodom and Gomorrah is so great and their sin so grievous" (Genesis 18:20). Many people believe the cities of Sodom and Gomorrah were judged because of their sexual immorality. That is one of the reasons (see Jude 1:7), but it was not the only reason. Ezekiel explains:

> Now this was the sin of your sister Sodom: She and her daughters were **arrogant, overfed and unconcerned**; they **did not help the poor and needy.** They were **haughty** and **did detestable things** before me. Therefore I did away with them as you have seen. (Ezekiel 16:49-50, emphasis added)

It is also helpful to note the meaning of the Hebrew word translated "outcry" (*zeaqah*) in Genesis 18:20. The word implies that oppression was taking place in the cities. "The term zeâqah, or seâqah, is a technical word for the cry of pain, or the cry for help, from those who are being oppressed or violated. It is the word used for Israelites crying out under their slavery in Egypt (Exodus 2:23)."[5]

Genesis 18–19 presents a clear contrast between the righteousness and justice of the people of God and the sin and oppression in the cities of Sodom and Gomorrah. The two contrasting peoples/cities is a theme that runs throughout the Bible and culminates in Revelation 17–22. Revelation 17–18 describes the evil city of Babylon, which experiences God's judgment, and Revelation 19–22 describes "the Holy City," which experiences God's blessing (Revelation 21:10; 22:19).

There are two types of justice emphasized in the Bible—the justice between God and humanity (vertical) and the justice between humans (horizontal). The second type of justice (horizontal) can be referred to as "social justice." Despite the Bible's strong emphasis on social justice, we often hear comments like the following with our work and research.[6]

> The church should not devote its time and effort to social justice. The church should be more focused on changing the hearts of people, which is the real problem. If people have accepted what Jesus has done for them there will be a heart transformation. No they will not be perfect but they will hopefully be trying to avoid being racist because God calls us to love everyone. (White, male, 18–19)

Notice in the comment above that the individual believed "changing the hearts of people" and "heart transformation" is separate from, or even in opposition to, social justice. They seem to believe that the Bible only addresses "heart transformation" in regard to our vertical relationship with God; but the Bible also addresses "heart transformation" in regard to our horizontal relationships with one another. As the apostle John wrote:

> We love because he first loved us. Whoever claims to love God yet hates a brother or sister is a liar. For whoever does not love their brother and sister, whom they have seen, cannot love God, whom they have not seen. And he has given us this command: Anyone who loves God must also love their brother and sister. (1 John 4:19-21, emphasis added)

THE BIBLE'S TEACHINGS ON SOCIAL ETHICS

After God freed Israel from slavery in Egypt, he commanded them to follow a collection of laws recorded in the first five books of the Bible (the Torah). These laws are referred to as "the Law" throughout the Bible. The Law contains about six hundred laws on a wide variety of topics including religion, economics, crime, justice, family dynamics, medical practices, animal treatment, etc. The Law is very helpful in understanding God's intentions for social relationships and flourishing. No one understands humanity and social systems better than God, so it is wise for us to study the principles God revealed to his covenant people of ancient Israel and discern how they might guide us today in our pluralistic culture.

The Bible is clear that Christians do not need to obey the Law in order to receive forgiveness for their sins or have a relationship with God (Acts

15:6-11; Romans 7; Galatians 3; Hebrews 10:1), but that doesn't mean that the Law is *irrelevant* for us today. Jesus often connected the work he was doing to the teachings in the Law. He taught, "Do not think that I have come to abolish the Law or the Prophets; I have not come to abolish them but to fulfill them" (Matthew 5:17). Similarly, the New Testament authors frequently affirm the trustworthiness and benefits of the teachings in the Old Testament, including the Law.

In Romans 7:5-6, Paul explains that we have died to the Law, we have been released from the Law, and we now serve in the new way of the Spirit. But a few verses later, Paul explains that the Law is "holy, righteous and good" (Romans 7:12). Paul also wrote to Timothy, "All Scripture is God-breathed and is useful for teaching, rebuking, correcting and training in righteousness, so that the servant of God may be thoroughly equipped for every good work" (2 Timothy 3:16-17). As Christians, we do not seek to follow the Law in our own strength or in order to gain salvation, but the Law remains holy, righteous, good, God-breathed, and useful. Christopher Wright describes some key questions we need to ask when seeking to apply principles from the Law in our current society.

- What kind of situation was this law intended to promote or to prevent?
- What change in society would this law achieve if it were followed?
- What kind of situation made this law necessary or desirable?
- What kind of person would benefit from this law, by assistance or protection?
- What kind of person would be restrained or restricted by this law, and why?
- What values are given priority in this law? Whose needs or rights are upheld?
- In what way does this law reflect what we know from elsewhere in the Bible about the character of God and his plans for human life?
- What principle(s) does this law embody or instantiate?

Wright explains how asking these types of questions can help to inform our social ethics. He continues,

> Now we won't always be able to answer these questions with much detail or insight. Some laws are just plain puzzling. But asking questions

like these leads us to a much broader and deeper grasp of what Old Testament laws were all about: forming the kind of society God wanted to create.

Then, having done that homework as best we can, we step out of the Old Testament world and back into our own. Ask the same kind of questions about the society we live in and the kind of people we need to be, and the kind of personal and societal objectives we need to aim for in order to be in any sense "biblical."

In this way, biblical law can function sharply as a paradigm or model for our personal and social ethics in all kinds of areas: economic, familial, political, judicial, sexual, and so on. We are not "keeping it" in a literalist way like a list of rules. But more important, we are not ignoring it in defiance of what Paul says in 2 Timothy 3:16-17. We are studying and using it as guidance, light for the path, in the joyful way of Psalms 1, 19, and 119.[7]

The Law contained many provisions focused on preventing rich/powerful individuals from exploiting poor/vulnerable individuals. God repeatedly commanded the Israelites to show special concern for the most vulnerable groups in their society (widows, orphans, foreigners/immigrants, and the poor). See examples in Leviticus 19 and Deuteronomy 24.

Of course, the Bible's call to restrain the rich and powerful and protect the poor and vulnerable did not end with the Law. In the book of Ruth, we are given a beautiful example of God's heart for the poor and vulnerable being lived out through the marriage of Ruth (a poor, widowed, Moabite outsider) and Boaz (a wealthy, Jewish insider). The psalmists implore, "Defend the weak and the fatherless; / uphold the cause of the poor and the oppressed. / Rescue the weak and the needy; / deliver them from the hand of the wicked" (Psalm 82:3-4). Similarly, the Proverbs declare, "Speak up for those who cannot speak for themselves, / for the rights of all who are destitute. / Speak up and judge fairly; / defend the rights of the poor and needy" (Proverbs 31:8-9).

Unfortunately, the Israelites did not heed God's call to protect the vulnerable and oppressed. Prophets like Isaiah, Jeremiah, Amos, and Micah served the role of prosecuting attorneys on God's behalf. They pointed to the Law, provided evidence of Israel's violations, and then declared God's righteous judgment upon their nation. The prophets presented "three major types of indictments against Israel: idolatry, social injustice, and religious ritualism."[8] A good example of God's indictment of Israel, through the prophets, is found in Isaiah 1. God declared that he had closed his eyes and ears to the Israelites because of their evil and lack of justice. When God closes his eyes and ears to us, we are in a desperate situation!

> When you spread out your hands in prayer, I hide my eyes from you; even when you offer many prayers, I am not listening. Your hands are full of blood! Wash and make yourselves clean. Take your evil deeds out of my sight; stop doing wrong. Learn to do right; seek justice. Defend the oppressed. Take up the cause of the fatherless; plead the case of the widow. (Isaiah 1:15-17)

The Old Testament ends with a sobering example of the painful consequences of refusing to follow God's plan. Israel did not listen to the rebukes of God and the prophets and turn from their idolatry, social injustice, and religious ritualism. As a result, God allowed them to be driven from their land and placed in exile. They suffered spiritually, socially, emotionally, physically, and economically.

The New Testament picked up where the Old Testament left off and continued to emphasize the need for justice and special protections and care for the vulnerable and the oppressed. Jesus described his ministry by reading excerpts from Isaiah 59 and 61: "The Spirit of the Lord is on me, because he has anointed me to proclaim good news to the poor. He has sent me to proclaim freedom for the prisoners and recovery of sight for the blind, to set the oppressed free, to proclaim the year of the Lord's favor" (Luke 4:18-19). He described his ministry as an extension and fulfillment of the Law and the Prophets (Matthew 5:17) and affirmed their emphasis on special compassion for the oppressed and vulnerable in society.

James, the brother of Jesus, also echoed the words of the Law and the prophets and emphasized themes like greed, worker exploitation, self-indulgence, twisting justice, and violence.

> Now listen, you rich people, weep and wail because of the misery that is coming on you. . . . You have hoarded wealth in the last days. Look! The wages you failed to pay the workers who mowed your

fields are crying out against you. The cries of the harvesters have reached the ears of the Lord Almighty. You have lived on earth in luxury and self-indulgence. You have fattened yourselves in the day of slaughter. You have condemned and murdered the innocent one, who was not opposing you. (James 5:1-6)

We will look at additional examples of the New Testament's emphasis on special protections and care for the vulnerable and the oppressed throughout this book.

Are Christians Willing to Apply the Bible's Teachings on Social Justice?

In our 2019 RRJP survey, we asked, "How often should the Bible be used to determine what is right or wrong?" Respondents could choose *always, sometimes*, or *never*. Not surprisingly, a large percentage of Christians in all racial groups selected *always* or *sometimes*, including 90% of White Christians, 87% of Hispanic/Latino Christians, 94% of Black Christians, and 84% of Asian Christians. We will refer to these individuals as "Biblical Morals Christians."

In the survey, we also asked if respondents *agreed* or *disagreed* with the statement, "We should have laws that protect foreigners/immigrants[9] from being treated unjustly." In figure 2.2 you can see the percentages of Biblical Morals Christians who selected *strongly agree, agree*, or *somewhat agree*.

Figure 2.2. Biblical Morals Christians, who agreed there should be laws that protect immigrants from being treated unjustly (RRJP Survey, July/Aug 2019, n=2797)

Toward the end of the survey, we posed a similar statement, but included a Bible reference to see if it would change the response of individuals who selected *neutral* or *disagree* for the question above. The second version of the statement was, "In the system of laws that God gave the Israelites to follow, there were laws that protected foreigners from being treated unjustly (Deuteronomy 24:14). Therefore, it is good to have laws that protect foreigners from being treated unjustly." In figure 2.3 you can see the percentages of Biblical Morals Christians who changed their response from *neutral* or *disagree* to *strongly agree* or *agree* for the second question.

Figure 2.3. Biblical Morals Christians who changed their responses regarding laws that protect immigrants when a Bible reference was included (RRJP Survey, July/Aug 2019, n=2797)

Notice that a large percentage of the Biblical Morals Christians who selected *disagree/neutral* for the first version of the question (without the Bible verse) selected *agree* for the second version of the question (with the Bible verse). In other words, simply mentioning a Bible reference seems to have had a very powerful influence on a significant percentage (46%–69%) of the respondents. That should motivate us to teach *all* of the Bible!

It is also important to note that approximately half of the Biblical Morals Christians *did not* change their mind even though a reference to the Bible's teachings on protecting foreigners/immigrants was included. The following are a few of the reasons Biblical Morals Christians gave for disagreeing, even when Deuteronomy 24:14 was mentioned:

- "As long as people come here legally, there should be laws to protect them."

- "Legal immigrants deserve protection illegal aliens do not."

- "Illegal immigrants were not the foreigners being referred to. LEGAL immigrants are what the Bible was referring to."

- "We should apply the law equally to legal immigrants; I don't believe illegal immigrants are necessarily entitled to special protections."[10]

As you can see from the comments, many Christians argued that we should not have laws that protect foreigners and immigrants who are not legal residents—in their view, foreigners who are not legal residents do not deserve or qualify for protection. But protecting individuals that are especially vulnerable, like foreigners who are not legal residents, *was the purpose* of commandments like Deuteronomy 24:14 in the Law. The Law recognized that explicit, extra protection for widows, orphans, and foreigners was essential because they were so vulnerable to exploitation. Arguing that foreigners do not qualify for protection unless they are already protected as legal residents is like arguing that widows don't qualify for protection unless they have a husband, or an orphan doesn't qualify for protection unless they have parents.

We realize that many readers will likely object to the idea of providing special protections for foreigners for pragmatic reasons. They may ask, "But wouldn't it be expensive and difficult to provide all foreigners with protection? Isn't that unrealistic?" Yes, it would require some sacrifices to provide foreigners with protection. But not providing foreigners with protection also requires sacrifices. The US government has spent well over *$330 billion* enforcing its immigration policies since 2003.[11] The provisions for the vulnerable and oppressed in the Old Testament Law required some sacrifices, but God knew that those sacrifices would improve the Israelite's society in ways that would far outweigh the cost. If we ignore God's will for social justice because it is too costly, we will inevitably discover that our systems are far more costly than God's. No one has a better or more efficient plan for social systems than God.

Applying the Bible's Teachings on Social Ethics in Our Current Context

Racial injustice, as it exists in the United States today, did not exist when the Bible was written. However, there are many principles in the Bible that apply to racial injustice in our society. Let's look at an example. Please read Deuteronomy 24:17-22. In that passage, God gave instructions regarding taking a widow's garment in pledge and what to do when one is harvesting olives. Those are situations we don't find ourselves in very often today. But that does not mean that we can't apply those verses in our lives. Let's consider some of the questions that Christopher Wright encouraged us to ask about Old Testament laws and ask them about Deuteronomy 24:17-22.

What kind of situation was this law intended to promote or to prevent? It would prevent vulnerable people (foreigners/immigrants, fatherless, widows) being treated unjustly or having what little they have taken from them, and prevent vulnerable people from going hungry because they do not have access to land or other means of providing for their family.

What change in society would this law achieve if it were followed? Vulnerable people would be treated with justice and compassion. They would have their physical needs met. It would allow them to provide for themselves (harvesting wheat, picking olives, gathering grapes). Landowners would share the cost of helping the poor and vulnerable. It would increase the moral, spiritual, and economic strength of their society.

What kind of person would be restrained or restricted by this law, and why? Landowners were restrained from harvesting every last grain or olive for their own benefit. They were also restricted from exploiting vulnerable workers for inexpensive labor.

What values are given priority in this law? Whose needs or rights are upheld? The values of justice and compassion are given priority. Individuals that are the most vulnerable to exploitation and injustice are given special protections and shown special kindness.

Now let's consider how we can apply the principles in Deuteronomy 24:17-22 in our society today. One of the groups that is most vulnerable to exploitation in the United States is immigrant workers. If they are not legal residents, they often cannot risk appealing to local law enforcement or the court system for protection.

Unauthorized workers are often afraid to complain about unpaid wages and substandard working conditions because employers can retaliate by taking actions that can lead to their deportation. This gives employers extraordinary power to exploit and underpay them. . . . This exploitation is not just theoretical. A landmark study found that 37 percent of unauthorized immigrant workers were victims of minimum wage violations. An astounding 84 percent who worked full-time were not paid time-and-a-half for overtime when they worked more than 40 hours in a week.[12]

In light of Deuteronomy 24:17-22 and many similar passages, we believe it is important to protect foreign workers, including those who are not legal residents, from being exploited by employers. A practical way to apply that in our society today would be to support local, state, and national policies and laws that are designed to protect foreign workers.

OTHER PRINCIPLES IN THE BIBLE THAT APPLY TO RACIAL JUSTICE TODAY

If we follow similar steps with other Bible passages, we can determine many principles that apply to racial justice in our society today. Here are a few examples:

- All humans are made in God's image (Genesis 1:26-27) and loved by God (John 3:16; Romans 5:8). God does not show partiality (Deuteronomy 10:17) or favoritism (Acts 10:34). God forbids showing partiality (Deuteronomy 1:17; Malachi 2:9). Christ died for people "from every tribe and language and people and nation" (Revelation 5:9). Therefore, **no groups/cultures should be viewed or treated as superior or inferior to other groups/cultures.**

- Greed is against God's will (Luke 12:15). Greed is a form of idolatry because it is relying on the hoarding of wealth to supply our needs rather than on God (Proverbs 11:28; Matthew 6:24; 1 Timothy 6:17). Therefore, **we should look for ways to restrain greed in our lives and society.**

- The Bible repeatedly calls us to love our neighbors and look out for the interests of others even if it requires us to make significant sacrifices (Mark 12:31; Luke 10:25–37; 1 Corinthians 10:24; Philippians 2:3). Therefore, **we must be willing to love our neighbors in practical, sacrificial ways.**

- God stands for the oppressed and against oppressors (Zechariah 7:9-10; Psalm 146:7-9). Therefore, **we should stand for the oppressed and against oppressors.**

- God condemns people with resources and power who are indifferent toward injustice and the needs of others (Ezekiel 16:49; 1 Timothy 6:17-19). Therefore, **those with resources and power should use their resources and power to help the vulnerable and oppressed.**

- In Christ, social hierarchies (Jew/Gentile, old/young, male/female, rich/poor, owner/slave, citizen/foreigner, etc.) are abolished and must not be a source of exploitation or division (Galatians 3:23-29). Therefore, **we should work against social hierarchies in our society and Christian organizations.**

- If we have unjustly received benefits at the expense of others, we must do our part to make it right (Exodus 21:33–22:15; Leviticus 6:1-7; Numbers 5:5-8; Proverbs 14:9; Matthew 5:23-24; Luke 19:1-10). Therefore, **if we have unjustly benefited from the racial hierarchy in the United States, we must do our part to make it right.**

Discussion/Reflection Questions

1. Why do you think missionaries published the "Slave Bible" in 1807 rather than confront the economic and political systems that were oppressing the people who were enslaved? Do we have similar reasons for teaching "edited" versions of the Bible today?

2. In the Christian traditions and organizations you have been a part of, was there a greater emphasis on the Bible's teachings on the vertical (God←→humanity) or horizontal (humanity←→humanity) facets of the gospel? If so, how has that impacted your view of the gospel?

3. In the Christian traditions and organizations you have been a part of, were the Bible's teachings on social justice downplayed or emphasized? If so, how has that impacted your view of social justice?

4. Do you agree with the example application of Deuteronomy 24:17-22? Why or why not?

5. Read Leviticus 19:34 and then ask the four application questions that we asked about Deuteronomy 24:17-22. Can you give some examples of how that passage could be applied in our society today?

6. In the section above, we listed examples of biblical principles that apply to racial justice today. Can you think of some specific examples of how those principles could be applied?

7. How do you plan to apply the content in this chapter?

Recommended Prayer

We recommend that you pray this prayer of David.

The law of the Lord is perfect, refreshing the soul. The statutes of the Lord are trustworthy, making wise the simple. The precepts of the Lord are right, giving joy to the heart. The commands of the Lord are radiant, giving light to the eyes. The fear of the Lord is pure, enduring forever. The decrees of the Lord are firm, and all of them are righteous. They are more precious than gold, than much pure gold; they are sweeter than honey, than honey from the honeycomb. By them your servant is warned; in keeping them there is great reward. But who can discern their own errors? Forgive my hidden faults. Keep your servant also from willful sins; may they not rule over me. Then I will be blameless, innocent of great transgression. May these words of my mouth and this meditation of my heart be pleasing in your sight, Lord, my Rock and my Redeemer. (Psalm 19:7-14)

CHAPTER THREE

FAITHFUL ANTIRACISTS STAND FOR JUSTICE

IN 2017, TIMOTHY ISAIAH CHO was serving as director of operations for a Christian website. After seeing some disturbing examples of racism in the news, he wrote an article titled, "Is Racism a Social Issue or a Gospel Issue?" that challenged Christians to take a stand for racial justice. He assumed there would be some pushback, but was surprised by the intensity of what he and his organization experienced. He later shared the following:

> In the comments section on social media, people threatened to pull their financial support for the organization. Pastors sent letters threatening to do the same. One of my former professors decided to dedicate an article on his blog in response to my piece without naming me or even linking back to the article. . . . I continued to receive hateful comments, further complaints, and more articles responding to what I had written.[1]

Rather than supporting the article, some of the members of his organization distanced themselves from him and the topic. He wrote:

> I made it clear to the other leaders of [the organization where I worked] that we had a responsibility to help guide Christians toward seeing the gospel's application in many important topics, including racial justice. But I saw content pulled after publication due to complaints. I saw blacklists of topics we were no longer able to talk about (e.g., race, racism). I saw blacklists of individuals we were no longer able to associate with.[2]

In the previous chapter, we looked at passages in the Bible that motivate us to stand for racial justice. However, many Christians choose to remain silent or passive on the issue. One of the primary reasons is fear that they will face negative ramifications like the ones Cho described above. When Christians stand for racial justice they often experience anger, pushback, and alienation from friends, family, coworkers, church members, and others. In many cases they also face professional and economic consequences such as losing a leadership position, not being considered for promotions, or even losing their job.

With our research, Christians often share that fear hinders them from taking a stronger stand for justice, for example:

There is always fear. Fear that if I speak out, something might happen to me, or my family, people I know, etc. (Hispanic/Latina/Native American, female, 20s)

As a White ally to my brothers and sisters of color, I am very careful about what I say and who I say it to because I am afraid that it will impact my job and my ability to get tenure. (White, female, 30s)

I don't want to share my culture with white students for fear that my culture will be stolen and the little security I have will be taken away. (Black, male, 20s)[3]

I am so afraid of fulfilling a stereotype [of] "angry Black woman." People always think I need to say something as a Black woman, but I don't want to be that stereotype. (Black, female, 20s)[4]

PARTIALLY STANDING FOR RACIAL JUSTICE

We find that many Christians feel pulled between not wanting to take a stand because of the potential consequences and a desire to live out the Bible's teachings on standing for justice. They find a compromise with their inner struggles by taking a limited or partial stand. Here are a few common approaches:

- *Secret stand.* Internally they support promoting racial justice, but they rarely, if ever, communicate that to others.

- *Theoretical stand.* They verbalize support for racial justice to others, but they rarely, if ever, act on their theoretical support.

- *Selective stand.* They are careful to only verbalize and act on their support for racial justice when it does not require significant sacrifices.
- *Limited stand.* Their stand for racial justice is limited to a specific group or cause. For example, a Hispanic/Latino Christian may stand for justice for undocumented Hispanic/Latino immigrants, but not stand for justice for Black Americans in the criminal justice system.

JESUS STOOD FOR JUSTICE

Jesus' stand for justice was not secret, theoretical, selective, or limited. Let's look at one example. In chapters 20 through 22 of Matthew, we learn about Jesus' final journey to Jerusalem for his death and resurrection (Matthew 20:17-19). While in Jerusalem, Jesus cleansed the temple of merchants and declared, "'My house will be called a house of prayer,' but you are making it 'a den of robbers'" (Matthew 21:13). In his rebuke of the merchants, Jesus quoted from Isaiah (Isaiah 56:7) and Jeremiah (Jeremiah 7:11), two Old Testament prophets who decried the injustice and oppression of the poor taking place in Israel. Jesus followed in their footsteps by rebuking the theft and exploitation that was taking place in the temple.

While in Jerusalem, Jesus also rebuked the religious leadership (scribes and Pharisees) for their hypocrisy, pride, hunger for recognition, misguided evangelistic zeal, superficial religiosity, greed, self-indulgence, and neglect of justice. His rebuke included:

> Woe to you, teachers of the law and Pharisees, you hypocrites! You give a tenth of your spices—mint, dill and cumin. But you have neglected the more important matters of the law—justice, mercy and faithfulness. You should have practiced the latter, without neglecting the former. You blind guides! You strain out a gnat but swallow a camel. Woe to you, teachers of the law and Pharisees, you hypocrites! You clean the outside of the cup and dish, but inside they are full of greed and self-indulgence. (Matthew 23:23-25)

Of course, Jesus took an enormous risk by pointing out the ways that the powerful religious leaders in his day were leading people away from God's will. In fact, soon after he made those comments, the religious leaders played a central role in having him arrested and crucified. But that did not stop Jesus from taking a stand for righteousness and justice.

PAUL OPPOSED SOCIAL HIERARCHIES IN THE CHURCH

In Paul's letter to the Galatians, he wrote, "But when Cephas came to Antioch, I opposed him to his face, because he stood condemned" (Galatians 2:11). Cephas was another name for the apostle Peter. What could have possibly caused Paul to publicly oppose Peter? Why would Paul say that Peter was "condemned"? Let's read the reason why in the next verses.

> For before certain men came from James, he used to eat with the Gentiles. But when they arrived, he began to draw back and separate himself from the Gentiles because he was afraid of those who belonged to the circumcision group. The other Jews joined him in his hypocrisy, so that by their hypocrisy even Barnabas was led astray. When I saw that they were not acting in line with the truth of the gospel, I said to Cephas in front of them all, "You are a Jew, yet you live like a Gentile and not like a Jew. How is it, then, that you force Gentiles to follow Jewish customs?" (Galatians 2:12-14)

Based on historical context provided in the book of Acts, it is likely that Peter separated himself from the Gentile Christians because of pressure from Jewish Christians who believed that the Gentile Christians did not have the same status as Jewish Christians or that it was essential for the Gentiles to follow the Mosaic Law (or "Jewish customs" as Paul puts it in verse 14). Peter's actions were very dangerous because they called into question the authenticity of the faith of the new Gentile Christians and they threatened to create a social hierarchy in the early church. Fortunately, Paul recognized the enormous dangers and took a stand for the gospel and against divisions and hierarchies.

It is important to realize that Peter was well aware that salvation is through faith and not obedience to the Law (Acts 2:38-39; 1 Peter 1:3-12). God had revealed to Peter that the Gentile Christians were not "unclean" and that the Holy Spirit was powerfully bringing them into God's new family (Acts 10). But when he faced criticism from other Jews, Peter's actions went against the truth of the gospel. His actions were an example of the "selective stand" or "limited stand" described above.

In chapter eight, we will reflect more on Galatians 2 and principles we can learn from Paul's willingness to speak up (despite the great risk) and Peter's willingness to receive Paul's correction.

Introduction to Historical Examples

In the following section, we share a few historical examples of Christians and Christian organizations who took a stand for justice during the 1500s to 1700s. Here are a few things to keep in mind.

Why did you choose these examples and not others? We chose these few examples because they had a significant impact on US Christianity and they model the complex nature of standing for justice. Unfortunately, we only have space to highlight a few of the thousands of examples that could be given. We primarily focus on Western (European) male Christians because of their influence during this time period, not because we believe that Western (European) male Christians have more credible or important voices than other Christians. Later in this chapter, we share examples of contemporary people standing for racial justice that include more racial and gender diversity.

Are these all good examples? All of the examples have positive aspects, but some of them also have negative ones. We intentionally include the imperfections because no one's life is completely for or against justice. Acknowledging an individual's weaknesses and failures helps us realize that we do not need to be perfect in order to stand for justice, and that no matter how boldly we declare a commitment to justice and how strong our track record, we are still susceptible to fall into sinful mindsets and actions. In order to remain strong and effective in our stance for racial justice we must continually compare our life to Scripture, rely on the power and leading of the Holy Spirit, and surround ourselves with Christians who can provide encouragement and accountability.

Being honest about the failures and limitations of individuals also helps us have a healthy perspective on the Christian traditions we are a part of. In order to be faithful antiracists, we must critically discern whether the teachings and actions of leaders in organizations (past and present) are aligned with the moral will of God. The history of the church is flooded with "clay feet" leaders who are beloved within their traditions but deeply flawed in character, theology, and actions. With the help of the Holy Spirit and other Christians, we must practice careful discernment. We also must be brave enough to lament, confess, and repent for the sins in our Christian tradition's past.

HISTORICAL EXAMPLES DURING THE 1500S TO 1700S

1500s: Martin Luther. As a priest and theologian in a society with powerful religious forces, Martin Luther took a great risk when he nailed his Ninety-Five Theses to the Castle Church in Wittenberg, Germany. His Ninety-Five Theses emphasized two central beliefs. First, that Scripture, not tradition, is the central religious authority. Second, that humans may reach salvation only by their faith and not by their deeds. The practice of *indulgences* (paying for remission of sins) obscured the teaching of salvation through faith alone and it exploited the poor. It gave rich and powerful individuals the impression that they could treat the poor and powerless with immutability. Here are a few of the points Luther made in his Theses:

36. Any truly repentant Christian has a right to full remission of penalty and guilt, even without indulgence letters.

42. Christians are to be taught that he who gives to the poor or lends to the needy does a better deed than he who buys indulgences.

43. Because love grows by works of love, man thereby becomes better. Man does not, however, become better by means of indulgences but is merely freed from penalties.

44. Christians are to be taught that he who sees a needy man and passes him by, yet gives his money for indulgences, does not buy papal indulgences but God's wrath.

Luther stood for the rights and dignity of certain impoverished people, but he was also notoriously anti-Semitic. Luther wrote that Jewish houses should "be razed and destroyed," that "safe-conduct on the highways be abolished completely for the Jews," and "their rabbis [should] be forbidden to teach on pain of loss of life and limb." Tragically, during the time of Adolf Hitler and his regime, "National Socialists used Luther to support their racist anti-Semitism, calling him a genuine German who had hated non-Nordic races."[5]

1500s: *Protestant Christians.* The Belgic Confession is one of the most important and oldest doctrinal statements of the Protestant Reformed tradition. Guido de Bres, the chief architect of the statement, was later deemed a rebel and martyred by Catholic political authorities. The statement declared that the true church extends beyond the culture or nationality of one people group. It condemned leaders who added and subtracted from the Bible as they pleased. It also condemned greed and idolatry in the church.

> And so this holy church is not confined, bound, or limited to a certain place or certain people. But it is spread and dispersed throughout the entire world, though still joined and united in heart and will, in one and the same Spirit, by the power of faith. (Article 27)

> As for the false church, it assigns more authority to itself and its ordinances than to the Word of God;
> > it does not want to subject itself to the yoke of Christ;
> > it does not administer the sacraments as Christ commanded in his Word;
> > it rather adds to them or subtracts from them as it pleases; it bases itself on humans, more than on Jesus Christ; it persecutes those who live holy lives according to the Word of God and who rebuke it for its faults, greed, and idolatry. (Article 29)[6]

1500s: *John Calvin.* John Calvin's *Institutes of the Christian Religion* had an enormous influence on Western theological thought. Calvin argued that all people have value because they are made in the image of God. He also affirmed that Christians are called to "do what in us lies" to oppose violence and injustice.

> Since the Lord has bound the whole human race by a kind of unity, the safety of all ought to be considered as entrusted to each. In general, therefore, all violence and injustice, and every kind of harm from which our neighbour's body suffers, is prohibited. Accordingly, we are required faithfully to do what in us lies to defend the life of our neighbour; to promote whatever tends to his tranquillity, to be vigilant in warding off harm, and, when danger comes, to assist in removing it. (Book 2, Section 39)

Calvin explained that there are many ways that people steal from one another, all of which are evil. Calvin stressed that God's moral law is more binding than the laws of the land. Theft is under God's judgment, even if it is legally sanctioned. Laws or practices that oppress and crush our neighbor for our own benefit are seen by a holy and just God as theft.

> There are very many kinds of theft. One consists in violence, as when a man's goods are forcibly plundered and carried off; another in malicious imposture, as when they are fraudulently intercepted; a third in the more hidden craft which takes possession of them with a semblance of justice; and a fourth in sycophancy (self-seeking flattery), which wiles them away under the pretence of donation. . . . [God] sees the long train of deception by which the man of craft begins to lay nets for his more simple neighbor, until he entangles him in its meshes—sees the harsh and cruel laws by which the more powerful oppresses and crushes the feeble—sees the enticements by which the more wily baits the hook for the less wary, though all these escape the judgment of man, and no cognisance is taken of them. (Book 2, Section 39)

Calvin stood against unjust gain, but his break with long-held Christian views regarding lending money for interest (also known as usury) contributed to the development of unjust economic systems. For the first fifteen hundred years of Christianity, there was general consensus among Christians that lending money for interest (especially to the poor) was evil. Church councils as early as AD 325 explicitly forbade usury based on prohibitions in the Bible (Exodus 22:25; Leviticus 25:36-37; Deuteronomy 23:19; Psalm 15:5; Luke 6:35). In the fourteenth century, Saint Albert the Great wrote, "Usury is a sin of avarice (greed); it is against charity because the usurer without labor, suffering or fear gathers riches from the labor, suffering and vicissitudes (bad circumstances) of his neighbor."[7] John Calvin was one of the first influential theologians to teach that all forms of usury were not evil. In a *Letter of Advice on Usury* in 1545, he wrote, "We need not conclude that all usury is forbidden."[8]

1600s: Presbyterian and Puritan theologians. The Westminster Standards were drawn up in the 1640s by an assembly of 151 mostly Presbyterian and Puritan theologians. The Standards contain some of the most influential theological statements ever written. In the excerpt below, the Standards explain that the sixth commandment (do not murder) requires more than not killing someone else. It requires us to avoid all actions that result in the unjust taking of the life of anyone. It also encourages comforting and succoring (helping) the distressed and protecting and defending the innocent.

Q. 135. What are the duties required in the sixth commandment?

A. The duties required in the sixth commandment are, all careful studies, and lawful endeavors, to preserve the life of ourselves and others by resisting all thoughts and purposes, subduing all passions, and avoiding all occasions, temptations, and practices, which tend to the unjust taking away the life of any; by just defense thereof against violence, patient bearing of the hand of God, quietness of mind, cheerfulness of spirit . . . comforting and succoring the distressed, and protecting and defending the innocent.[9]

1600s to 1800s: Christians who were enslaved. One of the most inspiring examples of Christians standing for justice in US history were the African American spirituals (also known as Negro spirituals) that were sung by people who were enslaved.

The songs expressed a yearning for a better life, claimed identification with the children of Israel, named the slave owner's deceit and hypocrisy, underscored the need for a closer walk with God, identified the reality of Satan and emphasized the slave's hope for freedom and the future.[10]

The spirituals were also used to undermine the brutal control of the slave owners.

Many of the spirituals carried dual meanings and symbolic messages unknown to slave owners. The lyrics of "Steal Away" alerted people who were enslaved that a religious meeting would occur that night; they sang the song all day until they notified everyone. Underground Railroad conductor Harriet Tubman used the spirituals "Wade in the Water" and "Deep River" to warn people who were enslaved to travel in the water to throw off their scent from the bloodhounds.[11]

One of the most beloved spirituals, "Down by the Riverside," declares:

Gonna lay down my burden
Down by the riverside, down by the riverside, down by the riverside
Gonna lay down my burden
Down by the riverside
I ain't gonna study war no more
Study war no more
Ain't gonna study war no more[12]

The song captures the heavenly imagination and embattlement of the Africans who were enslaved. It also serves as a homage to all those believing in Christ and subjugated by racial oppression. The imagery of no longer "studying war" and exchanging it all for peace is profoundly biblical and cathartic. In the Old Testament, we see the foretelling of a peacemaking judge of the nations who turns warriors into gardeners. Under his leadership, the sword—a symbol of destruction and domination—is beaten into a tool of cultivation. The song declares that Christ will judge between the nations and bring an end to violence and injustice.

He will judge between many peoples and will settle disputes for strong nations far and wide. They will beat their swords into plowshares and their spears into pruning hooks. Nation will not take up sword against nation, nor will they train for war anymore. (Micah 4:3)

1700s: Jonathan Edwards. Jonathan Edwards (1703–1758) was one of the most influential pastors and theologians in US history. The following is an excerpt from a sermon he preached in 1734 (in simplified, modern English):

Christians often place more emphasis on religious practices than they do on how they treat other people. But, how we treat other people is much more important. Jesus criticized the religious leaders during his time for emphasizing religious practices while also neglecting justice, mercy, and faithfulness—even though they were 'the more important matters of the law' (Matthew 23:23). (Paragraph 64)

When Christians do not follow God's will, their heart and actions become corrupted. They start to care only about their own interests. They are unwilling to make sacrifices for the benefit of others. They are indifferent toward injustice, oppression, and conflict in society. (Paragraph 69)

A humble Christian is willing to examine themselves and acknowledge their own sinfulness. They focus on their own sins and how they have disobeyed God. But, in times of spiritual darkness, people are not sensitive to their own sins. They condemn the pride, coveting, and injustice of other people, but are not attuned to the same things in themselves. (Paragraph 70) [13]

It was a powerful sermon. But a study of Edwards's life reveals a combination of support for and opposition to racial justice. On one hand, Edwards criticized the slave trade and took countercultural stands against racism. For example, his Northampton congregation was one of the first in colonial America to allow Black and Indigenous people as members. Toward the end of his life, Edwards spent time living and working among Indigenous peoples and advocating for them to be treated fairly. On the other hand, historical records show that "Edwards was a slave owner who purchased a number of slaves in the course of his lifetime . . . he bought his first slave in the auctions at Newport, Rhode Island, the major northern hub of the Atlantic slave trade." In 1731, Edwards purchased three enslaved individuals named "Joseph, Lee and a woman named Venus." [14] When Edwards died, there was an enslaved boy named Titus listed in his estate.

The clearest written record we have of Edwards's views of slavery are found in the draft of a letter he wrote to defend a pastor named Benjamin Doolittle. Doolittle was being criticized by his congregation because he owned enslaved people. [15] In the letter, Edwards rebuked the congregation for criticizing Doolittle. He explained why he believed owning enslaved people was justifiable. As one author explains, "Edwards himself never called what he and his other colonists were doing 'sin.' To Edwards, slavery was a necessary evil that served some positive good in the natural order that God had decreed." [16] Reflecting on Edwards's life can help us to realize that even the most influential Christians can decry injustice while also supporting injustice. How could he participate in the slave trade and spend twenty-seven years benefiting from the forced labor of other people and not connect his actions with his own preaching on Jesus' desire for "justice, mercy, and faithfulness"? If an esteemed theologian like Edwards can have such a disconnect in his life, none of us are immune to falling into similar traps. His place in the racial hierarchy increased his likelihood of being blind to the racial injustice being experienced by the people around him. Edwards's example should challenge us to reflect on how our social location may increase our likelihood of being "selectively blind" to the injustice around us today.

1700s: Benjamin Banneker. Benjamin Banneker was born in 1773 in Maryland to a free African American woman and a former slave. He attended a Quaker school, one of the first racially integrated schools in the United States. His obituary stated, "To no books was he more attached than the scriptures."[17] His letter to Thomas Jefferson in 1791 is one of the first recorded examples of justice activism in the United States. He was only eighteen years old when he wrote it. The entire letter is well worth reading. In this excerpt, he points out the ironic contradiction between the ideals that Jefferson wrote in the Declaration of Independence and the treatment of slaves.

> Sir how pitiable is it to reflect, that although [*sic*] you were so fully convinced of the benevolence of the Father of mankind, and of his equal and impartial distribution of those rights and privileges which he had conferred upon them, that you should at the Same time counteract his mercies, in detaining by fraud and violence so numerous a part of my brethren under groaning captivity and cruel oppression, that you should at the Same time be found guilty of that most criminal act, which you professedly detested in others, with respect to yourselves.[18]

1700s: Jonathan Edwards Jr. Jonathan Edwards Jr. was the son of Jonathan Edwards. He "possessed a deep, abiding, and all-too-rare compassion for the most marginalized people in 18th-century society: Native Americans and enslaved Africans and African Americans." He "rejected racist assumptions that Indian languages were primitive . . . challenged the biblical arguments often used to defend slavery . . . challenged his congregation to question their basic assumptions about morality and racial difference." He was also a political activist and leader in the first wave of American abolitionism. He wrote, "I assert that every Man is born free. No Man is or can be born a Slave."[19]

CURRENT EXAMPLES

While we were writing this book, we had the opportunity to interview thirty Christian leaders who are standing for racial justice in our society today. We selected the individuals because we or others on our research team had worked with them previously. Of course, there are many more champions for racial justice that we did not have the opportunity to talk with.

In the interviews, we asked them to share about their current work and their recommendations for Christians who desire to take a stand for racial justice today. They shared an incredible wealth of wisdom and practical tips. To watch excerpts from the interviews, visit faithfulantiracism.com. For a list of the interviewees and a summary of some of the topics we discussed in each interview, see appendix B.

A FEW HIGHLIGHTS FROM THE INTERVIEWS

"We're in an extraordinarily tribal moment in our society. We're all tribed up . . . We all feel it. The idea of standing up to our own fills us with fear, because the tribe is where we belong, where we are safe. There are real penalties when we transgress our tribe, and I think it's incredibly important to recognize, rather than belittle, people's fears."—Alexia Salvatierra

"It's been just in the past four or five years that I've begun to see how white supremacy has covertly invaded all our ways of life from top to bottom. Not all at once, but there have been important markers along the way. I remember hearing Christina [Edmondson] say that there's an enormous difference between a love of diversity and a love of justice—and a light broke through. I still get chills thinking about that moment of painful conviction. Because I've always loved diversity! . . . But that's not the same as loving justice. It's entirely possible to love the diversity and differences among God's people and, at the same time, maintain habits and systems that favor people in your comfort group who look and think like you. I know because I've done it—not knowingly, not with intention, but I've done it all the same."—Beth Moore

"I believe the Church must practice remembrance, just as Israel was commanded to do. Like Israel, we too easily forget who we are and

Whose we are, making us prone to create systems and structures that marginalize some and privilege others. But remembering, regularly and corporately, is a spiritual practice that grounds us in reality and compels us to confession and repentance. It re-roots us in our identity as people who are called to walk the narrow way and live into our citizenship that is not of this world."—Dominique Gilliard

Reflection Exercise

Before we wrap up this chapter, we encourage you to do the following exercise to reflect on whether your organization is standing for racial justice. If you are going through this book with other individuals in your organization, consider having each person pick a different item and then discuss your answers.

1. Does your organization, denomination, or faith tradition have a doctrinal statement that they hold to today? If so, does it mention topics related to social justice or racial justice?

2. Has there been racism in your organization, denomination, or faith tradition? If so, what are some examples and is it still ongoing?

3. Does your organization have a policy for how to handle individual incidents of racism and racial bias within the organization? If so, do you know what the policy is? Is it effective?

4. Do your organization's leaders take a stand for racial justice? If so, can you give some examples?

5. Who are some of the past and present "heroes" and "villains" in your organization? What were their views on racial justice?

Discussion/Reflection Questions

1. Does fear prevent you from standing for racial justice? If so, how?

2. We looked at four common ways that people take a partial stand for justice: secret stand, theoretical stand, selective stand, and limited stand. Do any of them describe your stand for justice? If so, why?

3. We looked at ways that Jesus and Paul took a stand for justice, mercy, faithfulness, and the gospel. What are some words you would use to

describe their stands? Do Christians in our society today take similar stands? If not, why do you think that is?

4. In the historical examples, what types of sacrifices did the individuals or groups need to make in order to stand for justice? Do Christians today face similar consequences when they stand for justice? If so, why do you think the risks have been similar for thousands of years?

5. Watch at least one of the interviews we conducted with current-day champions for justice and then discuss: How are they taking a stand for racial justice? What kinds of obstacles are they facing? How are they overcoming them?

6. How do you plan to apply the content in this chapter?

Recommended Prayer

Dear God, Help us to learn for the sake of love.

Help us to learn as an act of repentance.

Help us to become more educated in mercy, compassion, and justice.

Help us to see rightly our traditions and denominations—their strengths and weaknesses.

Your word reminds us that knowledge puffs up, but love builds up (1 Corinthians 8:1).

Break our dependency of worldly knowledge used only to puff up. Break our dependency of theological knowledge apart from love, as if we can educate our way to righteousness.

Instead let us boast in your wisdom and your love—alone.

Help us honestly reflect on the traditions and organizations we are a part of.

Help us to not fear what we find or cover up the truth.

We cling to the promises that you hold for us.

We know that they are secure.

CHAPTER FOUR

FAITHFUL ANTIRACISTS UNDERSTAND OUR PAST

HAVE YOU EVER HAD a conversation with a friend or family member that went like this?

You: Honestly, it was difficult for me when you made that comment earlier today.

Friend: What do you mean?

You: I felt like your tone was pretty harsh when you said ___.

Friend: What do you mean? That's not what I said or how I said it.

You: Well, that's how I remember it.

Friend: I don't remember it like that at all.

We are both parents of teenagers, so we have those types of conversations on a pretty regular basis. Isn't it amazing how often two people can have very different memories of the same event? Without a shared understanding of what took place in the past, it is very difficult to have productive dialogue and work through an issue.

This is true in everyday conversations between people; it is also true in regard to dynamics between racial groups in our society. If we have different perspectives on the history of our country, it is nearly impossible to make progress toward addressing racial injustice. As aboriginal leader George Erasmus explained, "Where common memory is lacking, where people do not share in the same past, there can be no real community. Where community is to be formed, common memory must be created."[1]

Similarly, author and Native American activist Adrian Jacobs wrote:

> We must embrace our history. To "do justly" we must tell our story and express all the pain of our history. You will hear our bright hopes and our painful deaths. Weep with us and sing with us. The pain will be so deep its only consolation is in our Creator. The great sin against our dignity is answered by a love that brings arrogant violence to its knees. This is the message of the blood of Jesus that speaks better things than that of Abel.[2]

It is often difficult and painful to "embrace our history," but it can also be healing and empowering. In this book, we only have space to highlight a few key events related to the history of racial injustice in the United States.[3] In this chapter we will focus on events from 1452 through 1963. In the next chapter we will look at some events from 1963 through today.

A Few Common Objections

Before we begin, let's consider a few common questions and objections that often come up when we lead training programs on the history of racial injustice in the United States.

Does focusing on the past do more damage than good and hinder progress? Many people believe talking about the past is counterproductive or a hindrance to progress. Here are a few examples from our research:

> Some ethnic groups were persecuted in the past but that needs to be left in the past. Move on! We can't change the past but we CAN act in the present and learn from our past mistakes. (White, female, 50s)

> We can't move forward if we are always holding on to the past. (White, male, 40s)

> We need to keep having this conversation but to come up with a solution and not keep talking about the pain and sufferings we were dealt in the past. We need to move on from the past; why keep talking about the past? (Asian, female, 20s) [4]

Another common comment is, "I don't want to dwell on the past. Just tell me what I need to do in order to make progress." But what they do not realize is that understanding and acknowledging the past is an essential part of making progress. We can't move forward if we refuse to look back. Reflecting on the past is not a barrier, it is a door to freedom, growth, and healing.

Doesn't the Bible teach that we shouldn't focus on the past? It is true that the Bible describes situations where God chooses to forget sins (Isaiah 43:25) and Paul talks about "forgetting what lies behind" (Philippians 3:13). But as a rule, the Bible doesn't discourage reflecting on the past. In fact, a very large portion of Bible is historical narrative, a record of the past. The Bible is filled with encouragement to remember the past.

Should we talk about the past even if it makes people feel uncomfortable? Imagine you had a friend who had hurt you deeply in the past. It would be difficult to build a strong relationship with that person if they were unwilling to acknowledge and discuss what took place. Similarly, acknowledging historic racial injustice is essential in order to make progress toward racial unity. It can help us to push through the discomfort of reflecting on the past if we consider how small our pain is in comparison to the pain of the people who had to live through the historical realities we are studying. For example, it is uncomfortable to talk about slavery, but it is far more uncomfortable to live trapped in slavery. The discomfort we feel discussing it pales in significance to the reality they experienced living it.

A Few Key Events from 1452 to 1963

In the following brief summary of key historical events, we will focus on three of the primary forces that have built and sustained racial injustice in the United States: economics, politics, and religion. We highlight some of those forces in the following summaries to make them easier to identify. Of course, many other forces have played a powerful role in sustaining racial injustice, including science and academic institutions. But, for the purposes of this book, we will primarily be focusing on economics, politics, and religion.

1452: Pope Nicholas V issues the Doctrine of Discovery. In a series of statements, the pope granted the king of Portugal the right to conquer and subdue non-Christians, seize their property, and turn them into perpetual slaves. As Mark Charles and Soong-Chan Rah write:

The Doctrine of Discovery served as theological justification for European Christian atrocities. One of the central explanations for the rightness of European conquest was the correlation of Christian evangelism and conversion with the expansion of European power as outlined in the Doctrine of Discovery. Enslavement could be justified because heathens would come to Christian faith.[5]

1492: Columbus claims the "New World" for Spain. Christopher Columbus's expedition to the "New World" was funded by the king and queen of Spain, motivated by economic gain, and sanctioned by the Christian institutions of the time. The European colonists generally did not view the Indigenous peoples in the Americas as human beings with equal value who were entitled to their own freedom, health, land, and beliefs. Many of the colonists believed they were sanctioned by God to kill, exploit, or enslave the Indigenous people for their own gain. Regarding his first encounter with the Indigenous people, Columbus wrote, "They would make fine servants. . . . With fifty men we could subjugate them all and make them do whatever we want."[6]

In 1542, a Spanish priest living in the colonies recorded a candid, horrific description of the atrocities experienced by the Indigenous people:

> The island of Hispaniola was the first to witness the arrival of the Europeans and first to suffer the wholesale slaughter of its people and the devastation and depopulation of the land. It all began with the Europeans taking native women and children both as servants and to satisfy their own base appetites. . . . (The Europeans) forced their way into native settlements, slaughtering everyone they found there, including small children, old men, pregnant women, and even women who had just given birth.[7]

1620: Puritans bring beliefs about white superiority from England. Many of the first Christians in the Americas brought beliefs about white superiority along with them from Europe. They believed that they were a superior people that were chosen by God to tame the spiritual darkness and wild wilderness of the Americas. In 1620, on a ship to America, influential Puritan leader John Winthrop wrote, "We must consider that we shall be as a city upon a hill. The eyes of all people are upon us, so that if we shall deal falsely with our God in this work we have undertaken, and so cause Him to withdraw His present help from us, we shall be made a story and a byword through the world."[8] But in 1641, as a government leader in Massachusetts, "Winthrop went against the recent trend of accepting Native Americans and Africans into the church . . . and helped write the Massachusetts Body of Liberties, the first legal sanctioning of slavery in North America. Indeed, Winthrop owned at least one Native American slave, taken during the Pequot War (1636–37)."[9]

1637: Colonists wage "total war" and enslave Native Americans. Almost all of the early European colonists would have described themselves as Christians, but in many cases, their treatment of Native Americans was in stark contrast to the Bible's teachings on love for neighbor and protection for the vulnerable. For example, in 1637, soldiers in the Colony of Connecticut and their Native American allies attacked a Pequot village at Mistick and killed 400 Pequot, including around 175 women and children. Then,

> in the following months, the English of Connecticut and Massachusetts Bay pursued the fleeing Pequot communities, executing leaders and fighting men and enslaving women and children. . . . The massacre of the Pequot at Mistick demonstrated to all observers, in southern New England and elsewhere, the English ability and will to wage total war against their Indian enemies.[10]

1676: Bacon's Rebellion and the beginning of African slavery. In the Colony of Virginia in the early 1600s, social dynamics were still fluid. Poor White and Black people shared relationships and common bonds as they both struggled to make a living. From 1661 to 1682, European indentured servants as well as free, poor White and Black workers rose up in a series of revolts over their mistreatment by wealthy tobacco plantation owners. Bacon's Rebellion was the most significant of the revolts. The workers laid siege to the capitol in Jamestown, burned it, and drove Governor William Berkley into exile. The plantation owners worked out a solution that met their desire for inexpensive labor and also prevented the dangerous allegiance of poor White and Black workers. Over the next few decades, the plantation owners shifted their labor force almost entirely to African slaves. They also established a wide range of policies and laws designed to keep

White and Black workers divided. Black people were punished more harshly than White people for the same crimes. A White person caught escaping with a Black person was punished more severely than if they escaped with a White person. Interracial marriage was outlawed. Poor White people were selected to patrol the slaves and enforce pro-White laws.[11] During the decades when these changes took place, all but one of the government leaders in the Colony of Virginia were Anglican Christians.[12]

1787: *Three-fifths clause in the US Constitution.* Advantages for White people were written into the earliest laws of the United States. For example, Article I Section 2 of the US Constitution stated that slaves could be counted as three-fifths of a person when determining the political power (representatives) of states. But the slaves themselves were given no political power whatsoever. The unjust laws were not surprising in light of the fact that approximately three out of four of the signers of the Declaration of Independence owned slaves, and many, if not all, of them held beliefs in white superiority.[13] For example, Thomas Jefferson, author of the Declaration of Independence, wrote in 1781, "Blacks, whether originally a distinct race, or made distinct by time and circumstances, are inferior to the whites in the endowments both of body and mind."[14] The large majority of the individuals who founded the United States were also Christians who were "baptized, listed on church rolls, married to practicing Christians, and frequent or at least sporadic attenders of services of Christian worship."[15]

1793: *Baptist Committee declares slavery a government issue.* A decision by the Baptist General Committee of Virginia in 1793 is a good example of the many ways that Christians passively sustained slavery during the 1600s to 1800s. The committee was pressured by pro-slavery members to endorse slavery and by abolitionist members to condemn slavery. After deliberation, they decided to dismiss the issue because they determined it was an issue for the government to decide rather than their committee. As a result, Baptist pastors were empowered to maintain the status quo by dismissing abolitionism as a "political issue."[16]

1861: *The Civil War begins over slavery and religious rights.* The bloodiest war in US history was fought for economic, political, and religious reasons. Disagreements about slavery and states' rights fueled the conflict, but so did the South's belief that the Bible approved slavery. Many Southerners viewed the war as a battle for their religious freedom.

Southern theologians challenged their abolitionist opponents to produce the chapter and verse where Jesus, or the Bible generally, condemned slavery. They gave extended treatises on the scriptural validity of slavery. Southern Methodist preacher J. W. Tucker said to Confederates in 1862, "Your cause is the cause of God, the cause of Christ, of humanity. It is a conflict of truth with error—of Bible with northern infidelity—of pure Christianity with northern fanaticism."[17]

1865: A thwarted attempt to empower freed slaves. Toward the end of the Civil War, as Northern armies won victories across the South, thousands of freed slaves followed the Northern troops. In 1865, President Lincoln sent his secretary of war, Edwin Stanton, to Savannah to meet with General Sherman to discuss plans for the freed slaves. On January 12, Sherman and Stanton met with twenty Black Baptist and Methodist ministers to discuss a plan. Representing the Black ministers, Brother Frazier asked that the freed slaves be given land and the freedom to govern themselves. Four days later, Sherman issued Special Field Order No. 15 that designated the redistribution of four hundred thousand acres of land to the freed slaves. By June of 1865, forty thousand freed slaves had been settled on four hundred thousand acres and were forming self-governing communities. After Lincoln's assassination, Andrew Johnson, a vocal white supremacist and former slave holder, became president and overturned Sherman's Field Order. In one of the most tragic moments in the history of our nation, the acres that were given to the slaves were returned to the wealthy plantation owners who originally owned them.[18] If Field Order No. 15 had stayed in effect, it would have provided much needed economic empowerment and a small measure of justice for the incalculable suffering of the people who were enslaved.

1860s–1950s: Many White Christians support unjust laws and participate in hate groups. In the period after the Civil War, the dominant status of White people was threatened in ways it had not been since the earliest days of European colonization. In the South, formerly enslaved people were free and pursuing a new role in society. In the Southwest, the

US government had greatly expanded its South and West borders through a war with Mexico. The military seizure of huge amounts of land resulted in a large new population of Mexican American citizens. In the West, the number of Chinese immigrants was increasing. In the East, immigrants from many countries were flowing into New York City and other metropolitan areas.

During this period, many White people reasserted their status at the top of the racial hierarchy through political action, violence, and intimidation. For example, in the South ex-slaves could be arrested for not being able to prove that they had a job. They were then forced to work as sharecroppers in conditions that were often worse than when they were slaves because they were no longer the valuable "property" of the plantation owners. This period also saw the rapid rise of hate groups such as the KKK. Rather than standing against these injustices, many White Christians actively or passively supported them. Tragically, White pastors and church leaders often served as leaders in the hate groups. Gruesome lynchings were often "terror festivals" that took place after church on Sunday and were well attended by church members.[19] Over 4,300 lynchings in states across the United States between 1877 and 1950 have been documented.[20] Very few of the people who carried out the lynchings ever faced any legal consequences.

1879: Christian boarding schools force Native Americans to assimilate.
The Carlisle Indian Industrial School was formed in 1879 and became the most famous of the over 350 Native American boarding schools. Carlisle's founder, Richard Henry Pratt, declared the purpose of the schools was to "kill the Indian in him, and save the man." Tragically, the schools were "a collaboration of the Christian churches and the federal government since its earliest inception, beginning with the Indian Civilization Fund Act of March 3, 1819."[21]

At the schools,

> Indian children were separated from their families and cultural ways for long periods, sometimes four or more years. The children were forced to cut their hair and give up their traditional clothing. They had to give up their meaningful Native names and take English ones. They were not only taught to speak English, but were punished for speaking their own languages. Their own traditional religious

practices were forcibly replaced with Christianity. They were taught that their cultures were inferior.[22]

1882: The Chinese Exclusion Act. Throughout the United States, "the influx of newcomers resulted in anti-immigrant sentiment among certain factions of America's native-born, predominantly Anglo-Saxon Protestant population. The new arrivals were often seen as unwanted competition for jobs."[23] The Chinese Exclusion Act of 1882 was the first significant law passed by the federal government that prevented immigration. Although Chinese immigrants were a very small group (.002 percent of the nation's population), they were blamed for declining wages and economic problems. "Congress passed the exclusion act to placate worker demands and assuage prevalent concerns about maintaining White 'racial purity.'"[24]

1890s–1920s: Many White Christians view "social action" as a dangerous distraction. During this period, an increasing number of White Christians became skeptical and fearful regarding "social action." Many pastors taught that it was a distraction from the more important work of "saving souls."

> The result in conservative evangelicalism was what theologian John Stott has called "the Great Reversal." This term was applied to the strange reversal of many Christian strands from their historical acts of social engagement—acts of charity, the building of hospitals, the abolition of slavery, and more. Suspicious and fearful of being associated with liberal theology, whole groups of Christians came to largely avoid work to redress worldly injustices or social ills. This trend was exacerbated by the emergence of dispensational theology, with its emphasis on end times, which became increasingly popular in evangelical circles through the 1900s.[25]

It is important to realize that the aversion to social action and the end times theology that developed during this period did not happen in a vacuum. At the time, millions of formerly enslaved Black people, Mexican Americans, and immigrants were struggling to find their place in US society. The racial hierarchy was being challenged, and White Christians had to decide whether they would follow the Bible's teachings on love and justice, give up their preferential status, and work to dismantle the racial hierarchy. Sadly, only a small percentage of White Christians were willing to do so. The shift away from social engagement and toward evangelism provided a theological justification for maintaining the racial hierarchy.

1930: Deportations in the Southwest. In the 1930s, Mexican Americans were blamed for the economic hardships of the Great Depression. Between 1930 and 1935, the US government repatriated or deported over three hundred thousand individuals to Mexico. Having legal residency in the United States did not prevent Mexican Americans from being targeted. In California, over 80 percent of the deportees were legal residents of the United States.[26]

1934: The National Housing Act of 1934. The National Housing Act of 1934 established the Federal Housing Administration (FHA). The FHA used color-coded maps to designate Black neighborhoods as undesirable. This practice of "redlining" prevented Black individuals from purchasing homes and acquiring wealth. Redlining powerfully reinforced racial housing segregation and the racial hierarchy.[27]

1944: The GI Bill. The GI Bill of 1944 was structured and administered in ways that allocated **billions of dollars in benefits** (college tuition, low-cost home loans, unemployment insurance) to White veterans. Lawmakers intentionally made it difficult or even impossible for the 1.2 million Black veterans to receive the same benefits as White veterans. There was "no greater instrument for widening an already huge racial gap in postwar America than the GI Bill."[28]

Prosegregationist Mississippi congressman John E. Rankin was the chair of the House Veterans Committee when the GI Bill was created. In the House of Representatives in 1952, he made the following statement regarding an immigration bill that was proposed. Notice the way he weaves together politics, prejudice, and Christianity:

> This is another dangerous amendment that tends to wreck our immigration laws and flood this country with undesirable elements. We have had too many questionable characters swarming into this country already, bringing with them communism, atheism, anarchy, infidelity, and hatred for American institutions. Instead of bringing in more of that ilk we had better begin to deport some who have already arrived. If we want to save this country from destruction at the hands of the enemies within our gates. If certain individuals who

have spoken for this and other similar amendments had the power to write the immigration laws of this country, and to govern our people generally, I would say, "God save America." They whine about discrimination. Do you know who is being discriminated against? The White Christian people of America.[29]

1963: Alabama clergymen appeal for "law and order." In April 1963, eight Alabama clergymen wrote the following in a public statement in response to civil rights demonstrations in Birmingham:

> However, we are now confronted by a series of demonstrations by some of our Negro citizens, directed and led in part by outsiders. We recognize the natural impatience of people who feel that their hopes are slow in being realized. But we are convinced that these demonstrations are unwise and untimely. . . . We further strongly urge our own Negro community to withdraw support from these demonstrations, and to unite locally in working peacefully for a better Birmingham. When rights are consistently denied, a cause should be pressed in the courts and in negotiations among local leaders, and not in the streets. We appeal to both our white and Negro citizenry to observe the principles of law and order and common sense.[30]

In his *Letter from Birmingham Jail*, Reverend Martin Luther King Jr. wrote the following in response to the letter from the clergymen (excerpt):

> I must make two honest confessions to you, my Christian and Jewish brothers. First, I must confess that over the past few years I have been gravely disappointed with the white moderate. I have almost reached the regrettable conclusion that the Negro's great stumbling block in his stride toward freedom is not the White Citizen's Counciler or the Ku Klux Klanner, but the white moderate, who is more devoted to "order" than to justice; who prefers a negative peace which is the absence of tension to a positive peace which is the presence of justice; who constantly says: "I agree with you in the goal you seek, but I cannot agree with your methods of direct action"; who paternalistically believes he can set the timetable for another man's freedom; who lives by a mythical concept of time and who constantly advises the

Negro to wait for a "more convenient season." Shallow understanding from people of good will is more frustrating than absolute misunderstanding from people of ill will. Lukewarm acceptance is much more bewildering than outright rejection.[31]

1968: Civil rights legislation remains unenforced and unimplemented. The civil rights movement brought many signs of hope in regard to racial justice in the United States, but leaders such as King remained frustrated by the ways that President Lyndon Johnson and other political leaders verbalized support for the movement but were unwilling to address the systemic forces that prevented change.

The civil rights measures of the 1960s engraved solemn rights in the legal literature. But after writing piecemeal and incomplete legislation and proclaiming its historic importance in magnificent prose, the American government left the Negro to make the unworkable work. Against entrenched segregationist state power, with almost total dependence economically on those they had to contend with, and without political experience, the impoverished Negro was expected to usher in an era of freedom and plenty.[32]

THE 1960S AND THE BIRTH OF *COLORBLINDNESS*

Like the period after the Civil War, the civil rights movement was a time of racial upheaval. White people's status at the top of the racial hierarchy was significantly challenged. The old tactics of overt violence and fear through intimidation, lynchings, and forced segregation were being opposed by a growing percentage of the public. A new approach was developed to maintain the racial social hierarchy: *colorblindness*. As Eduardo Bonilla-Silva explains:

It is my contention that despite the profound changes that occurred in the 1960s, a new racial structure—the new racism for short—is operating, which accounts for the persistence of racial inequality. The elements that comprise this new racial structure are the increasingly covert nature of racial discourse and racial practices; the avoidance of racial terminology and the ever-growing claim by whites that they experience "reverse racism"; the elaboration of a racial agenda over political matters that eschews direct racial references; the invisibility of most mechanisms to reproduce racial inequality; and, finally, the rearticulation of some racial practices characteristic of the Jim Crow period of race relations.[33]

In the above quote, Bonilla-Silva lists the following elements of colorblindness:

- Racial conversations and practices are hidden
- Racial terms are avoided
- White people claim they are experiencing "reverse racism"
- Race and politics are connected in hidden or coded ways
- New terminology is used for Jim Crow–like practices

EVERYDAY WAYS THAT THE RACIAL HIERARCHY WAS MAINTAINED

In the previous historical examples, we highlighted economic, political, and religious forces to emphasize how they work together to sustain racial injustice. Here are two fictional (but likely) examples that illustrate how those forces influenced behavior in common, everyday ways.

A tobacco plantation owner and Africans who were enslaved. Imagine a tobacco plantation owner in Virginia in the 1600s. He is afraid for his safety because of the recent worker riots in Jamestown; he also wants to maximize his profits. Therefore, he decides to change his labor force from indentured servants to Africans who were enslaved. He subconsciously feels a burden because he is dehumanizing and exploiting other human beings. He mentions his concern to his pastor. The pastor has been taught to believe that God has cursed the Black race and destined them for servanthood to superior White men. The pastor knows that the Bible teaches the importance of justice, but he feels it is misguided to apply those principles toward the treatment of Black people. Even if the pastor believes that slavery is against God's will, it is likely he will remain silent on the topic for fear of backlash from the slave owner (who is powerful and wealthy), the members of his congregation, and the local government. Therefore, the pastor tells the owner that he is doing God's will by owning slaves. When the owner sits on his front porch watching other people doing grueling and inhuman labor for his benefit, he tells himself: *I am living out my divine destiny and they are living out theirs.*

A frontier family and Native Americans. Imagine a frontier family heading west during the 1800s. They have befriended a number of Native Americans on their journey and have always considered themselves to be "friendly toward Natives." They come across a beautiful section of land near a stream that looks like an ideal place for a homestead. They know selecting a good location is essential for their survival. However, they are aware that the land is owned by a Native American tribe. They contact the local government and receive permission to settle on the land even though they know it is in violation of a treaty. When the Native Americans complain, the frontier family justifies their actions by telling themselves: *God placed the White race here to subdue these untamed lands and reach the Natives with the gospel. We are simply following God's will and doing what is best for everyone.*

Building and Sustaining the Racial Hierarchy

It is important to recognize that the racial hierarchy in the United States was not created by chance or because White Americans are better people, have more natural ability, or work harder. The racial hierarchy was intentionally created by White Americans who wanted to structure society for their own benefit. Some of the benefits they sought were money, power, status, health, land, and security. The following tactics were used to build and sustain the racial hierarchy:

- *Fear-driven rhetoric.* People were told they must support the racial hierarchy or they would be attacked or oppressed by people of color. They were told their only options were between white dominance and chaos, instability, and the overthrow of society.

- *Violence.* Physical violence through hate groups, mobs, military, private/local militias, police, and more was used as a public display of power meant to strike fear into anyone that challenged white dominance.

- *Psychological manipulation.* Pro-White, anti-Black, anti-Indigenous (and other persons of color) propaganda was communicated through avenues such as preaching, political speeches, news media, and entertainment.

- *Economics.* Economic practices that advantaged White people were created, strengthened, or expanded.

- *Politics.* Laws and political policies that advantaged White people were created, strengthened, or expanded at national, state, and local levels.

- *Religion.* Religious leaders ignored or minimized the Bible's teachings on social justice. In some cases, they also provided "biblical support" for white superiority and the racial hierarchy.

In order to maintain and justify oppression and the racial hierarchy, White people developed a lie that they are superior to people in other racial groups and therefore deserving of more resources and power. The lie of white superiority is in direct opposition to the Bible's teachings that all people are created in God's image (Genesis 1:27) and therefore have equal value and worth. As social justice activist Bryan Stevenson stated in a 2020 interview:

> I think what happened to Indigenous people when Europeans came to this continent was a genocide. . . . And we didn't really address the consequences of that era. We said that native people are savages. We created a narrative of racial difference to justify the violence that we imposed on those populations. . . . And we've been silent about what I believe was the great evil of American slavery, which wasn't involuntary servitude and forced labor. I think the real evil of slavery was the narrative of racial difference that we created to justify enslavement. White enslavers didn't want to feel immoral or un-Christian or unjust, so they had to create this ideology of white supremacy. They said that Black people are not the same as White people. Black people are less human, Black people are less evolved, Black people are less deserving, Black people are less capable. And that ideology of white supremacy, that narrative of racial difference wasn't something that we addressed. We fight the Civil War and the North wins the Civil War, but the South wins the narrative war. We pass the 13th Amendment, which talks about ending involuntary servitude and forced labor but says nothing about ending this ideology of white supremacy, ending racial hierarchy. And as a result of that, I don't think slavery ends in 1865, it just evolves. It turns into a century of racial violence and lawlessness where Black people are pulled out of their homes and they're beaten and they're tortured and they're lynched.[34]

BELIEF IN WHITE SUPERIORITY IN OUR SOCIETY TODAY

Many Christians feel they are free from any beliefs in white superiority. When they think of belief in white superiority or white supremacy they may have an image in their head of a KKK member or of George Wallace yelling, "Segregation now, segregation tomorrow, segregation forever."[35] Unfortunately, belief in white superiority continues to fester in much more subtle ways in our society today.

When we work with Christian organizations we often observe three dynamics that are expressions of the white superiority developed in our nation's history. They are especially common in predominantly White organizations but can also be found in organizations where people of color are in the majority.[36] We frequently observe:

- *White dominance.* White people control the policies, activities, and dynamics in ways that primarily cater to the preferences of White people.

- *White normativity.* The views and practices of White people are treated as the norm or standard. The views and practices of people in other racial groups are treated as special, unusual, or dangerous.

- *White transparency.* White dominance and white normativity powerfully influence dynamics, but their effects remain invisible or unacknowledged.

As Korie Edwards writes:

White normativity reinforces the normalization of whites' cultural practices, ideologies, and location within the racial hierarchy such that how whites do things; their understandings about life, society, and the world; and their dominant social location over other racial groups are accepted as "just how things are." . . . It is difficult for them to see how race affects their lives and to cultivate a racial consciousness. For these reasons, whiteness is a powerful, yet elusive force in the construction of race and racial hierarchies. As such, it shapes the structure of and interrelations within any organization, including interracial churches.[37]

Here are a few of the many negative ramifications of white dominance, white normativity, and white transparency:

- They affirm the false view that White people's perspectives are better and more valuable.

- They create an oppressive environment for people of color.

- They teach people of color that their perspectives are less important and valuable.

- They contribute to Christians associating White views with "Christian views."

- They place pressure on people of color to assimilate or code-switch (we will define these terms in chapter eight).

THE IMPORTANCE OF TRUTH TELLING

In this chapter we have explored some difficult truths about our country's past. It can be painful and disorienting to honestly acknowledge those realities, but it is essential if we want to work toward racial justice in our society today. We cannot "just move on" without looking back.

Being willing to honestly acknowledge our past is sometimes referred to as *truth telling*. As Christians, we are called to be truth-telling people. As Paul writes:

> So Christ himself gave the apostles, the prophets, the evangelists, the pastors and teachers, to equip his people for works of service, so that the body of Christ may be built up until we all reach unity in the faith and in the knowledge of the Son of God and become mature, attaining to the whole measure of the fullness of Christ.
>
> Then we will no longer be infants, tossed back and forth by the waves, and blown here and there by every wind of teaching and by the cunning and craftiness of people in their deceitful scheming. Instead, *speaking the truth in love*, we will grow to become in every respect the mature body of him who is the head, that is, Christ. From him the whole body, joined and held together by every supporting ligament, *grows and builds itself up in love*, as each part does its work. (Ephesians 4:11-16, emphasis added)

Truth telling and historical reflection are a powerful way we can help to promote growth and the building up of one another in love.

Discussion/Reflection Questions

1. George Erasmus said, "Where community is to be formed, common memory must be created." What do you think he meant? Do you agree?

2. Select a few of the historic examples and answer these questions: Who did what? Why did they do it? What were they trying to accomplish?

3. The racial hierarchy in the United States could not have been built and sustained without the active and passive support of millions of Christians. Why do you think so many Christians have supported racial injustice throughout US history?

4. What are some ways racial dynamics changed in the United States during the civil rights movement? What are some ways they stayed the same?

5. Can you think of a current dynamic in our society that has been influenced by one of the historical examples?

6. Read the list of tactics used to build and sustain the racial hierarchy. Can you think of other examples throughout history where those tactics have been used?

7. Why is truth telling essential in order to make progress toward racial justice? How can you promote truth telling in the relationships and groups you are a part of?

8. How do you plan to apply the content in this chapter?

Recommended Prayer

Forgive our nation and the Christian church when we have stood for greed, corruption, and exploitation rather than compassion, honesty, and justice. Give us wisdom, strength, and courage to promote your righteousness and justice in our society. Give us eyes to see what we can do and the willingness to do it. We recognize in our own strength we will never be able to change the powerful religious, economic, and political forces that continue to perpetuate injustice. We need your help. Please move, by your grace, and change the unjust systems that produce devastation in so many people's lives. Please allow justice to roll down like waters and righteousness like an ever-flowing stream (Amos 5:24). Amen.

CHAPTER FIVE

FAITHFUL ANTIRACISTS UNDERSTAND OUR PRESENT

ON AUGUST 31, 1962, A GROUP of seventeen Black neighbors traveled from Ruleville to Indianola, Mississippi, to register to vote. When they arrived at the county building, all of the passengers were denied the right to register. Demoralized, they began their return trip. On the ride home, their bus was stopped by police and the bus driver arrested. The reason provided by the police was their bus was too yellow. As the passengers nervously waited to find out if they would be jailed, or worse, one of the women on the bus began to sing.

> This little light of mine
> I'm gonna let it shine
> This little light of mine
> I'm gonna let it shine
> This little light of mine
> I'm gonna let it shine
> Let it shine,
> Let it shine,
> Let it shine
> Everywhere I go . . .
> I've got the light of freedom . . .
> Jesus gave it to me, now . . .
> Shine, shine, shine, shine . . .
> All in the jailhouse . . .[1]

When the passengers scraped together enough money to pay the driver's fine, they were allowed to return home. The woman who began the song was Fannie Lou Hamer, one of the great champions for justice during the civil rights movement.[2]

Fannie Lou Hamer traveled across the United States speaking in church after church. She gave powerful challenges that inspired disenfranchised Black Americans to register to vote.

> Her magnificent voice rolled through the chapel as she enlisted the Biblical ranks of martyrs and heroes to summon these folk to the Freedom banner. Her mounting, rolling battery of quotations and allusions from the Old and New Testaments stunned the audience with its thunder.[3]

Overviews of the history of racial dynamics in the United States (like the ones in this book) often focus on statistics and major events. Those details are important, but it is also important to know the "behind the scenes" stories of courageous individuals like Fannie Lou Hamer. The progress that has been made toward racial justice in the United States has been accomplished through their prayers, courage, blood, sweat, and tears. As faithful antiracists, we have the privilege of walking in their footsteps.

LOOKING AT MORE RECENT EVENTS

In this chapter, we will pick up where we left off in the last chapter and focus on more recent events and dynamics. Some readers may find this chapter more difficult because the closer we get to our current context, the more it impacts us personally. If this section is difficult for you, we encourage you to not tune it out. When we are presented with uncomfortable facts or views we disagree with, there's a strong temptation to skip that section or walk away. With modern technology, we can filter any voices that don't agree with our perspectives, but that only perpetuates groupthink and confirmation bias. Be brave and teachable enough to consider different perspectives.

Keep in mind, it is much easier to see injustice in previous generations than it is in ourselves. There are very few, if any, Christians who currently attempt to justify slavery or hate crimes by the KKK. Today it is easy for almost all of us to see those actions were immoral and against God's will. But at the time, many White Christians participated in, condoned, or passively supported them. Their moral compass was broken. It is essential for us to ask, What am I doing or supporting today that future generations will look back on and wonder why I couldn't see that it was evil? How is my moral compass broken in similar ways?

One of the patterns we hope you will recognize throughout these historical accounts is the tendency for people to justify injustice for their personal and collective gain. As John Newton, a slave trader who became a pastor and abolitionist, recognized, "The slave trade was always unjustifiable, but inattention and interest prevented for a time the evil from being perceived."[4] Tragically, "inattention and interest" continue to blind people to injustice today. When people, organizations, and governments are benefiting from injustice, they are willing to make incredible psychological and moral "accommodations" in order to attempt to justify those actions.

WHY WE ADDRESS POLITICS IN THIS BOOK

Few topics raise stronger emotions and opinions than politics. That is one of the reasons the topic is often avoided in books, discussions, and training programs on racial dynamics. Understandably, authors, training facilitators, and leaders do not want to deal with the controversy. But, as we saw in the previous chapter, politics have a very powerful impact on racial dynamics in our country. Therefore, we believe it is essential for Christians to understand past and present political dynamics and use our political influence wisely in order to effectively work toward racial justice. We believe we are doing a disservice to our readers if we ignore politics in this book.

One of the primary points we attempt to make is that we must not allow our political views or alliances to take precedence over the teachings of the Bible. As Pastor Tim Keller explains, we must avoid package-deal ethics.

Another reason Christians these days cannot allow the church to be fully identified with any particular party is the problem of what the British ethicist James Mumford calls "package-deal ethics." Increasingly, political parties insist that you cannot work on one issue with them if you don't embrace all of their approved positions. This emphasis on package deals puts pressure on Christians in politics.... So Christians are pushed toward two main options. One is to withdraw and try to be apolitical. The second is to assimilate and fully adopt one party's whole package in order to have your place at the table. Neither of these options is valid.[5]

Consider the following excerpt of a teaching by Jesus:

What comes out of a person is what defiles them. For it is from within, out of a person's heart, that evil thoughts come—sexual immorality, theft, murder, adultery, greed, malice, deceit, lewdness, envy, slander, arrogance and folly. All these evils come from inside and defile a person. (Mark 7:20-23)

Some of the items that Jesus mentioned may be emphasized by some political parties and other items not emphasized by any political party.

Table 5.1. Example emphases of political parties

Party 1 emphasizes	Party 2 emphasizes	Neither party emphasizes
Sexual immorality	Theft	Adultery
Murder	Greed	Malice
Lewdness	Deceit	Slander
Folly	Envy	Arrogance

Christians lose their ability to be salt and light in the world when they allow their political party or politicians to determine which social issues are important and a high priority. Which of the issues in table 5.1 are important? All of them. Which of the issues should Christians focus on? All of them.

A Few Key Events from the 1960s to Today

In the examples below, we again highlight economic, political, and religious forces to make it easier for readers to see how those forces are continuing to sustain racial injustice.

1960s–1970s: A tale of two friends. Evangelist Billy Graham and theologian Carl Henry were good friends and very influential leaders in the rise of evangelicalism in the 1960s and 1970s. David Neff, former editor of *Christianity Today*, said, "If we see Billy Graham as the great public face and generous spirit of the evangelical movement, Carl Henry was the brains."[6]

Henry has been described as "evangelicalism's theological architect."[7] Henry helped to start several influential evangelical organizations including Fuller Theological Seminary, the National Association of Evangelicals, and *Christianity Today*. Graham and Henry shared many things in common, but they had different approaches to social justice.

Carl Henry's stand for social justice was not flawless,[8] but generally speaking, he passionately advocated for Christians to confront social evils like racial hatred. For example, he gave a challenge at a gathering of evangelical pastors.

> [He asked] "How many of you, during the past six months, have preached a sermon devoted in large part to a condemnation of such social evils as aggressive warfare, racial hatred and intolerance, the liquor traffic, exploitation of labor or management, or the like—a sermon containing not merely an incidental or illustrative reference, but directed mainly against such evils and proposing the framework in which you think solution is possible?" Not a single hand was raised in response.[9]

In 1972, Henry was invited to attend Expo 72, a large evangelistic conference, but declined the offer after he learned that social justice would not be a focus. He wrote the conference organizer, "I am persuaded that evangelical evangelism today disadvantageously walks on crutches if it does not, along with the banner of grace, carry the flag also of truth, and of righteousness or justice, in the name of the Living God of revelation."[10]

In 1976, he wrote:

> Christian silence and inaction in the face of such miscarriage of God's purpose in government obscures much of what makes evangelical good news truly good. It needlessly thins the gospel to internal experience only. . . . It even encourages those who profess to speak in the name of justice, even if they may not truly know what justice is, to reject believers as socially insensitive, just as when Christians speak up some consider them politically dangerous. No Christian incisively proclaims that gospel unless he is as explicit and urgent about the justice God demands as he is about the justification God offers.[11]

Billy Graham's views on social justice were less clear. In 1952 he told a Jackson, Mississippi, newspaper, "We follow the existing social customs in whatever part of the country in which we minister. As far as I have been able to find in study of the Bible, it has nothing to say about segregation or nonsegregation. I came to Jackson only to preach the Bible and not to enter into local issues."[12] But the following year, he famously removed ropes dividing White and Black attendees during an evangelistic crusade. In 1957, he invited Martin Luther King Jr. to pray at one of his rallies. However, after King was arrested for protesting in 1961, Graham told reporters, "I am convinced that some extreme Negro leaders are going too far and too fast."[13]

As Graham's ministry extended across the United States, so did his political involvement and influence. In 1967, Graham encouraged Richard Nixon to run for president while they were on vacation together. Although Graham (who described himself as a Democrat who voted independently) never officially endorsed Nixon, he made favorable statements about him during his campaign. For example, during a Portland Crusade in May 1968 he introduced Nixon's wife and stated, "There is no American I admire more than Richard Nixon."[14]

During the 1960s to 1980s, many evangelicals began to be more politically engaged. For example, a strong political alliance was formed between White Christians and Republicans through the efforts of Jerry Falwell, who founded the Moral Majority. Ironically, Billy Graham spoke out about the dangers of the alliance. In a 1981 interview he explained, "It would disturb me if there was a wedding between the religious fundamentalists and the political right. The hard right has no interest in religion except to manipulate it."[15] In a 2011 interview Graham was asked, "If you could, would you go back and do anything differently?" Graham explained, "I . . . would have steered clear of politics. I'm grateful for the opportunities God gave me to minister to people in high places; people in power have spiritual and personal needs like everyone else. . . . But looking back, I know I sometimes crossed the line, and I wouldn't do that now."[16]

1971: Nixon attacks "hippies and Black people" through a "war on drugs." During his campaign, Nixon criticized the civil rights movement and claimed that their leaders were causing anarchy and unrest. With the strong support of Billy Graham and other evangelical leaders, Nixon received 69 percent of the evangelical vote in 1968 and 84 percent of the evangelical vote in 1972.[17] In 1971, Nixon declared a "war on drugs." His domestic policy chief, John Ehrlichman, later explained that they were actually targeting hippies and Black people:

> We knew we couldn't make it illegal to be either against the war or blacks, but by getting the public to associate the hippies with marijuana and blacks with heroin and then criminalizing both heavily, we could disrupt those communities. We could arrest their leaders, raid their homes, break up their meetings, and vilify them night after night on the evening news. Did we know we were lying about the drugs? Of course we did.[18]

Recorded conversations in the Oval Office in 1971 revealed Nixon's prejudice toward African Americans and Mexican Americans:

> We're going to [put] more of these little Negro bastards on the welfare rolls at $2,400 a family. . . . I have the greatest affection for [blacks], but I know they're not going to make it for 500 years. They aren't. You know it, too. The Mexicans are a different cup of tea. They have a heritage. At the present time they steal, they're dishonest, but they do have some concept of family life. They don't live like a bunch of dogs, which the Negroes do live like.[19]

1978: School integration galvanizes evangelical political involvement.
One of the primary issues that galvanized White evangelicals as a political force during the 1960s–1970s was school integration.

The IRS's guidelines about racial integration in 1978 sparked national outrage among many Christian conservatives. Department officials as well as members of Congress received tens of thousands of messages in protest. In an interview Weyrich explained, "What galvanized the Christian community was not abortion, school prayer, or the [Equal Rights Amendment] . . . What changed their minds was Jimmy Carter's intervention against the Christian schools, trying to deny them tax-exempt status on the basis of so-called de facto segregation." While it would be wrong to suggest that racist resistance to integration was the single issue that held the Religious Right together in these years, it clearly provided an initial charge that electrified the movement.[20]

1970s–1980s: Coded racism is used to gain political support. Political strategists recognized the effectiveness of using "coded racism" to motivate White voters to support political candidates. Lee Atwater served as a campaign strategist for Ronald Reagan and George H. W. Bush. He became the Chair of the Republican National Committee in 1988. In a 1981 interview with a political science professor that he thought was off the record, Atwater explained how focusing on economic and political policies can be used as coded racism. Here is an excerpt of the interview:

> You start out in 1954 by saying nig——, nig——, nig——. By 1968 you can't say nig——: that hurts you, backfires. So you say stuff like forced busing, states' rights, and all that stuff, and you're getting so abstract. Now, you're talking about cutting taxes, and all these things you're talking about are totally economic things and the byproduct of them is, blacks get hurt worse than whites. And, subconsciously maybe that is part of it. I'm not saying that. But I'm saying that if it is getting that abstract and that coded, uh, that we are doing away with the racial problem one way or the other.[21]

1970s–1980s: Reagan condemns "welfare queens" and escalates the "war on drugs." During his 1976 election campaign, Ronald Reagan frequently referred to an African American woman he alleged was gaming the welfare system.

> There's a woman in Chicago. She has 80 names, 30 addresses, 12 Social Security cards and is collecting veterans' benefits on four nonexisting deceased husbands . . . And she's collecting Social Security on her cards. She's got Medicaid, getting food stamps and she is collecting welfare under each of her names. Her tax-free cash income alone is over $150,000.[22]

At the time, reporters looked into the details of the woman's case and determined she was charged with fraud of $3,000 (not $150,000).[23] But, regardless of the facts, Reagan used attacks on the "welfare queen" and poor and Black people to fuel his rise in politics. Reagan was elected in 1980, in large part due to the support of White evangelicals. Jerry Falwell described the election of Reagan as "my finest hour."[24]

One of the central focuses of Reagan's presidency was a "war on drugs." The war on drugs disproportionately targeted Black men for strict enforcement and harsh sentencing.[25] To enforce the war on drugs, the budgets for law enforcement were dramatically increased.

> Practically overnight the budgets of federal law enforcement agencies soared. Between 1980 and 1984, FBI antidrug funding increased from $8 million to $95 million. Department of Defense antidrug allocations increased from $33 million in 1981 to $1,042 million in 1991. During that same period, DEA antidrug spending grew from $86 to $1,026 million, and FBI antidrug allocations grew from $38 to $181 million. By contrast, funding for agencies responsible for drug treatment, prevention, and education was dramatically reduced. The budget of the National Institute on Drug Abuse, for example, was reduced from $274 million to $57 million from 1981 to 1984, and antidrug funds allocated to the Department of Education were cut from $14 million to $3 million.[26]

1994: Clinton signs the largest crime bill in US history (which was written by Joe Biden). A decade later, Bill Clinton also recognized the political power of being "tough on crime." Clinton followed through on his campaign vow that no Republican would be tougher on crime than he. In 1994 he signed the largest crime bill in US history. The bill was written by Joe Biden (a senator at the time). The Clinton administration's policies proved devastating for people of color.

> As the Justice Policy Institute has observed, "the Clinton Administration's 'tough on crime' policies resulted in the largest increases in federal and state prison inmates of any president in American history." . . . In so doing, Clinton—more than any other president—created the current racial undercaste . . . During Clinton's tenure, Washington slashed funding for public housing by $17 billion (a reduction of 61 percent) and boosted corrections by $19 billion (an increase of 171 percent), "effectively making the construction of prisons the nation's main housing program for the urban poor."[27]

Criminal justice policies by the US government over the last sixty years have led to huge disparities in incarceration rates for Black and Hispanic people. As Michelle Alexander wrote in 2012:

> More African American adults are under correctional control today—in prison or jail, on probation or parole—than were enslaved in 1850, a decade before the Civil War began. The mass incarceration of people of color is a big part of the reason that a black child born today is less likely to be raised by both parents than a black child born during slavery. The absence of black fathers from families across America is not simply a function of laziness, immaturity, or too much time watching Sports Center. Thousands of black men have disappeared into prisons and jails, locked away for drug crimes that are largely ignored when committed by whites.[28]

1995–2021: Fox News Channel influences many Christians' understanding of racial dynamics. Fox News Channel (FNC) was launched in 1995. Since that time it has become one of the most popular news sources for Christians. In our 2019 RRJP survey, we asked respondents which news outlets they believed provided the most reliable information. 53% of Christians selected the FNC followed by CNN (32%), *New York Times* (18%), and MSNBC (18%). By racial group, we found 58% of White Christians, 49% of Hispanic/Latino Christians, 38% of Black Christians, and 48% of Asian Christians believed that FNC provided the most reliable information.

Unfortunately, the programming on FNC frequently presents inaccurate and misleading information on racial dynamics. The information is often presented in the form of an urgent warning about how our country is being attacked by evil actions motivated by political agendas. The following is an example from FNC's *Tucker Carlson Tonight*, currently one of the most viewed cable news shows in the nation.[29] In the show, aired on September 2, 2020, Carlson opens with a clip of a Catholic mass where a priest leads a responsive prayer "denouncing White privilege." Carlson then states, "Wow, that's 2020 in 20 seconds. This is a religion. The left has won. For years they have tried to replace God with political orthodoxy, and now they've succeeded."[30] Later in the segment, Carlson nods in agreement as his guest explains,

The people who are using these new terms 'systemic racism' or 'white privilege,' these are Marxists. These people not only don't believe in God, they hate God. . . . When you're using these kinds of terms I want to say to every pastor, every Christian in America, this is something, if you do not reject this with everything you have you are bringing about the death of Christian faith in America.

With programming like the example above, it is not surprising that our research has shown that Christians who trust FNC typically have less accurate racial views and less motivation to address racial injustice than Christians who do not trust FNC. Figure 5.1 shows a few examples from our RRJP survey.[31]

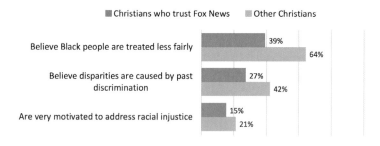

Figure 5.1. Christians who trust Fox News in comparison to other Christians (RRJP Survey, July/Aug 2019, n=2797)

2011–2021: Trump's political career powerfully impacts racial dynamics in the United States. The relationship between US Christianity, race relations, and the political career and presidency of Donald Trump is a complex topic that is well beyond the scope of this book. However, we believe the following are some important realities to be aware of.

Trump's words and actions have supported racial injustice and prejudice. In 2011, Donald Trump began his political career by leading the "birther" movement, which questioned whether President Barack Obama was born in the United States.[32] When Trump announced his presidential candidacy in 2015, he declared he would build a wall between the United States and Mexico and demand that Mexico pay for it. He stated, "When Mexico sends its people, they're not sending their best. . . . They're bringing drugs. They're bringing crime. They're rapists. And some, I assume, are good people."[33] As president, in a meeting about immigration with top officials, Trump asked why the United States should accept more immigrants from "s—-hole" countries such as Haiti and countries in Africa.[34] When NFL players took a knee to protest racial injustice he called them "sons of b——-" and said they should be fired.[35] Trump frequently referred to Covid-19 as the "Chinese virus" and "Kung flu" even though it encouraged anti-Asian sentiment.[36] On June 1, 2020, Trump gave a speech at the White House where he described individuals protesting for racial justice as "anarchists, violent mobs, arsonists, looters, criminals, rioters, antifa, and others."[37] Trump frequently criticized antiracism training as divisive and unpatriotic and worked to remove it from the government and schools.[38]

Many Christians of color are frustrated by the high percentage of White Christians who support Trump. White Christians, especially White evangelicals, continue to provide some of Trump's most faithful and enthusiastic support. According to national polls, Trump received 81 percent of the White evangelical vote in the 2016 presidential election[39] and 81 percent in the 2020 presidential election.[40] In our 2019 RRJP survey, 61% of White Christians, 32% of Hispanic/Latino Christians, 8% of Black Christians, and 48% of Asian Christians indicated that they voted for Trump in 2016. With our research, Christians of color often express pain and frustration over the high percentage of White Christians who have supported Trump. One of our respondents had this to say:

> There was a large, white, Christian voter turn-out for Donald Trump and people of color have been suffering from a rise in hate crimes since the election. However, when this statement is brought up in social settings (both online and in person) with facts and examples, Christians are always the first to pull out a Bible quote to either justify the hate crime or to say that everyone is equally wrong and we all just need to love each other, thereby completely ignoring the hurt of entire populations of people. (Hispanic, female, 20s) [41]

Trump has influenced many Christians' belief in facts and truth. Unfortunately, it is not uncommon for politicians to bend the truth. But Trump has been especially prolific in making statements that are not true. The *Washington Post* documented 30,573 false or misleading claims by Trump during his presidency.[42] That is more than twenty false or misleading claims a day. Seminary professor Karen Swallow Prior described her concerns about Trump's impact on the concept of truth:

> [Donald Trump] is a textbook example of a demagogue, a leader who appeals to the masses by tapping into common fears and prejudices and employing false promises and disinformation to gain power. One of a demagogue's primary tool's is gaslighting, a form of manipulation which includes reversing then denying previous words and actions, making it difficult to distinguish truth from lies. . . . Trump is the embodiment of the Nietzschean will to power that replaces truth within a postmodern mindset, the very worldview Christians used to warn about. Because he operates in a post-truth reality, truth isn't even a category, and thus lies can't exist.[43]

Some readers may ask, "The Democrats say things that are false and misleading, as well. Why are you focusing on Trump?" We agree that both Democrats and Republicans make false and misleading statements, but we are focusing on Trump in this book because of the strong support he received from many Christians and the many ways he has propagated misinformation and perpetuated racism.

Trump has frequently denied racial realities. Throughout his political career, Trump has repeatedly denied past and present racial realities. For example, in an interview on June 18, 2020, Bob Woodward and Trump had the following exchange:

> **Woodward:** "We share one thing in common. We're White, privileged. . . . My father was a lawyer and a judge in Illinois, and we know what your dad did. Do you have any sense that that privilege has isolated and put you in a cave to a certain extent, as it put me, and I think lots of White, privileged people in a cave? And that we have to work our way out of it to understand the anger and the pain particularly Black people feel in this country?"

> **Trump:** "No. You really drank the Kool-Aid, didn't you? Just listen to you. Wow. No, I don't feel that at all."[44]

Trump's political career has demonstrated the influence of Fox News. Since its founding in 1995, Fox News has had a powerful influence on US elections.[45] The 2016 election of Trump was a clear example. Fox News provided some of Trump's strongest and most consistent support. A 2016 Pew Study found that individuals who voted for Trump named Fox News as their "main source for news about the 2016 campaign" five times more frequently than any other news source.[46] A 2019–2020 Pew Study found, "Fox News consumers tend to have an especially positive view of the president." Our 2019 RRJP survey found that a high percentage of individuals who voted for Trump in 2016 also indicated that they trust Fox News, including 77% of White Christians, 68% of Hispanic/Latino Christians, 66% of Black Christians, and 55% of Asian Christians.

2021: The impact of the Biden presidency remains to be determined. At the time we are writing, the Biden presidency is in its first year. Biden has stated that his role in the creation of the 1994 crime bill was a "mistake."[47] During his candidacy, he acknowledged the reality of systemic racial injustice in our country. In his inaugural speech, Biden denounced white supremacy and declared that working toward racial justice would be a primary emphasis for his administration.[48]

Unfortunately, the Biden administration already has a mixed record when it comes to racial justice. For example, on January 26, 2021, Biden signed an executive order aiming to end the use of private prisons by the Justice Department, but it did not apply to private facilities contracted by the Department of Homeland Security to detain immigrants.[49]

On September 21, 2021, leaders of thirty-nine human and civil rights organizations challenged the Biden administration's handling of Haitian asylum seekers at the US-Mexico border and the continued use of private prisons. They wrote:

> We fear that commitments made on the campaign trail—to uphold the United States' domestic and international legal obligation to asylum, to end privatized detention, and to disentangle federal immigration enforcement from local law enforcement—are being shredded before our eyes . . . your Administration, like its predecessors, is utilizing harsh and illegal policies to attempt to deter people, particularly Black migrants, from seeking refuge at the border.

Your Administration has promised to uphold tenets of racial equity, but is unleashing immigration policies infused with anti-Black racism.[50]

As the above examples show, having a presidential administration that is more supportive of racial justice efforts does not eliminate the need to hold the administration accountable for its actions. It is essential for Christians to continue to stand for racial justice at local, state, and national levels regardless of which political party is in power.

COMMON BARRIERS TO RACIAL JUSTICE EFFORTS TODAY

In chapter one, we explored several barriers to racial justice efforts by Christians today, including nonstructural understandings of racial disparities and viewing racial injustice as a lower priority than other moral issues. The following are a few of the many additional barriers that are common in our society today.

New (old) forms of opposition. In chapter four, we looked at a variety of forces that opposed racial justice efforts from the 1600s to the 1900s. Unfortunately, similar forces continue to be very active in our society. As you reread this list from chapter four, consider, What are some examples of these forces today? Why haven't they gone away?

- *Fear-driven rhetoric.* People were told they must support the racial hierarchy or they would be attacked or oppressed by people of color. They were told their only options were between white dominance and chaos, instability, and the overthrow of society.

- *Violence.* Physical violence through hate groups, mobs, military, private/local militias, police, and more was used as a public display of power meant to strike fear into anyone that challenged white dominance.

- *Psychological manipulation.* Pro-White and anti-Black (and other persons of color) propaganda was communicated through avenues such as preaching and sermons, school lessons, political speeches, news media, and entertainment.

- *Economics.* Economic practices that advantaged White people were created, strengthened, or expanded.

- *Politics.* Laws and political policies that advantaged White people were created, strengthened, or expanded at national, state, and local levels.

- *Religion.* Religious leaders ignored or minimized the Bible's teachings on social justice. In some cases, they also provided "biblical support" for white superiority and the racial hierarchy.

Superficial support. If you talk with someone about racism, it is likely that they will share with you evidence that they are not a racist person nor contributing to racism. Their evidence may be an action they have been a part of, for example, "Our business hires a number of Black people" or "We adopted a child from another country." It may be a declaration of their lack of prejudice, for example, "I don't have a racist bone in my body" or "I don't even see color." Or it can be a person or group they are associated with, for example, "My sister-in-law's father is Hispanic" or "Our church is one of the most racially diverse in our city." Those types of statements are often an attempt to communicate, "See, I can't be a racist person because of ___." It is possible for the above items to be true while the person still harbors racial prejudice and sustains racial injustice. Superficial actions and verbalized support for racial justice that does not translate into substantive, effective action often hinders rather than promotes progress. That is why we chose the subtitle *Moving Past Talk to Systemic Change* for this book.

Tokenism. Tokenism is a common type of superficial support. Tokenism refers to symbolic gestures used to demonstrate "progress" rather than more substantive, systemic, and sacrificial changes. For example, tokenism often takes place within the leadership structures of organizations. Individuals who are not in the majority are selected for leadership teams and committees, but they are not given the authority to produce significant changes within the organization. We will explore that more in chapter eight. Tokenism provides a misleading sense of progress, and it can be used to justify not taking additional, more effective action.

Political allegiances that take precedence over the teachings of the Bible. Many Christians are unaware of how powerfully their political views affect their moral views. A recent study of the influence of political views on religious beliefs found:

> The single biggest takeaway [from our study] is that your partisanship or your political outlooks can actually affect religious decisions that individuals make. So rather than thinking about religion

affecting politics, how you view the political world and what party you align with can shape religious decisions and how active you want to be in a religious community and which community you want to be involved in.[51]

In other words, if people have to choose between their religious views and political views, they often choose their political views. When that takes place, political leaders or media outlets can take on the role of pastors and spiritual mentors for Christians. Politicians and media outlets shape the person's views and actions as much, or more so, than their Christian faith or the Bible. This tragically common scenario is one of the primary reasons many Christians continue to support racial injustice, even when they are presented with Scripture that should motivate them to do otherwise.

Bothsidesing. In this chapter, we have shared examples of both Republicans and Democrats supporting racial injustice. Many individuals use that reality to justify supporting any political candidate. For example, they may say, "See, both political parties have a bad track record on racial justice. Therefore, I choose the politicians I vote for based on other criteria like ___." That type of argument is sometimes referred to as *bothsidesing* or *both-sides-ism*. According to bothsidesing, "Both sides are not perfect. Therefore it is wrong to judge either side. It doesn't really matter which side you choose." Bothsidesing is often based on the false idea that both parties and all political leaders have equally supported racial injustice, but that is not the case. In order to be effective faithful antiracists, we must take the time to learn about the views and actions of political

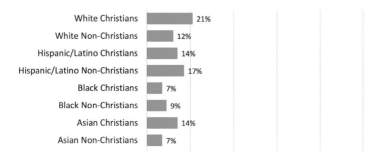

Figure 5.2. Respondents who selected "I don't believe it is true that Black people have lower jobs, housing, and income" (RRJP Survey, July/Aug 2019, n=2797)

parties and candidates and not assume, "All of them are equally good or bad choices."

Denial of racial realities. When we facilitate training on racial dynamics, it is common for some participants to question the accuracy of the information we are sharing, even when it is based on reliable historical sources and current research. They will often mention experiences they had in the past (e.g., "I attended a diverse school when I was growing up") or information they read in a book, heard in a talk, or watched on a media outlet. They have "alternative facts" that make it very difficult for them to accept what we are sharing.

We also frequently observe a denial of racial realities with our research. For example, in our 2019 RRJP survey, we asked, "Based on statistics, on average Black people have lower quality jobs, housing, and income than White people. Why do you think this is?" Figure 5.2 shows the percent of respondents who selected *I don't believe it is true*. Notice that White and Asian Christians were nearly twice as likely to select this option as non-Christians in their racial group.

It is very difficult to help individuals grow in their understanding of past and present racial dynamics in the United States if they refuse to accept information that does not align with what "they know is true." We find that denial of facts, motivated reasoning, and groupthink are powerful barriers that prevent many Christians from supporting racial justice efforts.

Christian nationalism. Christian nationalism is an important, complex, and emotional topic, which can easily fill a book on its own. For an explanation of the concept we recommend the article "What is Christian Nationalism?" by Paul Miller. In summary,

> Christian nationalism is the belief that the American nation is defined by Christianity, and that the government should take active steps to keep it that way. Popularly, Christian nationalists assert that America is and must remain a "Christian nation"—not merely as an observation about American history, but as a prescriptive program for what America must continue to be in the future. . . . Christian nationalism takes the name of Christ for a worldly political agenda,

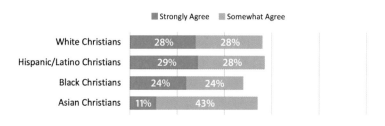

Figure 5.3. Respondents who agreed with the statement "The federal government should declare the United States a Christian nation" (Barna Group, Jan/Feb 2021, n=2007)

proclaiming that its program is the political program for every true believer. That is wrong in principle, no matter what the agenda is, because only the church is authorized to proclaim the name of Jesus and carry his standard into the world. It is even worse with a political movement that champions some causes that are unjust, which is the case with Christian nationalism and its attendant illiberalism. In that case, Christian nationalism is calling evil good and good evil; it is taking the name of Christ as a fig leaf to cover its political program, treating the message of Jesus as a tool of political propaganda and the church as the handmaiden and cheerleader of the state.[52]

There is a strong connection between Christian nationalism, White nationalism, and racism. Unfortunately, Christian nationalism is currently very common in the United States, especially among evangelicals. Researchers Andrew Whitehead and Samuel Perry estimate 40 percent of evangelicals are "ambassadors" (active advocates) for Christian nationalism and 38 percent are "accommodators" (passively supportive) of Christian nationalism.[53]

A study conducted in early 2021 by the Barna Group confirmed that a large percent of Christians hold views that align with Christian nationalism. Figure 5.3 is one example. It shows the percentage of Christian respondents who agreed with the statement "The federal government should declare the United States a Christian nation." Notice that approximately half of the Christians in all racial groups agreed with that statement.

Label, mischaracterize, dismiss. Oftentimes, efforts to promote racial justice are opposed using a "label, mischaracterize, dismiss" approach. Here is an example:

> Teresa says to a Christian friend, "I just heard a great sermon on how Jesus' command to love our neighbor should motivate us to work toward racial justice."
>
> Christian friend: "I would be careful with that whole social justice movement."
>
> Teresa: "What do you mean?"
>
> Christian friend: "I've heard that the leaders who are pushing for social justice are really motivated by socialism and Marxism."
>
> Teresa: "Really?"
>
> Christian friend: "Yes, it's scary stuff. I think it is best that we stick with the gospel and not fall into those types of traps."

Notice that Teresa's Christian friend did not ask for more details about the sermon or the Bible passages that the pastor used. She didn't provide an explanation why those Bible passages were being interpreted incorrectly or in harmful ways. She made the case that the sermon was a part of a movement (labeling), the movement was motivated by socialism/Marxism (mischaracterization), and therefore it should be avoided (dismissing). The "label, mischaracterize, dismiss" approach has been frequently used throughout US history to support the racial hierarchy. It hinders teachability and prevents honest, productive dialogue on important issues like racial justice.

THE OBSTACLES ARE LARGE AND COMPLEX, BUT WE CAN OVERCOME THEM

Every generation of individuals who have worked for racial justice have faced large, complex barriers that are similar, and even greater, than the ones described above. Fortunately it is possible to overcome them. We will look at ways to do so throughout the remainder of this book.

Discussion/Reflection Questions

1. In what ways do politics influence racial dynamics in our country?

2. Why is it easier to see injustice in previous generations than in our own generation?

3. We briefly looked at some differences between Carl Henry's and Billy Graham's approaches to social justice in the 1950s. Do you think that either of their approaches was more aligned with the Bible? If so, why?

4. We looked at some ways that economics, politics, and religious forces have sustained racial injustice. How are those forces interrelated and interdependent?

5. Can you think of a current dynamic in our society today that has been influenced by one of the historical events that were mentioned?

6. We looked at some common obstacles to racial justice today. Have you experienced those obstacles in your life or organization?

7. How do you plan to apply the content in this chapter?

Recommended Prayer

Please give us an accurate understanding of the past and present realities in our country. Help us to see the realities as you see them. Help us to be able to discern truth from lies. We confess the many ways that Christians in the United States have not followed your will in regard to love, mercy, and justice. Please forgive those sins and bring righteousness, justice, and restoration to our country and Christian communities. Please give us the faith, courage, love, and determination that are required to bring about racial justice in our society. Please show us the path we need to take and give us the strength we need to take it. Help us to shine your light to the world.

CHAPTER SIX

FAITHFUL ANTIRACISTS UNDERSTAND RACIAL TRAUMA

NOTE TO READERS: *The content in this chapter was written by Christina unless noted otherwise. We felt she was best equipped to address this topic because of her doctorate in counseling psychology and her extensive experience working with trauma victims.*

Something seemed to tap Michael on his shoulder, gently compelling him to leave his college campus and check on his family. There, in a small, wooden-framed house in a Baltimore alleyway, he was greeted by his deeply distressed mother. Earlier that day, Michael's grandmother, Madessa, had been assaulted with a brick by an intruder in their family home. Michael's mother sent her two sons to the university hospital to check on their beloved and deeply injured grandmother. Accompanied by his ten-year-old brother, they made their way to the university hospital. They left the environment of crushing and vulnerable poverty to enter into the unknown medical center. The receptionist in the integrated hospital gestured for them to go to the basement to find their loved one. Their beloved grandmother lay still, with stitches on her head and forehead without any bandaging and barely a blanket to keep warm.

Michael is my father. Memories escape him about all that followed that day, but he can still hear the cries and wails of his twenty-year-old self and ten-year-old brother. Madessa survived, but their family was changed. Within a year Madessa would die of pneumonia after a year of mental decline that was likely related to the untreated brain injury in the hospital that day. My father, reflecting on that tragic day, lamented, "They treated my grandmother, your great-grandmother, worse than a dog."

In this chapter, we will explore the complex and important topic of racial trauma. First, let's cover a few key terms.

- *Psychological trauma*: The result of an event or multiple events or circumstances that are experienced as physically or emotionally threatening or deleterious, which has lasting effects on an individual's functioning or well-being.[1]

- *Cultural trauma*: A collective or communal response to a shared life-threatening and identity-altering event that metaphorically leaves the group timestamped and directionally rerouted. The event has become a part of the group's cultural story. In other words, the group's sense of collective consciousness is bookmarked with a *before and after trauma* page holder.[2]

- *Racial trauma*: The cumulative effects of personal and systemic racism. Remember, racism is race-based discrimination and stratification produced by racial prejudice and social power. Racial trauma impacts mental, physical, and spiritual well-being and health.[3]

INTRODUCTORY EXERCISE

1. Think of a moment from your life's history marked by a cultural trauma. Some people may recall an assassination of an influential leader, a social uprising, a terrorist attack, a pandemic, or even repeated images of death on social media.

2. Do you remember where you were during this moment? What else was happening? How did it make you feel and how do you feel now as you reflect on the event?

3. In what ways did this event reframe how you see the world and yourself?

4. Take a moment to pray for the faith and love to be able to empathize with others overwhelmed by cultural traumas.

PAIN, FROZEN IN TIME

I remember exactly where I was when I discovered . . .

Rodney was beaten;
Tamir was shot;
Sandra never left the cell.

Like a polaroid camera photo, stopping time and freeze-framing us in the pain, shock, and anger, trauma truly captures a moment. By capture I mean holds it hostage. Yet at the same time, it's *almost* funny how traumatic moments can offer incomplete memories. The oddest things at times are retained, like the smell of a room, the sound of shoes clicking down a hall, or the taste of the last meal you had eaten. On the other hand, a facial feature might be a blur or time of day is irretrievable.

I can still remember the way the trees shaded the walkway and the fluorescent lights bounced off the cash register in the department store where I experienced blatant personal racism as a teenager. A White woman, angered that her credit card was declined, muttered the "N-word" at the teenaged me. In that moment, I was beckoned back to when a White police officer threatened my group of Black elementary school friends with physical force for playing outside. He matter-of-factly stated, "You know I have the right to beat you," with his hands on his hips, one placed near his walkie talkie and the other near his gun. That was his response after a call from a neighbor about a group of kids laughing in front of our apartment building after school let out. Yet even before these events of my youth, in the first grade I had experienced a group of White boys chasing and taunting me as I ran home in what was supposed to be a "good" integrated suburban neighborhood in Columbia, Maryland.

These types of events plucked from my fairly limited direct experiences with White Americans as a kid growing up in Baltimore, Maryland, are less severe, frequent, and enduring than many of my peers. Maybe you have your own stories? Even as you read my memories, your stories and emotions start bubbling up. Maybe stories were passed like hand-me-down clothes from one generation to another. Like the one I received from my father about his grandmother, left alone with a bloody, bandaged head in the hallway of a segregated hospital where she would later die. That story would tap me on my shoulder as I trained in a medical center, oftentimes only acknowledged in the hallways by the mostly older, African American janitorial staff.

For some readers, your memories may relate to the other side of the story—the chasing school kids, the angry customer, the power-drunk officer, or the disconnected and aloof White hospital staff was a family member, respected mentor, or even you. Maybe as you hear these stories, you find yourself torn about where to place empathy based on who is most like you in the narrative. Our lack of empathy and disbelief only work to further cement and traumatize others, yet it is so easy to do. Christian empathy is risky in a racist society because it demands we humanize others and treat them as we would want to be treated. Christian empathy isn't merely a feeling but a social and political response to suffering.

Finally these experiences build on each other, creating a compounded racial trauma wall. Brick by brick, memory by memory, indignity by indignity—erecting a wall of guardedness, false identity, or anxiety. While we all have experiences of mistreatment and pain, targeted trauma based on stagnant factors—characteristics that will not change within our social context—offer an additional burden. While it is very true that I will not always be an elementary schooler, retail worker, or resident of a certain neighborhood, I will always be African American, a cultural marker and racial category that won't change and I would not want to change. However, this also means that the variable that made me a target is with me every day, as a daily reminder reinforced by vicarious racial trauma experiences in the media and among friends and neighbors.

Examples from Research

Understandably, people do not open up about racial trauma experiences unless they are having a conversation with someone they trust. Therefore it can be difficult to capture the extent of racial trauma with traditional research methods like online surveys. We found a few exceptions, one recounted below.

I have experienced a lot of 'joking around' concerning my race and the culture I identify with. I actually had a situation freshman year in which the girls on my floor were joking around about my race and it ended up hurting me very badly. They were talking in the group text and just making jokes about me being Asian (as if it's supposed to be something I'm ashamed or unaware of) and it ended up being so hurtful to me I cried. Other than that specific situation it is mostly people just calling me Asian, then when I call them White they get offended. It's slightly amusing but mostly annoying. (Asian, female, under 20)

RACIAL TRAUMA SHAPES PEOPLE

Trauma happens when an experience results in a psychological impact that seems to reshape personality and mood, physiological functioning, and future decisions. All forms of untreated and persistent psychological trauma cause us to see the world through changed lenses; these lenses are now cracked, barbed, or muddied. While our emotional sight is distorted it's possible that our emotional hearing is heightened, as tone, silence, and rhetoric are megaphone loud, popping into our psyche even while we long for stillness and escape. Exhausted by it all, longing to just be, we can find ourselves inescapably paranoid and hypervigilant, or numb and even self-loathing. The external world around us may read our trauma and wounds as performative or insincere, especially when the catalyst of the pain complicates their own story, identity, or privileges.

When crisis, confusion, or trauma happens, the brain longs for answers: "Why me?" "Why us?" Our psyche is a meaning-making machine that fills in the blanks with what it already knows and assumes. For Christians, the call to renew our minds with the truth is both a biblical exhortation and, from a clinical standpoint, the beginning of a reparative response to sin's distortive work and burden. Responding to trauma without an acceptance of the truth is not only ineffective but, at worst, retraumatizing.

As humans, we distinctly make meaning and use story to ground and root ourselves in reality. I believe storytelling is a communicable attribute of God. In other words, the Creator of all things also created story, and those made in God's image are both a part of God's story and also storytellers. We tell stories about ourselves and the world using creative materials like voice, body, and art. Even the parts that we dare not utter, personally or socially, become a loud blank chapter in our storybook. Yet unlike the God of the eternal story, only some of our stories are truth, while others are convenient or socially imposed lies. People of color who are traumatized by systemic and personal racism piece together narratives—borrowing from inherited stories, filling in holes with numbness or self-blame, and making meaning while attempting to cope.

Clinically speaking, trauma results in a change in how we relate to ourselves, others, and our vocations after the painful event(s). Trauma doesn't replace the original us, although it can seem that looming and powerful. Rather, it places a before-and-after page holder in our stories. For me, this divider separated a childhood of racial ignorance from a childhood with lived knowledge that Black people were mistreated, ignored, and/or vilified in the world.[4] This is a page holder that was placed in my very early childhood. Where is the page holder of racial trauma located in your story? Is there a place holder of racial awareness? Or racial injustice? Or racial privilege? How long did you move through your story of life and meaning-making before that page holder appeared?

Our encounters with severe racial trauma, like being threatened or attacked personally because of one's racial group, often leave the residue of feeling trapped, having recurring nightmares, panic attacks, irritability, hypervigilance, and even depression. These symptoms mirror post-traumatic stress and acute stress disorders.[5] Trauma is so pervasive and impactful that indirect traumatic experiences via what is known as *secondary trauma* can leave us demonstrating lesser but nevertheless agitating symptoms. Take, for example, the Black mother who is now reeling after watching a bereaved Black mother interviewed by the news networks about the death of an unarmed son playing in a park, shopping at a Walmart, or eating ice cream on his couch. Each story told by the media of police or communal violence picks at a painful scab or punches at a sore hip. The bereaved mother's raw grief-rich pain lights the fire of the observer, who now goes from deep empathy to surrogacy. She now carries an anticipatory trauma that impacts her world and parenting.

From generation to generation, the crimson fingerprint of racial trauma can change our self-identities, brain development, and social narratives.[6] The Western world, the United States specifically, has long groaned with the historical and present-day traumas of racialized injustice. It is a trauma often denied yet unavoidable in its historical, biological, systemic, and psychic scope. Trauma is not merely a difficult experience or encounter, but it is the "inescapable-ness," the loss of control and agency, and the dreaded near-death of personhood and purpose that grips the individual or community. I imagine this description seems so big that it is hopeless—but for generations people have coped to various degrees and often relied on faith for identity, freedom, and healing.

Racial Trauma and Christianity

In my mind's eye, I can vividly see the race riots of Oklahoma, Chicago, St. Petersburg, and Atlanta during the 1900s. These events are woven together for many families, spurring the Great Migration that caused my own family to journey from Mississippi to Maryland. Acclaimed psychologist the late Dr. Olivia Hooker tells of being a small girl during the riot and deadly assault on Tulsa's Black Wall Street district in the early 1920s.

A group of White men stormed her home where her mother and siblings stood in fear. In a fit of jealousy and covetousness, her family's beloved piano was broken into pieces by the White men after they gently removed and placed aside the Bible that was positioned on the top of the family's prized possession.

Dr. Hooker's family as well as hundreds of others were targeted because they were Black and middle class. The notion of the shared religion between the Black family and the White rioters protected an unopened Bible but not the family's property and the mind of a little Black Christian girl. The assault against the people and the city destroyed over thirty city blocks, leveled more than 1,200 homes, and took the lives of some 300 people. The governor declared martial law and utilized the National Guard to imprison every Black person that was not yet in jail.[7]

This sinful dance that white supremacy waltzes so boldly with Christianity, where it swaps Klan sheets for clergy robes, further pains and plagues the Christian of color. They, the traumatized Christian of color, find themselves seeking relief in the arms of Jesus of Nazareth, while being threatened, traumatized, or disbelieved by the "mythological Jesus" of nationalism and white supremacy. Consider for just a moment the depths of pain when one experiences trauma at the hands of a family member.

Significant segments of those who claim membership in God's family have traumatized or denied the trauma of other members of the family of believers. Not an enemy or a neighbor, but a so-called brother or sister in Christ is the traumatizer, and that very religion, or an expression of it, is used to justify, hide, or exacerbate the trauma.

Often this results in a psychological loop providing minimal relief and no escape. From the genocide of countless Indigenous families, to the human trafficking and forced breeding of West Africans, to the fabrications and myths made to tolerate such—America from its onset made clear that involuntary human suffering was worth the earthly freedom and moral bankruptcy of many. Yet the reality of our tragic history is replaced by a fictitious and heroic account, complete with notions of bravery and freedom for all. The historic mythologies only further deny the trauma of millions of ancestors and the present-day systemic and psychological out-workings.

We need healing. However, healing requires honesty; healing assumes the acknowledgment of harm, and it demands the acknowledgment of the worth of the harmed.

Prayer Questions for God

Now is a good time to stop and take a breath—literally a short breathing and prayer activity before we go on to some reflection questions. With the psalmist we cry out, "How long, O Lord?" Let's raise these questions of reflection before God while taking a deep breath after each line.

Oh God, must racial trauma be fully healed for relief to come?

How can one be healed where denial is rampant?

The truth sets us free, and conversely lies keep us in bondage. Have mercy, Lord.

God of all wisdom, how does one seek out and grasp healing in spaces that reinforce the trauma?

From the trauma of dehumanization, threats of violence—a necessary element to maintain racism—and the activity of silencing voices of truth. Deliver us.

We long for answers, but even more we need your presence.

Come, Jesus, come. Amen.

THE "DRAFT A NICER BLACK PERSON" STRATEGY

Too often White Christian spaces, even when well intentioned, draft people of color to offer their skills, suffering, and selves to the advancement of White racial enlightenment. The request to "share your perspective" is often retraumatizing and White-centric. When done poorly, it becomes voyeuristic, dehumanizing, and entitled. Christians must guard against this practice of traumatic performative storytelling by people of color. Credible data, brilliant autobiographies, and many documentaries exist to serve White people who are seeking to understand racial trauma and racism. This route is a much more loving step than inviting someone to coffee with the good intention of hearing their racial pains or to gather free diversity and equity consultation.

Nearly twenty years ago, I attended a graduate school class with a small group of future therapists. The classes were most often majority White, but on that day we had a visiting postgraduate student, a middle-aged African American woman. I was excited that she was there. Having attended a Historically Black College and then a predominantly White graduate school, I was happy I wasn't "the only one" even if it was just one hour of class. Our class discussion focused on culture and how the therapist's identity impacts the clinical work.

The postgraduate student began to highlight what she described as "Western beliefs of property and ownership." She used humor to carefully point out the rugged individualism, God-complex-dominion, and property-as-identity in Western ideologies. "See," she said with a chuckle, "look at how you are sitting on that chair with your feet placed up as if you own it. We [likely referring to Black people] know we could never sit like that without enduring judgement." She noted how this might look to other cultures outside of White middle-class ones. With a matter-of-factness and a grin she stated, "You all think you own everything and this body language shows it. That's not even your chair and you have misused it. What would that mean to the laborers who crafted this chair?"

Needless to say, the tension in the room bubbled up. The grad student didn't just name her perception of a cultural difference but critiqued the dominant culture represented in the room—and did so without much cultural accommodation or empathy for the dominant group.

In the next moment, many things *could* have happened. My White peers could have sat in silence; they could have let her points rest without response, allowing the class to move to the next statement—a few attempted to do that. Some *could* have articulated how they felt, whether judged, confused, angry, or ashamed. After all, this was a group of therapists in training; feelings talk was a daily ritual. One could have asked for the academic and experiential sources of her observations and offered a counterpoint. Instead, however, what did break the silence (but not the tension) was something I have seen happen in many forms since that moment. The oldest White classmate said to me, "Christina, I would like to hear what you think. Would you share your perspective?"

Some readers might see this as a fairly innocent request, maybe even charitable—but drafting a person of color to respond to another person of color's statement was ill-intentioned and tokenizing. I sensed the problems in a moment, but before I could speak or decline, the postgraduate student spoke up and named those observations and more: "If she wanted to speak, she would have said something. You should speak for yourself instead of trying to get this young Black woman to correct me." The optics were not lost on either of us.

My classmate, an incredibly smart, assertive White woman, had sought to manage the discomfort of the guest's words. In this case, her request boiled down to asking a young light-skinned Black woman to challenge an older dark-skinned Black woman in order to soothe her white fragility. That did not happen that day.

Have you seen this dynamic before? Have you been in any of the roles? The White woman appealing to her "Black friend" to cut the tension? The Black postgraduate woman offering a provocative racial reflection, and being met by avoidance, minimization, or distraction? Maybe you were the person of color, observing until drafted into a conversation to reduce White anxiety about racial tensions.

I lift this story up because it was not the first time the postgraduate student had been minimized and the opportunity for productive dialogue had been squelched by the "draft a nicer Black person" strategy. Additionally, it would not be the last time someone would attempt to draft me to diffuse a hard truth. This moment in the early 2000s was not the first time either of us had been faced with the burden of hard race conversations or experiences. Children of color experience race consciousness much earlier than White children, and they carry with them a host of experiences of race and racism shaping them by the time they get to any graduate school classroom.[8]

So how do we learn from each other and in our antiracism efforts guard against retraumatizing those with racial trauma? As mentioned earlier, we must *let a written biography tell the story, let data tell the story, let Scripture tell the story.* We do not have the moral right to demand engagement from those who have been wounded by our complicity, apathy, or flagrant abuses. We do, however, have the duty to do what is right by centering suppressed voices in ourselves and asking introspective questions: *Why have these voices been ignored? What does it cost when they speak? As a White person, why don't I have much to say about my whiteness?*

REDUCING RACIAL TRAUMA IN TRAINING AND ASSESSMENT

When I work with people of color, I often hear comments like the following:

> I don't like talking and never seeing action. It is good to have talks, however it gets exhausting for the people who share and the people who listen to it. It is repetitive and every time it is just magnifying the problem and never dealing with the problem. It's all about the talk and no action. (Hispanic/Latina, female, 20s)

> Sometimes it feels like you're just beating against the wind . . . an exercise in futility. . . . At some point you just get exhausted . . . tired of 'talking' about it! (Black, female, 60s)[9]

It's exhausting to keep talking about race and not see action. But people of color in predominantly White organizations are often singled out to share their perspective. This is important for progress, but it must be done in a way that doesn't exhaust and retraumatize the participants. This chapter concludes with some guidelines to support outcomes-oriented antiracism work while being mindful of reducing retraumatization for people of color.

Have a shared mission that produces a trauma-informed strategy. The more diverse a community, organization, or team, the more critical the shared mission becomes.[10] The *motivating why* behind the church's antiracism work deeply matters since it is the well that parties will draw from to fuel the work of repentance and structural change. For example, a motivating why for many might be: Christ has died and risen to tear down the wall of hostility that is maintained by idolatrous power, and we must honor the gospel itself by living into this eschatological reality now. Another motivating why might be Christ's final apologetic argument and strategy: "By this everyone will know that you are my disciples, if you love one another" (John 13:35).

Churches and denominations must find their motivating why rooted in a value system that is more than platitudes or clichés that will not hold up under the fierce resistance of racism. The motivating why moves from deeply held convictions to a source of identity. In other words, it goes from *this is what we know or believe* to *this is who we are*. Finally, mindful of the insights from this chapter and the growing body of research and practice regarding race and cultural trauma, the strategy that is produced from our mission cannot nullify itself by haphazardly replaying white dominance and themes of racial stratification in its strategy. This has immediate implications for who is at the table and how practical resources and positions are allocated and filled.

Acknowledge the harm, and develop an antiracist restorative justice focus. It is critical that the harms of racism are acknowledged not just "out there" but "in here" also. The harms of racism within your local church, denomination, or tradition must be confessed, lamented, and changed as a liturgy of life. A temptation will exist to minimize or avoid discussing the severity and frequency of incidents and ideologies that cause shame. It would not be surprising if paternalism dressed as well-meaning concern was used as reason to not record, discuss, and strategize against racial incidents. However, acknowledgment is essential to overall systemic health. There very well could be a person of color who articulates fatigue discussing such events or minimizes the impact personally. Be strategic in not drafting or becoming a minority voice that downplays dysfunction for the perception of peace and to avoid conflict. Conflict and difficult conversations are a sign of a healthy team or community.

Resist pitting groups against each other. Antiracism efforts in Christian communities are often thwarted by people of color being pitted against each other through polarized identities, in-group tensions, colorism, and a lack of solidarity. In an effort to reduce racial trauma, people of color can find themselves overstating that they are a "team player" and not like the "others." After the election of Donald Trump in 2016, I recall a woman of color declaring on social media that she just didn't get the frustration of people of color and that "we should just be united in Christ." Her decision to declare herself as supposedly above the fray and to pull on Christian jargon signaled a diffusing of unresolved, but necessary, conflict. She also established herself, at least temporarily, as trustworthy to White evangelicals.

While it is more than reasonable that within groups people will hold diverse beliefs, it is nonetheless problematic for a well-intentioned outlier in a group to signal allegiance and turn down the volume on the voices of others. Whether race, class, or gender, it is important that we appropriately challenge the dominant sentiment when necessary. Piety is not pretending that sociological factors don't affect the lived experiences of our group or neighbors. As majority and minority people, we have to watch for this in order to address real issues and resist the urge to promote or elevate voices that make us feel comfortable about the sin of racism. Can you imagine how the racially traumatized person of color would experience such a social media post followed by several statements of affirmation from White evangelicals?

Decenter the myth of the personal friendship approach. Many believe that in a country with a history of physical and psychological barriers to cross-racial relationships that the answer to racial injustice is friendship or togetherness. However, it is just not that simple. We will explore that more in the following chapter.

Integration and equity are necessary. But when we have relationships without equity, we wrongly promote the idea that White proximity can reduce Black suffering or that White friendship can resolve Hispanic/Latino trauma. People of color don't just want White friends, they want and need racial equity. Friendship without equity is a farce used to narcissistically manage the consciences of those who, if able to see it, would not divest of the system of stratification. Additionally, proximity without the correct translation of our experiences reinforces caricatures and can foster Messiah complexes for White people and codependency for people of color.

Create measurable goals and external systems of accountability. It is so easy for us to think we have the answers to the most difficult internal and external problems we face, especially when we don't want to reveal the depth of the wound. White culture does not have the answers to fix racial injustice within itself because, in many ways, White identity is designed to perpetuate injustice. This fixation on White solutions refuses to acknowledge the truth that White people have internalized and inherited a system that is bigger than even their best intentions and religious lingo. Dismantling it requires actual prayerful strategy, clear and measurable goals, and accountability outside of itself. We explore ways to effectively measure progress in chapter ten.

WE ALL NEED TO UNDERSTAND AND ADDRESS RACIAL TRAUMA (CHAD)

Until recently, I believed that conversations about racial trauma were mostly for people of color. But I now realize that they are essential for White people like me as well.

It helps us be more empathetic, patient, and helpful allies. Discussing racial trauma helps us to understand that the dynamics we have looked at so far in this book do not just produce "inaccurate and unbiblical mindsets," they produce stress, physical and emotional pain, and even death for many people. Racial injustice continues to exact a terrible human toll on individual lives, Christian communities, and society. Understanding this reality can help us to be more empathetic, patient, and helpful toward our brothers and sisters in Christ who are suffering due to racial injustice. Among other things, it should prevent us from ever asking the question, "Why can't people of color just get past this whole race thing?" That common question often flows from a lack of empathy and a lack of understanding about the physical and psychological impacts of racism.

It helps us work toward our own healing. Racial injustice hurts us all. Those of us who are White are not immune to the spiritual, emotional, psychological, and physical damage that racism inflicts. Our pain is often complicated by an awareness that we have contributed in some way to the damage. But wounds are still wounds, whether they are inflicted by ourselves or others. As I have grown in my understanding of racial injustice and my role in perpetuating it, I have wrestled with some difficult questions.

1. **Have I contributed to the pain of others**? Reflecting on my life, I can see how actions I have done (and not done) have contributed to

racial injustice and the pain of people of color. That is a painful reality that I wish I could undo, but sadly, I cannot. I must rest in Christ's limitless grace and do all that I can to avoid similar sins in the future.

2. **Have I internalized the lie of superiority?** Like most White people, I have been taught the lie that White people are safer, wiser, cleaner, more trustworthy, more pure, and more deserving than people in other racial groups. As Shannon Sullivan writes, "The enigmatic messages concerning race transmitted by white slaveholders to contemporary white people are real: they have real effects in the lives of white and nonwhite people today."[11] Sorting out the lies we have been taught and their "real effects" is often a difficult and painful journey that requires prayer, God's grace, and the help of others.

3. **What is the responsibility of those who benefit from unjust systems?** When we recognize that we are receiving advantages at other people's expense, it is essential to do our part to correct that injustice. But, even if we are working toward building a more just and loving society, there remains a psychological and spiritual burden that comes with receiving benefits unjustly. In my life, I find the burden can prompt denial ("It doesn't affect me."), anger ("I never asked for this!"), and guilt ("Why haven't I done more to fix it?"). I'm seeking to follow the more productive paths of acknowledging my privilege and the pain it produces in me and others, forgiving the propagators of injustice (including myself), and focusing on the freedom and forgiveness we have through Christ.

Special Support and Protections for People of Color

In light of the dynamics addressed in this chapter, we believe providing special support and protections for people of color is an important step for many Christian organizations. As Christians work to improve the racial dynamics in their organizations, it is important to recognize that change is unlikely to happen quickly. It may take years or even decades. In the meantime, it is often very beneficial to provide special support for people of color. The support can take many forms: prayer, relationships, racial affinity groups, retreats, and counseling.

Furthermore, it is important for leaders to recognize that Christian organizations are not immune to overt acts of racial prejudice, intimidation, and even violence. It is essential for organizations to have policies and procedures in place for how to handle these types of situations *before they happen*. We have frequently seen a tragic act of racial prejudice produce enormous organization-wide pain and division because there were no procedures in place for how to handle it. We have also seen organizations do a good job of handling racial bias incidents and turn them into teachable moments for the individuals involved and the organization. We highly recommend that every Christian organization have policies and procedures in place for handling racial bias incidents in productive ways.

Learning More About Racial Trauma

In this chapter we only scratched the surface on this important topic. For much more information we encourage you to read *Healing Racial Trauma* by Sheila Wise Rowe.[12]

Discussion/Reflection Questions

1. How would you summarize the concept of racial trauma? What causes it? What does it produce?

2. Why is it important for Christians who want to work toward racial justice to understand racial trauma?

3. What are the consequences of denying racial trauma? Have you denied or minimized it?

4. How does racial trauma affect our relationship with God? With one another?

5. What can Christians do to help heal racial trauma?

6. What can Christians do to help avoid creating additional racial trauma?

7. Were the guidelines at the end of the chapter helpful? If so, which ones and why?

8. Chad shared three questions he has wrestled with. Have you wrestled with those questions? If so, what are some of the conclusions you have reached?

9. How do you plan to apply the content in this chapter?

Recommended Prayer

Gracious God, you chose to be with us as our Emmanuel.

You are the God who empathizes.

Within your humanity, you know suffering.

You know what it means to be disbelieved even now.

You see our wounds; you remove shame and bottle every tear.

You give us the power to acknowledge the pain of our sin and how we have been sinned against.

Jesus, be a balm to our weary souls. Jesus, be a reconciler to our broken world.

As you make all things new, bring truth, light, justice, and resurrection to our trauma. Amen.

CHAPTER SEVEN

FAITHFUL ANTIRACISTS DO NOT RELY ON MAGIC

WHEN WE TALK WITH CHRISTIANS about racial dynamics, we often hear comments like, "It's not complicated. All we need to do is ___" or "It all comes down to ___." Many Christians believe there is an approach or technique that will "magically" bring about positive change. It would be nice if it were that simple, but unfortunately it is not. In this chapter, we look at inadequate or ineffective ways that many Christians seek to improve racial dynamics in our society and Christian organizations. We believe it is essential for readers to understand why these approaches are inadequate or ineffective before we look at effective approaches in the remainder of the book.

In our 2019 RRJP survey, we asked, "How can you, as an individual, improve racial/ethnic dynamics in our country? Select all that apply." Figure 7.1 shows the top four actions selected by Christians. Notice that *building cross-racial friendships* and *helping people become Christians* were two of the most common actions selected.

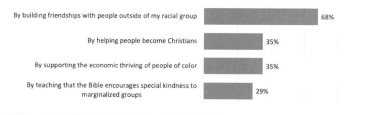

Figure 7.1. Responses to "How can you as an individual improve racial/ethnic dynamics in our country?" (RRJP Survey, July/Aug 2019, n=2797, Christians only)

The Magic of Cross-Racial Friendships

You may have watched a movie with this familiar plotline: a small town or neighborhood is burdened by racial divisions and tensions, but a courageous White person goes against the tide and forms cross-racial friendships. The town is saved, and unity and peace prevail. The magic of relationships saves the day! This plotline may be an effective way to sell movies, but it gives a misleading picture of what is required for racial justice to become a reality. (Also, it promotes the idea that White people must be the "savior," but that is a whole other topic.)

Cross-racial friendships and mentors can be very helpful. They have had a major, positive influence on both of our lives. Cross-racial relationships can help promote empathy, understanding, and motivation to combat racial injustice. In chapter nine, we will look at a few of the many benefits of having cross-racial relationships and mentors. Despite the benefits, it is important to realize that relationships do not magically produce the systemic changes required to eliminate racial injustice.

Sadly, cross-racial relationships often become a barrier to progress if used as justification for not supporting systemic changes. The phrase "I have a Black friend" has rightfully become a joke because it is frequently used when a person is challenged to consider their racial prejudice or to work toward systemic change. The "Black friend" is used as evidence that a person is not racist and doing everything that should be expected of them. But, of course, just having a friend in another racial group does not automatically mean that a person is helping to promote racial justice.

Sadly, we find that people who have many cross-racial relationships often have racial views that are more problematic than people who do not. The concept of *moral licensing* can help us understand why that is the case:

> [Moral licensing] explains how when people initially behave in a moral way, they are more likely to display behaviors that are immoral, unethical, or problematic in other ways later. . . . In other words, when we are confident we have behaved well in the past, and our actions demonstrate compassion and generosity, we are more likely to explain away acts that are selfish, bigoted, or thoughtless.[1]

When people have cross-racial relationships, moral licensing can prevent them from acknowledging and addressing their problematic racial views. Sadly, some of the most racially prejudiced comments we hear with our work come from people who start their comments with, "Don't get me wrong. I have many friends who are [Black, Latino, Asian], but I think . . ."

It is also important to be aware of the extra burden that cross-racial friendships can place on people of color. Many people of color have relationships with White people because they live, work, worship, or go to school in predominantly White environments. But most White people have few, if any, strong relationships with people of color. It is important for White people to be sensitive to that reality when seeking out friendships with people of color and not be offended if they don't have the time or relational capacity.

You may be asking, "Are you saying that cross-racial friendships are helpful or unhelpful?" Our answer: it depends on the situation and the motivations. If a person's motivations are to listen, be teachable, empathize, and work together toward racial justice, then relationships can be very helpful. However, if a person's motivations are to prove to themselves and others that they are not a "bad, racist person" or to justify not addressing systemic injustice, then they are unhelpful.

THE MAGIC OF HELPING PEOPLE BECOME CHRISTIANS

As Christians, we have the joy and responsibility of following Jesus' command to "go and make disciples of all nations, baptizing them in the name of the Father and of the Son and of the Holy Spirit, and teaching them to obey everything I have commanded you" (Matthew 28:19-20). Sharing our faith and helping people to grow in their relationship with Christ is one of the most important and enjoyable things we can do as Christians. But it is important to keep the following in mind as we consider the relationship between helping people become Christians and racial progress.

Sadly, identifying as a Christian does not correlate with views that promote racial justice. Periods of US history when very high percentages of people described themselves as Christians have not correlated with increased racial justice. For example, during the 1600s to 1700s a large percentage of the colonists would have described themselves as Christians. A large percentage of those same individuals also passively or actively supported the unjust treatment of Native Americans and the transatlantic slave trade.

Let's look at an additional example from our research that shows that identifying as a Christian does not correlate with views that promote racial justice. In our 2019 RRJP survey, we asked, "How motivated are you to promote racial justice?" The options were *very motivated, motivated, somewhat motivated, unmotivated, not at all motivated, not sure.* Our research partner, the Barna Group, asked the same question in the fall of 2020 to see if views had changed after the national racial justice protests in the spring of 2020. With the exception of Black Christians, we found there was a significant *decrease* in the percent of Christians who described themselves as "very motivated" between 2019 and 2020. During the same time period, the motivation among non-Christians in each racial group remained similar or significantly increased.

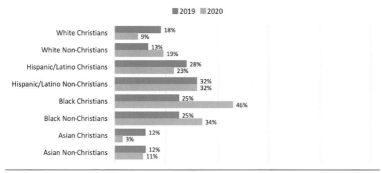

Figure 7.2. Respondents who indicated they are very motivated to address racial injustice in our society (RRJP Survey, July/Aug 2019, n=2797; Barna Group, Race Today, June/July 2020, n=1464)

According to Jesus, many people deceive themselves about being his followers. Jesus made it clear that many people claim his name who are not his followers.

Not everyone who says to me, "Lord, Lord," will enter the kingdom of heaven, but only the one who does the will of my Father who is in heaven. Many will say to me on that day, "Lord, Lord, did we not prophesy in your name and in your name drive out demons and in your name perform many miracles?" Then I will tell them plainly, "I never knew you. Away from me, you evildoers!" (Matthew 7:21-23)

Even if all of the people in the United States described themselves as Christians, based on Jesus' warning we should assume that "many" of those individuals will not really be followers of Christ. Some readers might say, "I understand that, but what if we help people become *authentic* Christians? Won't that lead to racial progress?" This leads to our next point.

Even authentic Christians do not automatically promote justice. Walking in obedience to God's will does not automatically happen the moment someone becomes a Christian. Otherwise there would be no need for teaching and mentoring on topics like love, compassion, prayer, forgiveness, self-control, and studying the Bible. In the same way, becoming a Christian does not automatically make a person equipped, motivated, or active in racial justice efforts. It typically requires help and accountability from other Christians.

Some people might ask, "What if we help people become *authentic* Christians and help them to be active in racial justice efforts? Wouldn't that help?" Yes! We believe that would be very helpful. That's why we wrote this book and do the work that we do. But unfortunately that is not what many people are referring to when they advocate for helping people to become Christians as essential for racial progress. They often believe that simply helping people becoming Christians will magically address racial injustice.

Sharing a justice-less version of the gospel hinders racial progress. Finally, we want to emphasize that the effectiveness of helping people to become Christians as a way to produce racial progress is dependent on the type of gospel we are sharing. In chapter two, we looked at the sad reality that many Christians seek to downplay or remove the Bible's teachings on justice and protections for the vulnerable and oppressed. When a justice-less gospel is shared, it leads to justice-less Christians. Justice-less Christians oppose or neglect racial justice efforts rather than support them.

The Magic of Colorblindness and Equal Treatment

Many Christians believe the best way to promote racial progress is by ignoring racial/ethnic differences (sometimes called *colorblindness*) or treating everyone the same. The two approaches are similar and often go hand-in-hand, so we will look at them together in this section.

As part of our RPCCS, we asked if respondents *agreed* or *disagreed* with the statement, "I think it is best to try to ignore a person's race/ethnicity."

Figure 7.3 displays the results. Notice that approximately one out of five Christians agreed with that statement.

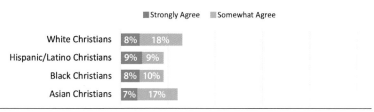

Figure 7.3. Responses to "I think it is best to try to ignore a person's race/ethnicity" (RPCCS, 2016-2020, n-13,580)

In our surveys, people frequently specify equal treatment as the key to progress.

I think the best way to combat racism is to just treat everyone in the same way. (White, female, 20s)

If we truly want to get rid of racism in our society, then we need to treat everyone the same. (White, male, 40s)

Race is only an issue if you make it an issue. Treat everyone the same. (White, female, 30s)

Let's just treat everyone the same. Not that hard to do. Treat someone else the way you want to be treated. Problem solved. (White, male, under 20)[2]

Let's look at a few reasons why colorblindness and equal treatment are not magical solutions.

An "equal treatment" approach often reveals a lack of understanding of racial dynamics. The following story illustrates how a colorblind or equal-treatment approach can be problematic.

Imagine you are on a soccer team with a shrewd coach who desperately wants to win games. Before the game, he pays the officials to not call penalties on your team. Your coach then encourages you and your teammates to cheat during the game—grab the other team's jerseys, trip them, and use your hands. After the first half, your team is winning 12-to-1. A friend of yours who plays on the other team comes over to you and says, "This is completely unfair. Your team is cheating!"

You feel sorry for your friend and her team and respond, "You're right. For the second half, I'm not going to cheat and I'm going to encourage my team to not cheat either."

Your friend would not believe that is a fair solution. If you and other players on your team decided to not cheat in the second half, it will not change the fact that the score is already lopsided. And the officials will continue to make calls in your favor. The only way to make the game fair is to acknowledge and address your team's unfair tactics, reset the score to zero, and bring in different officials. Similarly, pretending as though there has not been over four hundred years of racial injustice in our country is not an effective solution. It is impossible to make progress without acknowledging and addressing the racial injustice in our past as well as the systems and structures that continue to perpetuate it.

A colorblind approach often reveals an unconscious superiority mindset. A well-meaning White person might tell a person of color, "I look at you just like everyone else" or "I don't see you as a ___ person." These types of statements are often motivated by a desire to build relationship and communicate "I am not a racist person." But, for good reason, the person of color often interprets the statement as racially prejudiced. Why? Because underneath the good intentions, the statement often reveals a belief that the person of color's race/ethnicity is inferior.

It may be easier to understand why it is offensive to ignore a person's race/ethnicity if you think about it in terms of gender. Imagine if a husband told his wife, "You are so great. I don't even look at you like a woman." Of course, she would rightfully be offended. She would assume that he feels women are inferior to men. Why would he ignore or downplay the fact that she is a woman if he saw that as a positive attribute?

Does Galatians 3:28 encourage colorblindness? Christians who advocate for colorblindness and equal treatment will often refer to Paul's statement, "There is neither Jew nor Gentile, neither slave nor free, nor is there male and female, for you are all one in Christ Jesus" (Galatians 3:28) as evidence that the Bible teaches that it is best to ignore racial/ethnic differences.

In order to understand the point of Paul's statement in Galatians 3:28, we must understand the context. In Galatians, Paul helps Christians recognize that our common identity in Christ allows us to overcome hierarchies or divisions in our society. He did not, however, encourage his readers to pretend like social realities did not exist in society. In fact, just a few verses earlier, Paul wrote,

> James, Cephas and John, those esteemed as pillars, gave me and Barnabas the right hand of fellowship when they recognized the grace given to me. They agreed that we should go to the Gentiles, and they to the circumcised. All they asked was that we should continue to remember the poor, the very thing I had been eager to do all along. (Galatians 2:9-10)

If Paul and the early church leaders felt it was best to pretend like social realities didn't exist, why did they emphasize the importance of remembering the poor? They could have said, "In Christ, there are no longer rich or poor people. Therefore, we should treat poor people just like everyone else, no special treatment." Instead, they chose to emphasize the importance of showing special kindness to the poor. The early church leaders' priorities were aligned with the Old Testament teachings on special kindness and protections for the vulnerable and oppressed.

The Magic of Being Woke

People sometimes use the term *woke* to refer to a person who is knowledgeable and motivated in regard to racial justice efforts. Ironically, when people think that they are woke it can be a major barrier to them becoming a faithful antiracist. For example, Daniel Hill shares about a time when he was leading a training for a non-profit organization and the executive director interrupted his presentation. The director stated:

> I'm sure this material you are sharing is helpful for beginners, but that's not who you are talking to right now. You are actually speaking to an extremely woke group—we know all about the history of race, and we understand that it's a really big deal. We only have one day together, so I'm hoping you can maybe speed this up and get to some of the deeper stuff?[3]

After sharing that story, Hill writes:

I think most of us carry this fantasy that if we take the racial awakening journey seriously enough—if we read the right articles, study the right history books, listen to the right podcasts—we will eventually land at an arrival point where we can exhale and join the ranks of other woke White allies. It's a fantastical place where all major lessons have already been learned. It's a place where all blind spots have already been exposed. It's a place where I am on equal footing in my knowledge of the issue with those who represent the margins. It's a place where my credibility is solid enough that I can tell jokes about race without repercussions. It's a place where I no longer have to be sensitive to the multitude of cultural vantage points on an issue, because my own sense of instinct is so well developed. It is a place where I no longer have to worry about being corrected, because I never make mistakes anymore. It is a place where I no longer say anything stupid or say the wrong thing at the wrong time.[4]

Belief that "I am woke" reduces teachability and reliance on God and others. We never reach the fantastical place that Hill describes. This should be a source of motivation, rather than a source of discouragement. Recognizing we all have room to grow drives us to rely on God's power and leading; it motivates us to work in partnership with other Christians who can provide insight, help, and accountability; it releases us from the pressure of feeling like we have to get everything figured out before we can be effective advocates for racial justice.

THE MAGIC OF THE OPEN-MINDED, YOUNGER GENERATION

One of the most frequent comments we hear is "Young people seem to be so much more open-minded about racial issues. Don't you think racial injustice will go away as they grow older?"

It is important to realize that throughout US history many people have overestimated how quickly racial "progress" is being made. When George Washington was asked to join an antislavery petition campaign in 1785, he responded, "It would be dangerous to make a frontal attack on a prejudice which is beginning to decrease."[5] In 1785, slavery would not be abolished for another eighty years. A Philadelphia newspaper declared in 1888 that "prejudice against color is slowly but surely dying out."[6] However, in 1888, millions of people of color were suffering under Jim Crow Laws, mob violence, and voter disenfranchisement.

It is also important to understand how difficult it is to accurately measure a person's racial prejudice or support for racial injustice. For example, let's look at some historical data collected by the University of Illinois on racial views. Figure 7.4 shows the percentage of White Americans who approve of integrated schools and who approve of interracial marriage.[7]

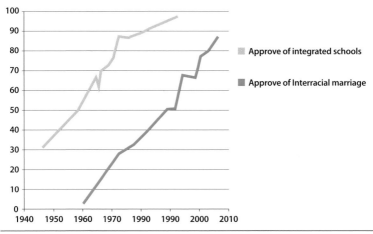

Figure 7.4. Percentage of White Americans who approve of integrated schools and who approve of interracial marriage

The data in figure 7.4 shows that support for integrated schools and interracial marriage has steadily increased over the last sixty years. We could look at those findings and think, *Racial discrimination is slowly being eliminated from our society. All we need to do is give it enough time.* But we must be careful to not assume support for those issues is an effective way to measure support for racial justice.

Let's look at some additional historic data. Figure 7.5 shows the percentage of White Americans who agree with the statement "Generations of slavery and discrimination have created conditions that make it difficult for Blacks to work their way out of the lower class." Agreement with that

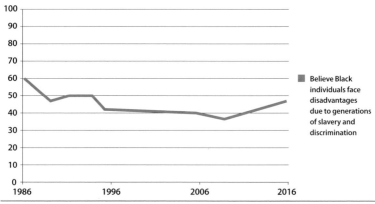

Figure 7.5. White Americans who agree with the statement "Generations of slavery and discrimination have created conditions that make it difficult for Blacks to work their way out of the lower class."

statement indicates a structural understanding of racial dynamics (see chapter one). Notice that agreement with that statement *decreased* by 13 percent between 1986 and 2016. Therefore, we should be careful to not assume that racial views among White Americans are trending in a more accurate or positive direction.

Similarly, we need to be careful to not assume that younger generations are more knowledgeable and supportive of racial justice than they are. Two scholars describe the racial views of White millennials (born between 1981 and 1996) in the following way:

> White millennials readily acknowledge racial inequalities, and few report feeling fearful about members of other racial groups. The overwhelming majority report feeling angry about the existence of racism and say they feel sad when they think about racial injustice. Additionally, 69% of white Millennials in our sample believed that "racism is a major problem in this country."
>
> On the other hand, when we ask about institutionalized racism and racial privilege, seven in ten young whites believe that hard work is all it takes to be wealthy. This group is no more likely than older whites to acknowledge that their racial identity is associated with certain advantages—even though factual research shows that whites enjoy greater wealth, better health outcomes, and greater employment

opportunities, and better treatment in the criminal justice system. Our respondents did not seem to notice these markers of systemic white privilege.[8]

To add to the complexity, we must keep in mind that people's racial views are not fixed. Research has shown that people often become more racially prejudiced as they age.[9] One cause of this is the desire to hold onto possessions and privilege. For example, a White teenager's support for the concept of racial justice costs them very little. As they age they consciously or unconsciously receive more of the benefits of being a White person. In addition, it is likely that their relational networks become increasingly composed of people who share their race and economic status. Therefore, supporting racial justice is more costly (economically, relationally, emotionally) than it was when they were younger.

It is problematic to assume that the magic of the open-minded, younger generations will eventually produce racial justice in our society. Extensive social science data and hundreds of years of US history make it clear that generational changes, on their own, are unlikely to eliminate racial injustice anytime soon.

MAGICAL SOLUTIONS IN CHRISTIAN ORGANIZATIONS

In the remainder of this chapter, we shift to magical ways that Christian organizations often seek to promote racial progress. In our 2019 RRJP survey we asked, "How can churches improve racial/ethnic dynamics in our country? Select all that apply." Figure 7.6 displays the top four actions selected by Christians. Notice that *welcoming people* and *teaching about race/ethnicity* were two of the top three actions selected. We will look at those approaches and a few others.

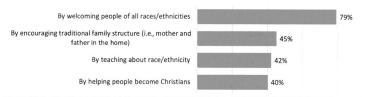

Figure 7.6. Responses to the question "How can churches improve racial/ethnic dynamics in our country?" (RRJP Survey, July/Aug 2019, n=2797)

THE MAGIC OF WELCOMING PEOPLE

Of course, it is good to have an organization that is striving to make every visitor feel welcome, regardless of their race/ethnicity. But *welcoming people* will not magically produce racial progress on its own. Many organizations pursue racial diversity through an open-door policy: "Everyone is welcome here." But simply opening the door to other groups is unlikely to result in racial diversity unless the organization is intentional in other ways. Extensive research has shown that Christians typically choose to be in Christian organizations with people who share their race/ethnicity.[10] Furthermore, increasing the racial diversity in an organization through an open-door policy or other approaches oftentimes does not produce "racial progress" or racial justice within an organization or our society. In fact, in many cases, it has the opposite effect. We will explore this in the next section.

In addition, a welcoming approach can contribute to an organizational climate where people who are not in the racial majority often feel like perpetual outsiders. Here are a few comments from the RPCCS:

> I've been at [our organization] twenty-plus years and I really do feel like an outsider. . . . I just don't feel a real part of the Community. (Black, female, 60s)

> I've never felt a sense of belonging in [our organization]. (Asian, female, 20s)

Jin Cho reflects on the limitations of a welcoming approach using a helpful metaphor involving a house built for giraffes.

> There once lived a well-respected giraffe living in the beautiful suburb of Giraffetown. This giraffe built a beautiful, aesthetically balanced house that won many awards. It had tall windows and long narrow hallways that accentuated all the right giraffe-y things; it was, he would beam, the "perfect home."
>
> One day, an elephant family moved into the neighborhood. The giraffe, being the neighborly sort, invited the elephant for tea: "Please make yourself at home!" he exhorted warmly.
>
> But the elephant found this not so easy to do—the proportions of the giraffe house were all wrong for him. He clumsily damaged

the thoughtfully architected walls, tipped over vases, and crushed the furniture as he attempted to "make himself at home." Horrified, the giraffe muttered that the elephant may need to be more mindful perhaps—that maybe he should lose some weight, or take a dance class, so that he could be nimble like the other giraffes in the community.

The elephant, however, wasn't so convinced. He replied on his way out, "I'm not so sure . . . that a house built for giraffes is good for an elephant."[11]

Our research frequently finds that people in the racial minority in an organization often feel like they are elephants in a house built for giraffes. Cho goes on to say,

> The act of inviting diversity into our community in itself is easy, but without the commitment to enter into the difficult conversations about our assumptions and values that are embedded in our systems— the way we "normally" do things—the experiment is bound to run into all sorts of trouble. . . . Dealing with someone else's norms makes us feel awkward, and places us at a disadvantage; having someone enter into our norms makes us anxious. Yet, our commitment to a racially diverse future must include the inward reflection to see how we may have unintentionally sent a message of un-welcome to those not like us.[12]

The Magic of Racial Diversity

Is it beneficial or detrimental for Christian organizations to be racially diverse? There are many strong opinions about this question. Some people believe racial diversity in Christian organizations is beneficial because it builds relational connections and empathy between people who are normally divided by society—it also demonstrates the unifying power of the gospel. Others believe it is detrimental because racially diverse organizations typically cater to the desires of White members and, therefore, perpetuate the racial hierarchy of our society—this is contrary to the Bible's teachings on justice and love, and a misrepresentation of God's plan for his people. Who is correct? They both are. We will explain our reasoning in later chapters. For now we point out that racial diversity will not magically produce racial justice on its own. Here are a few of the reasons why.

Tracking racial demographics is not an effective way to measure progress. *Racial demographics* refers to the statistical racial diversity within a group or organization. For example, if an organization has one thousand members and seven hundred are White, two hundred are Asian, and one hundred are Black, then the racial demographics of the organization is 70% White, 20% Asian, and 10% Black. Over the last decade, one of the most common racial demographic targets used by Christian organizations has been the "80/20 Standard." The 80/20 Standard was popularized by Michael Emerson in the book *People of the Dream*.[13] According to the 80/20 Standard, an organization is defined as "multiracial" if the largest racial group in the organization is no larger than 80 percent of the membership.

The 80/20 Standard can be helpful for research purposes, but it is essential to not use it as *a measure of progress*. As Emerson writes,

> The 80/20 Standard was used for two reasons. Mathematically, it is the point at which there is a high probability that people of different racial groups will meet each other. Sociologically, the 80/20 Standard is the point which research finds across different kinds of organizations that it is more likely that minority group members will have their voices heard. . . . A racially diverse congregation should not use the 80/20 Standard as an indication that they have achieved that goal.[14]

Furthermore, our research has shown that racial dynamics in Christian organizations often get *worse* as the racial diversity increases. Bringing together people of different races creates additional opportunities for relationships, empathy, and understanding, but it also creates additional opportunities for acts of racial prejudice, conflict, unhealthy power dynamics, and more. We must use more effective methods for measuring progress. We explore that more in chapter ten.

Participation in a multiracial organization does not correlate with more accurate racial views. Many people assume that participating in multiracial organizations will help Christians to become more knowledgeable about racial realities. However, our research and other studies have shown that is often not the case. For example, researchers who did an extensive study of dynamics in multiracial congregations found the following:

> We find that attending a multiracial congregation is unassociated with Whites' explanations for racial inequality, and Blacks who attend multiracial congregations are actually less likely to affirm structural explanations for Black/White inequality than Blacks in nonmultiracial congregations or Whites in multiracial congregations. We find little evidence that multiracial congregations promote progressive racial views among attendees of any race or ethnicity. Rather, our findings suggest that multiracial congregations (1) leave dominant White racial frames unchallenged, potentially influencing minority attendees to embrace such frames and/or (2) attract racial minorities who are more likely to embrace those frames in the first place.[15]

In other words, participation in multiracial organizations often affirms problematic views and actions in society rather than challenges them. *Racial diversity is often pursued for the benefit of the organization rather than to promote racial justice.* Over the last ten years, we have worked with many Christian organizations that are trying to become more racially diverse. We find a complex mix of motivations for focusing on racial diversity. The following are a few of the most common motivations. Notice that these items are primarily focused on the needs and desires of the organization rather than promoting racial justice among Christians or in society.

- Increasing the membership of the organization
- Remaining financially sustainable
- Demonstrating that the organization/leaders are not racially prejudiced or behind-the-times
- Appeasing members and employees that are encouraging the organization to focus on racial diversity
- Avoiding a negative public incident and/or a racial bias lawsuit
- Reducing racial conflict and tension within the organization

Motivations influence outcomes. The above motivations are not detrimental per se, but they often produce detrimental outcomes if they are not combined with efforts to promote racial justice. If leaders are primarily seeking the good of their organization, it isn't surprising that efforts to promote racial justice are viewed as an afterthought, or even a distraction.

THE MAGIC OF RACIAL DIVERSITY TRAINING PROGRAMS

When leaders of Christian organizations become motivated to focus on racial diversity, one of the most common approaches they take is to develop a racial diversity training program of some sort. Training programs can be very beneficial (we both frequently help lead them), but they can also be problematic. We explain a few of the reasons why below. For a more in-depth look at the dangers, we encourage you to watch Chad's interview with Brittany Wade (faithfulantiracism.com). In it, she shares about a six-week racial diversity training program that she helped coordinate in one of the largest churches in the United States. Approximately 20 percent of the congregation participated in the program. On the surface the program looked very successful, but Brittany explains how it produced a wide variety of unintended, negative outcomes, including the following.[16]

Overestimating the impact. One of the most problematic ways to measure the success of a diversity program is by the number of people who participate. Participating in a diversity program oftentimes does not produce a change in the participant's heart or their actions. People participate in activities for a wide variety of reasons (e.g., desire to grow, not wanting to appear racist, pressure from the leadership). Even if participants feel motivated and equipped after a training program, and take some initial steps, it is very likely their enthusiasm will fade if they do not receive ongoing support, coaching, assessment, and training as part of an organizational culture of focusing on racial justice.

Islands of racial justice. Diversity programs can contribute to the tendency of organizations to have "islands of racial justice." The large majority of the organization is disinterested or opposed to racial justice, but there is a small group (island) of members and leaders who are committed to working toward racial justice. Sometimes this can be a positive step, especially if the "islanders" are given power to lead organization-wide change. But oftentimes the members and leaders who are not on the island look at the island as problematic or "good for those who are motivated to be a part of that."

A significant (additional) toll on the people of color in the organization. In the interview with Brittany, she shares how it fell on the shoulders of the people of color in their church to repeatedly participate in the six-week training program so that the White participants could have people of color as a part of the discussions. That was time-consuming and emotionally exhausting for the people of color. It was especially draining and discouraging when the perspectives of the people of color were minimized or dismissed by the White participants. Before the training program, the people of color were already facing oppressive dynamics in the church. Rather than helping with those dynamics, in many ways the training program made them worse because it elevated the tensions without providing opportunities for ongoing healing and dialogue.

The Magic of Diversity Superheroes

We have both enjoyed working with hundreds of amazing leaders who are helping to lead racial diversity efforts in their organizations. Having a qualified and gifted diversity coordinator or committee can be a tremendous help with an organization's efforts, but it can become a liability if the organization has unrealistic expectations for the coordinator or committee. The following fictional scenario is very common.

Jose is a diversity professional at a Christian university that is predominantly White. His responsibilities include designing and facilitating training programs for students/staff/faculty, leading the diversity committee, recruiting people of color, measuring racial climate, and helping to provide support for students and employees of color. His efforts are limited by a small budget, lack of staff, and frequent pushback from students and fellow employees. The leadership of the institution has asked him to produce measurable change within three years.

Dynamics like the one above are some of the reasons why diversity leaders in Christian organizations have high levels of burnout and low levels of retention. In order for Christian organizations to effectively work toward racial progress there must be an "all hands on deck" mentality. Racial diversity efforts cannot be allocated to a few gifted individuals who must work under the pressure of high expectations and very limited time and resources.

So How Do We Make Progress?

In this chapter we looked at the limitations of common "magical" solutions that people often rely on to make progress toward racial justice. If you or an organization you are a part of are relying on these approaches, don't be discouraged. You are not alone. We find that most individuals and organizations are relying on at least one of the magical solutions. The good news is that shifting your approach to more effective methods will help to reduce frustration as well as wasted energy and resources. There are better paths forward! The Bible, the example of the early church, the input of experienced practitioners, and current research can help us to develop more effective approaches. That's what the next few chapters are all about.

Discussion/Reflection Questions

1. Which is a bigger barrier to racial justice: inaction or misguided action? Why?

2. Before reading this chapter, did you believe that any of the following magical approaches were effective? If so, which ones? Have your views changed?

   Individual Magic
       The magic of cross-racial friendships
       The magic of helping people become Christians
       The magic of colorblindness and equal treatment
       The magic of being woke
       The magic of the open-minded, younger generation
   Organizational Magic
       The magic of welcoming people
       The magic of racial diversity
       The magic of racial diversity training programs
       The magic of diversity superheroes

3. Are you a part of a Christian organization that believes that any of the magical approaches are effective? If so, which ones? Has that hindered their efforts to make progress? If so, how?

4. Review the list of magical approaches and consider, Why do many Christians assume this is effective? What do all of the magical approaches share in common? Reflect on the underlying beliefs and assumptions.

5. How do you plan to apply the content in this chapter?

RECOMMENDED PRAYER

Lord, we confess that we cannot effectively work toward racial justice and unity without your direction and help. If our efforts are misguided and ineffective, please open our eyes to those realities and show us how to change our mindsets and actions. Give us the courage to make changes even when they are complex and require sacrifice. Help us to follow your will rather than relying on ineffective "magical" approaches to progress.

CHAPTER EIGHT

FAITHFUL ANTIRACISTS FOLLOW THE EXAMPLE OF THE EARLY CHRISTIANS

IN THE FOLLOWING FOUR CHAPTERS, we look at practical ways that Christians can live out God's call to do what is right and just (Genesis 18:19) and to love our neighbors as ourselves (Mark 12:31) in regard to racial dynamics. In chapter eleven, we look at actions we can take to promote racial justice in society. But first, in the following three chapters, we focus on actions we can take within our lives and Christian organizations. If our lives and Christian communities do not reflect racial justice, it is unlikely we will be effective at promoting those realities in society. We must seek to remove the plank in our own eye before we try to remove the speck in our brother's or sister's eyes (Matthew 7:3-5).

Before we continue, we encourage you to do a quick exercise. The following are two recent examples of Christians standing for justice. As you read these stories, consider the following questions:

1. Do you believe their actions were in line with the teachings of the Bible? Why or why not?

2. Did their actions make it more or less likely that people would be attracted to the gospel? If so, why?

3. Would the Christian groups or organizations that you are a part of be willing to do these actions? Why or why not?

New Shiloh Baptist Church. In 2015, Freddie Gray sustained fatal injuries while being transported in a van by Maryland police officers. The incident sparked national outrage and local protests. New Shiloh Baptist Church is a historically Black congregation located less than a mile from the housing project where Freddie Gray lived. The New Shiloh congregation responded to the major social unrest in their neighborhood by using their building as a space to rally hurting people, help mediate conflict, challenge unjust law enforcement practices, and minister the gospel.

Asian American Christian Collaborative. In 2020–2021, Asian Americans experienced a staggering increase in hate crimes due to portrayals of Covid-19 being a "Chinese virus" and other anti-Asian rhetoric by government leaders and media outlets. Many Asian Christians rallied together and formed the Asian American Christian Collaborative (AACC). Since its launch, the AACC has organized prayer and protest rallies in over a dozen cities, issued a joint statement on the killings of Asian Americans in Atlanta in March 2021, advocated for policy and practice changes, and led efforts to promote interminority Christian solidarity.[1]

LEARNING FROM THE EXAMPLE OF THE EARLY CHURCH

In the remainder of this chapter, we look at a few key events from the first years of the growth of Christianity (approximately AD 30–60) and some principles they can teach us about being faithful antiracists. At the start of each section, we provide a fictional example based on dynamics we frequently observe with our work and research.

ACTS 1: THEY PRAYED AND RELIED ON GOD'S POWER

Common scenario: The leadership of New Covenant Church decides racial justice should be a stronger focus for their congregation. They read and discuss books. They form a diversity committee. They hire outside experts to help with their efforts. They teach several series on the topic. Two years later, despite all their efforts, they feel like they have made very little progress.

Working toward racial justice is typically a difficult, long-term process. We must navigate emotional topics and formidable economic, political, and religious barriers. Spiritual forces of darkness oppose our every step (Ephesians 6:12). In the scenario above, New Covenant Church engaged in many helpful activities, but they didn't see the results they hoped for. They were unsuccessful because they relied on their own ideas and efforts rather than on God's leading and power.

Let's consider the example of the first Christians. After Jesus ascended to heaven, his small group of followers had to find a way to sustain their fragile movement without Jesus physically being with them. They were a persecuted minority group within the Jewish community. They could be arrested at any moment by the religious and political leaders who crucified Jesus. Just weeks earlier one of their inner circle, Judas Iscariot, had betrayed Jesus, then ended his own life. Despite their many challenges, small size, and limited resources, Jesus had given them the enormous task of making disciples of all the nations (Matthew 28:19-20).

How did they respond to their overwhelming situation? They prayed.

- Acts 1:14—The early Christians "all joined together constantly in prayer"

- Acts 4:24—The early Christians "raised their voices together in prayer to God"

- Acts 12:12—"Many people had gathered and were praying"

- Acts 13:3—"After they had fasted and prayed, they placed their hands on them"

- Acts 20:36—"[Paul] knelt down with all of them and prayed"

Individual and collective prayer is essential for racial justice efforts. It does the following:

- *Gives power:* Only God can provide the power required to overcome the personal, structural, and spiritual barriers to racial justice.

- *Gives hope:* When we focus on God's limitless abilities, it gives us hope that we can overcome the challenges.

- *Gives direction:* Prayer is essential to discern an effective path through the complexities.

- *Gives peace:* As Paul wrote, "Do not be anxious about anything, but in every situation, by prayer and petition, with thanksgiving, present your requests to God. And the peace of God, which transcends all understanding, will guard your hearts and your minds in Christ Jesus" (Philippians 4:6-7).

ACTS 6: THE OPPRESSED SPOKE UP AND THE OPPRESSORS LISTENED

Common scenario: The leadership of Madison Christian College is confused because many students of color are leaving after only one or two years on campus. The leaders decide to launch a new tutoring program for students of color. They create racial affinity groups to provide support. They hire several new professors of color. Several years later, they are discouraged because students continue to leave.

Progress toward racial justice and unity is only possible if there is good communication. In the example above, the leaders assumed they understood the problem and could choose an appropriate solution. The action steps they chose could have been helpful, but they were ineffective because the leadership did not listen to the individuals who were struggling.

In Acts 6, Luke shares a brief but very helpful example of the early church effectively addressing systemic injustice in their community. First, let's look at his summary of the tension: "In those days when the number of disciples was increasing, the Hellenistic Jews among them complained against the Hebraic Jews because their widows were being overlooked in the daily distribution of food" (Acts 6:1).

The *Hellenistic Jews* were most likely Greek-speaking Jews who had resettled in Israel after living abroad. Their culture was a blend of Greek and Jewish elements. The *Hebraic Jews* were most likely Hebrew/Aramaic-speaking Jews who had always lived in Israel. Their culture was less influenced by foreign cultures. The linguistic and cultural differences between the Hellenistic Jews and the Hebraic Jews undoubtedly contributed to the injustice and the tension.

The Hellenistic Jews spoke up and the Hebraic Jews listened. Luke does not provide any details about how the Hellenistic Jews spoke up. They could have sent a representative to the leaders or stood up as a group during one of their gatherings. The important thing is they didn't remain silent.

When oppressed individuals share their concerns, they often risk the pain of minimization ("Are you sure it's really that bad?"), criticism ("I think you should be more grateful"), or alienation from other group members. The Hellenistic Jews in Acts 6 likely faced similar consequences, but they still spoke up because they recognized that there were also risks with remaining silent. When the oppressed remain silent, it hurts both the oppressed and the oppressors. As Kathy Khang explains, "Silence is complicity. Speaking out is often labeled as rocking the boat or causing trouble, but silence is just as dangerous."[2]

Just as important, the Hebraic Jews listened to their complaint. They were not too busy "doing God's work" to care about the experiences of the members of their community. They did not dismiss the concerns of the Hellenistic Jews as unreasonable or a distraction from more important things. They took the Hellenistic Jews' complaint seriously because they knew that injustice and disunity in their community was a poor reflection of the gospel and a hindrance to their efforts.

It is helpful to note that it was the oppressed (Hellenistic Jews) who spoke up and it was the oppressors (Hebraic Jews) who listened. Oftentimes, when Christians in the majority are asked to listen to the concerns of individuals in the minority, they will complain that the dialogue is "not a two-way street." They feel it is unfair for them to be asked to listen if they cannot express "their side of the story."

It is fair to want two-way dialogue, but in situations where one group is being oppressed it is essential for the oppressed group to speak up and the oppressors to listen. Our love for our fellow brothers and sisters in Christ should motivate us to first seek to listen and act on their concerns rather than seeking to turn the conversation to our own concerns. We need to apply Paul's instructions that "no one should seek their own good, but the good of others" (1 Corinthians 10:24).

The Hebraic Jews' willingness to listen in Acts 6 models the importance of being attuned to the voices of the oppressed and marginalized in our communities. As Jessica Nicholas explains, "To build a culture of justice and righteousness, you need to know how to integrate the people least likely to experience it."[3] Knowing how to integrate oppressed and marginalized groups requires healthy, honest communication.

We often work with Christian organizations where the oppressed are not speaking up and the oppressors are not listening. The following are actions that can help facilitate better communication.

- *Conversations:* Prayerfully look for ways to facilitate one-on-one or small-group conversations where individuals who are not in the majority can share their candid perspectives and experiences. Keep in mind, they may not speak openly if they feel they will be penalized for doing so. For example, a supervisor may ask an employee for their perspective, but the employee will not share it if they fear it may result in them not being promoted.

- *Racial affinity groups:* Racial affinity groups (e.g., Hispanic Student Association) can help oppressed groups share their concerns because it provides a forum for dialogue and collective communication. Many people are more open to sharing their concerns as a part of a group rather than as an individual.

- *Anonymous surveys:* Anonymous surveys can be a great way to help group members speak up without the fear of being punished. They also allow leaders to have a much broader perspective on the dynamics in their organization than can be gained through individual or small-group conversations.

- *Exit interviews:* Yes, we know, it can be awkward to ask people to explain why they are on their way out the door. But in situations where it is appropriate, exit interviews can be a very helpful way to capture honest feedback about your organization.

Acts 6: They Empowered Leaders to Address Injustice Within Their Community

Common scenario: Brian is the principal of a Christian K–12 school that would like to become more racially diverse. Some of the staff express concern that the school's board of directors is all White. So Brian adds Luis, who is Latino American, and Jada, who is African American, to the board. Months later, Luis and Jada begin to make recommendations for structural changes in the organization. Their suggestions are politely dismissed as "unrealistic" or "not a high priority." Jada schedules a meeting with Brian and expresses her concerns that their recommendations are not being implemented. Brian responds, "I don't think it would be fair to place greater emphasis on yours and Luis's perspectives than the rest of the board's. The majority of the board members don't think those items should be a high priority right now."

Working toward racial justice in Christian organizations requires a biblical, effective approach to power dynamics. *Power dynamics* refers to the ways that leadership or authority is distributed in an organization. You can detect who has power in an organization by asking questions like: Who determines the mission and vision? Who determines the priorities? Who determines the budget? Who determines the hiring and promotions?

Sometimes Christians are reluctant to talk about power dynamics because it feels "unchristian." However, building healthy multiracial communities requires acknowledging that power dynamics exist and then working to share power in just and Christ-honoring ways. As Drew Hart explains:

> [We Christians] must have that same mind of Christ, living in mutual submission to one another. This is not a powerless community, because no such thing exists. Such Jesus-shaped communities bear witness to the reign of God by intentionally giving, sharing, and dispersing power in the congregation in ways that make the Jesus story visible in their public witness. . . . We must participate in decentralizing anyone who takes the place of Christ in the community, because that is idolatry. . . . The task we have is to creatively discern how to disperse and redistribute power in the church while ultimately yielding to the power of God, who is able to deliver us from captivity and our distorted vision which is leading to domination and abuse.[4]

Power sharing in Acts 6. We can see a practical example of what Hart describes above in the way that the Christians in Acts 6:1-7 resolved the injustice taking place in their community.

> So the Twelve gathered all the disciples together and said, "It would not be right for us to neglect the ministry of the word of God in order

to wait on tables. Brothers and sisters, choose seven men from among you who are known to be full of the Spirit and wisdom. We will turn this responsibility over to them and will give our attention to prayer and the ministry of the word." This proposal pleased the whole group. They chose Stephen, a man full of faith and of the Holy Spirit; also Philip, Procorus, Nicanor, Timon, Parmenas, and Nicolas from Antioch, a convert to Judaism. They presented these men to the apostles, who prayed and laid their hands on them. (Acts 6:2-6)

The resolution is a good example of effective power sharing. Five important things took place.

1. *The apostles allowed others to be involved in the solution process.* Most, if not all, of the twelve apostles were a part of the oppressor group (Hebraic Jews). They had wisdom to recognize the need to seek out other people in order to determine an effective solution. Luke does not tell us, but it is likely that both Hebraic Jews and Hellenistic Jews were involved in the solution process.

2. *The apostles delegated authority to a group.* They chose to delegate power to a group of seven people rather than just one or two individuals. That is an example of *collective power sharing.*

3. *The apostles allowed others to select the appointees.* The twelve apostles determined a course of action (choosing seven leaders to appoint), but they allowed the larger group to select the individuals who would be appointed.

4. *The appointees were most likely members of the oppressed group.* It is interesting that Luke shares with us the names of all seven of the appointees. They all have Hellenistic (Greek) names. It is likely that all seven were a part of the oppressed group (Hellenistic Jews).

5. *The appointees were given the authority to lead change.* The twelve apostles "prayed and laid their hands on" the appointees and gave them the authority to lead change.

In contrast to the example in Acts 6, we often work with organizations who make the following errors when attempting to address racial conflict or injustice:

1. *The leaders do not involve others in the solution process.* As a result, the solution is more likely to sustain the status quo and not be supported by the larger group.

2. *The leaders delegate authority to only one or two appointees.* As a result, it is much easier for leaders to micromanage and limit the power of the appointees.

3. *The leaders select and remove appointees.* As a result, the appointee's perspectives often align very closely with those of the leaders. If they do something that goes against the status quo or wishes of the leadership, they are removed and another person is selected by the leadership.

4. *The appointees are not members of the oppressed group.* As a result, they do not understand the perspectives of the oppressed group and the oppressed group does not feel empowered to help lead change.

5. *The appointees are given very little power.* As a result, the appointees are an example of *superficial support and tokenism* (see chapter five) rather than effective efforts to share power and address injustice.

Many Christian organizations could benefit greatly from establishing a team similar to the group formed in Acts 6. In order to be effective, the team must be delegated authority to work directly with members and employees without having their decisions micromanaged by the leadership team. It is important for the team to maintain good communication and partnership with the organization's overall leadership, but it is also important that the team has independent decision-making ability and power to implement action steps, like the seven leaders did in Acts 6. Ideally, over time, the team and the organization's leadership can work together in complementary ways (see Acts 11–13 below).

We need colleges and seminaries led by people of color. Before continuing, we want to briefly point out a major barrier to healthy power dynamics in US Christianity. With our coaching and research, we have worked extensively with Christian colleges and seminaries. We consistently observe sacrificial and excellent work by administrators, staff, and faculty. There is much to celebrate. But we also consistently observe a lack of power sharing with leaders of color in Christian higher education. It is essential that we continue to work to increase leadership by people of color in existing

Christian colleges and seminaries. At the same time, we believe it is essential for Christians to support new colleges and seminaries that are founded and led by Christians of color. If you would like to make a financial contribution or donate land to support the launch of a college or seminary led by people of color, please contact the Racial Justice and Unity Center (rjuc.org) for help connecting with individuals who are working on those efforts.

ACTS 6: THEY PRIORITIZED SOCIAL JUSTICE

Common scenario: The national leadership of a campus ministry feels led to help their organization become more intentional about promoting racial justice. They communicate their vision for the new focus at their annual staff conference. Soon after, they hear from many concerned staff, students, and donors. One of the most common objections is "I'm afraid our organization is being distracted by social issues and drifting away from sharing the gospel." The leadership team struggles against this opposition for five years, but their efforts are unsuccessful. The Board of Trustees chooses to replace the leaders with individuals that believe "social issues should not be a high priority."

In Acts 6, the apostles recognized the importance of preaching the word of God (Acts 6:2) but they also prioritized maintaining justice in their community (Acts 6:3-6). As we shared in chapter two, one of the most common obstacles to racial justice efforts is the argument that it is a "distraction from the gospel." In passages like Acts 6, we can see that the early Christians believed maintaining justice in their relationships with one another was a high priority.

ACTS 11–13: THEY SHARED LEADERSHIP

Common scenario: Over the last ten years, the racial diversity at Hope Metro Church has increased rapidly. Despite the shift in demographics, the individuals of color express concerns that nearly all of the leadership continues to be white and the church continues to cater their worship services and other activities to the preferences of the White members. They do not feel like the church is truly "theirs."

In her helpful book *The Elusive Dream*, Korie Edwards shares about research she conducted in a church that transitioned from being 70 percent White to 65 percent African American over a period of several years. She summarizes some of the positive and negative outcomes that resulted from individuals of different races worshiping in the same congregation. She states:

> I contend that, in order to understand the cultural, structural, and social dynamics of interracial churches, race, particularly whiteness, needs to be situated at the heart of the explanation. Given that whiteness is the cornerstone of the racial system in the United States, it plays a fundamental role in how interracial churches function. . . . The interrelations, religious and cultural practices, and organizational structures of interracial churches will be more representative of the preferences and desires of whites than of the racial minorities in these organizations. . . . In short, I propose that interracial churches work, that is remain racially integrated, to the extent that they are first comfortable places for whites to attend.[5]

Our 2019–2020 research confirmed what Edwards found a decade ago. When Christians participate in interracial organizations, it is very common for the preferences and desires of White people to take precedence over the preferences and desires of other groups. Sadly, interracial Christian organizations typically mirror the racial hierarchy in our society rather than model a countercultural love, unity, and justice that is in line with the Bible's teachings.

In Acts, Luke helps us see that the early Christians shared their lives together in ways that did not reflect the cultural divisions and social hierarchies in their society. One of the best examples of this is the church at Antioch. Antioch was the third largest city in the Roman Empire, with nearly half a million people. At least eighteen different ethnic groups were living within the city at the time.[6] The ethnic groups largely kept to their own communities—but that was not true of the followers of Jesus. It is likely that their breaking down of the typical ethnic boundaries motivated outsiders to give them the new name *Christ-ian*, which literally means "those belonging to Christ" (Acts 11:26). It was probably used as a derogatory term because it implied that they were "slaves of Christ" and slaves/servants were low in the social hierarchy.[7] But the term was embraced by the early Christians because they recognized that they were, indeed, servants of Christ (Romans 1:1; 2 Peter 1:1; Revelation 1:1).

In Acts 13, Luke describes the Antioch leadership team a few years after the church began.

> Now in the church at Antioch there were prophets and teachers: *Barnabas, Simeon* called Niger, *Lucius* of Cyrene, *Manaen* (who had been brought up with Herod the tetrarch) and *Saul.* While they were worshiping the Lord and fasting, the Holy Spirit said, "Set apart for me Barnabas and Saul for the work to which I have called them." So after they had fasted and prayed, they placed their hands on them and sent them off. (Acts 13:1-3, emphasis added)

It is easy to breeze over Acts 13:1-3 and miss the significance. Luke pointed out that the leadership team in Antioch included individuals with a variety of ethnic, national, geographic, and socio-economic backgrounds (see below). Clearly, Luke thought this was significant, and so should we.

- *Barnabas* was from Cyprus, an island in the Mediterranean Sea.

- *Manaen* was "a lifelong friend of Herod the tetrarch," which implies he grew up in Israel with wealth and power.

- *Lucius* was from Cyrene, a city in Northern Africa.

- *Simeon* was "called Niger" (literally, "called black"), which implies he was most likely African.

- *Saul* (another name for the apostle Paul) was from Tarsus, a city in Central Asia along the Mediterranean Sea.

The Antioch leadership team sent out Paul and Barnabas on their first missionary journey, one of the most significant events in the history of the early church. The Christians in Antioch shared their financial resources across ethnic lines (see below). The church in Antioch played a central role in the expansion of Christ-followers in the Roman Empire. It is not a coincidence that their members and leadership were working together across ethnic lines—their unity in an ethnically divided city was a central part of God's plan and one of the reasons they had such a major impact on the world.

As we have stressed throughout this book, it is important to recognize that racial diversity can be helpful or problematic. This is true of racial diversity in leadership teams. Diversity is helpful when there is productive, open dialogue and mutual leadership sharing. It is problematic when tokenism and unhealthy power dynamics exist. As Jemar Tisby writes:

> Putting a token person of color on a leadership team does not ensure positive change. You may have desegregated your leadership team, but that does not mean you have an integrated team. Integration means incorporating diverse perspectives, people, and practices into an organization so that the culture expands to include diversity while maintaining unity. Desegregation simply means that people are not excluded from participation because of their race or ethnicity. Desegregation does not say anything about how racial and ethnic minorities are included in decision-making, how much power is shared with them, or how they are supported when exercising that power.[8]

ACTS 11: THEY SHARED FINANCIAL RESOURCES

Common scenario: Pastor Ricardo's church is attended by many undocumented immigrants. He decides to try to raise funds so three of the teenagers in his congregation can attend college. He reaches out to local churches and Christians in the area. Some respond generously, but most do not reply or explain that they do not feel it is appropriate to support individuals who are not legal residents.

In Acts 11, we see the church in Antioch model compassion and resource sharing across ethnic lines. The Christians in Antioch (mostly Gentiles) sent financial resources to Christians in Jerusalem (mostly Jews).

> During this time some prophets came down from Jerusalem to Antioch. One of them . . . predicted that a severe famine would spread over the entire Roman world. . . . The disciples, as each one was able, decided to provide help for the brothers and sisters living in Judea. This they did, sending their gift to the elders by Barnabas and Saul. (Acts 11:27-30)

The Christians in Antioch provided practical Christian love and compassion for their fellow Christians in Jerusalem. When they learned about the needs in Judea they didn't simply say, "We'll pray for you." They followed the Bible's instructions to provide tangible help for those in need, as James taught.

> Suppose a brother or a sister is without clothes and daily food. If one of you says to them, "Go in peace; keep warm and well fed," but does nothing about their physical needs, what good is it? In the same way, faith by itself, if it is not accompanied by action, is dead. (James 2:15–17)

GIVING AS AN ACT OF LOVE AND RESTORATION (CHAD)

The Antioch church's gifts in Acts 11 and many other Bible passages like the parable of the Good Samaritan (Luke 10:25-37) should motivate us to provide practical help for the financial needs of individuals outside of our racial or ethnic group as an act of love and compassion. The Bible also encourages giving or returning financial resources as an act of restorative justice or reparations (Exodus 21:33-22:15; Leviticus 6:1-7; Numbers 5:5-8; Proverbs 14:9; Matthew 5:23-24, Luke 19:1-10). If we have received benefits at the expense of someone else, our desire to "do justly" (Micah 6:8) should motivate us to correct the wrong that has been done, regardless if we were actively involved in the transfer of benefits or not.

A thorough exploration of restorative justice or reparations is well beyond the scope of this book. For that, I recommend that you watch my interview with Duke Kwon (faithfulantiracism.com) or read the book that he coauthored titled *Reparations: A Christian Call for Repentance and Repair*.[9] In the book, they emphasize that effective reparations are not just about restoring wealth. They are also about restoring truth and power.

> This book frames both theft and reparations in terms of three distinct categories: truth, power, and wealth. Though this distinction is historically true and useful practically, the fact of the matter is that each of these is in practice indivisible from and dependent on one another; they exist in a symbiotic system. . . . Those who take up the work of reparations must work diligently to address all of these: truth, wealth, and power.[10]

When we take practical steps to restore truth, wealth, and power, it honors God, it benefits those who have been wronged, it benefits those of us who carry the burden of receiving benefits unjustly, and it strengthens the church's witness in our society and the world. Everyone wins. When we refuse to take practical steps to restore truth, wealth, and power, it dishonors God, it hurts those who have been wronged, it fosters guilt and fear by those of us who receive benefits unjustly, and it hinders the church's witness in our society and the world. Everyone loses.

Acts 15: They Practiced Accommodation, Not Assimilation

Common scenario: Grace Academy is a Christian K–12 school in a racially diverse neighborhood. Their student population is 62% White, 18% Hispanic/Latino, 8% Black, and 12% Asian, but their teachers are 94% White. When they recruit individuals of color onto their staff, they typically leave after only a few years. Grace Academy's leaders are confused why the turnover is so high despite their efforts to make their school a welcoming place.

When we study the racial climate in organizations like Grace Academy, we often find that *cultural assimilation* and *code-switching* are taking place by the individuals of color. Assimilation takes place when individuals who are not in the majority group take on the values, behaviors, and beliefs of the majority group in order to fit in or be "successful" (e.g., maintain relationships, keep their job, be selected for leadership positions). Code-switching refers to "adjusting one's style of speech, appearance, behavior, and expression in ways that will optimize the comfort of others."[11] Code-switching is a type of situational assimilation. For example, a Latina woman may use passive or indirect communication with friends and family members, then switch to more assertive and direct communication with White coworkers in order to be successful at her job.

Adjusting our behaviors for the benefit of others can be healthy and beneficial (1 Corinthians 9:19-23), but it becomes detrimental when people in some groups are required to "adjust" more than people in other groups. When cultural assimilation and code-switching are taking place for the benefit of one group at the expense of others, it produces frustration, exhaustion, and division. It also diminishes the many benefits of cultural diversity. If people do not have the freedom to be themselves, then the group or organization cannot benefit from their unique perspectives, culture, experiences, and gifts.

In Acts 15, we see a key moment in the early church that can teach us about assimilation. When the church was first launched (Acts 2), almost all of the followers of Jesus were Jews. Then, through the leading of the Holy Spirit and the efforts of individuals like Philip (Acts 8) and Paul (Acts 13-14), the number of Gentile Christians began to grow rapidly. As a result, the Jewish Christians were debating, "Should we ask Gentile Christians to practice circumcision and follow other Jewish customs and laws in order to be Christians?"

The early Christian leaders gathered in Jerusalem to discuss a resolution to the "sharp dispute and debate" (Acts 15:2). The leaders determined that God had already accepted the Gentiles without discrimination (Acts 15:8-9) and that they would not burden the Gentiles with "a yoke that neither we nor our ancestors have been able to bear" (Acts 15:10). It is by grace through faith that we are saved (Acts 15:11). However, they did ask the Gentiles to "abstain from food polluted by idols, from sexual immorality, from the meat of strangled animals and from blood" (Acts 15:20).

There are many key principles we can learn from their decision. For the focus of this book, it is helpful to notice that both the Jews and Gentiles were required to make cultural accommodations, but neither of them were required to culturally assimilate. The accommodations in Acts 15:20 allowed Jewish and Gentile Christians to share meals in each other's homes and maintain the unity of the early church. As Warren Wiersbe writes:

> The legalistic Jews willingly gave up insisting that the Gentiles had to be circumcised to be saved, and the Gentiles willingly accepted a change in their eating habits. It was a loving compromise that did not in any way affect the truth of the Gospel. . . . This is not doctrinal compromise, for that is always wrong (Jude 3). Rather, it is learning to give and take in the practical arrangements of life so that people can live and work together in love and harmony.[12]

Like the early church, healthy Christian communities ask the Holy Spirit to help them find cultural accommodations where *everyone* is required to make sacrifices for the sake of justice and unity. They do not ask individuals in the cultural minority to sacrifice their cultural identity through assimilation or code-switching.

GALATIANS 2: THEY HAD COURAGEOUS CONVERSATIONS

Common scenario: The president of Brookville College attends a conference where racial justice is emphasized. She returns and informs the staff and faculty of her desire to help Brookville College become a "leading organization" in the area of racial justice. A Latina professor who has served on campus for over twenty years asks the president if they can go to lunch. Over lunch, she graciously explains some of the ways that the president's actions have made it difficult for the employees and students of color to thrive on their campus. The president responds, "I'm sorry you see it that way. In no way were those actions racially prejudiced. You are the only person who has expressed that opinion."

The only thing that is worse than conflict in a Christian community is no conflict. You're probably thinking, *Say what?* When there is no conflict, it is often a sign that there is a lack of open, honest communication. In many organizations there is an obsession with "niceness" and a commitment to conflict avoidance that makes it nearly impossible to have the courageous conversations that are necessary for improving racial dynamics.

In his book *The Five Dysfunctions of a Team*, Patrick Lencioni explains the need for productive conflict.

All great relationships, the ones that last over time, require productive conflict in order to grow. This is true in marriage, parenthood, friendship, and certainly business. . . . It is important to distinguish productive ideological conflict from destructive fighting and interpersonal politics. Ideological conflict is limited to concepts and ideas, and avoids personality-focused, mean-spirited attacks. . . . When team members do not openly debate and disagree about important ideas, they often turn to back-channel personal attacks, which are far nastier and more harmful than any heated argument over issues.[13]

In chapter three, we briefly looked at the time when Paul "opposed [Peter] to his face" (Galatians 2:11) because his actions were leading Jewish Christians to not associate with Gentile Christians. Paul was very concerned because "they were not acting in line with the truth of the gospel" (Galatians 2:14). Paul's confrontation of Peter is a good example of the type of courageous conversations that are essential in order to work toward racial justice and sustain healthy communities.

Speaking up like Paul. It was a risky move for Paul to confront Peter. Peter was part of Jesus' inner circle and one of the most influential leaders in the early church; Paul was a former persecutor of Christians and a less established leader. If Peter had chosen to, it is likely he could have made life very difficult for Paul. Peter could have gathered other Christians who had been persecuted by Paul or who disagreed with his teachings, publicly criticized him, and severely damaged Paul's position and influence in the early church.

When we speak up, it often involves risking our reputation, influence, financial security, and relationships. Some of us would rather walk a mile barefoot on hot coals before confronting a friend or coworker who does something we believe contributes to racial injustice. What an awkward conversation! It is very difficult, but it is also very important. Later in Galatians, Paul writes:

> Brothers and sisters, if someone is caught in a sin, you who live by the Spirit should restore that person gently. But watch yourselves, or you also may be tempted. Carry each other's burdens, and in this way you will fulfill the law of Christ. If anyone thinks they are something when they are not, they deceive themselves. (Galatians 6:1-3)

When we read passages like the one above, we may think of confronting someone regarding sins related to sexual immorality, stealing, greed, and so forth. But sins that perpetuate racial injustice are just as damaging to the individual and our Christian communities. When we observe such actions, we need to follow Paul's example and prayerfully speak the truth with grace.

Listening like Peter. In Galatians 2, Paul does not tell us Peter's response when he confronted him, but there is evidence in other passages that Peter acknowledged Paul was correct. We know that Peter and Paul continued to be allies and advance the gospel together. Later in his life, Peter wrote the following about Paul:

> Bear in mind that our Lord's patience means salvation, just as our dear brother Paul also wrote you with the wisdom that God gave him. . . . His letters contain some things that are hard to understand, which ignorant and unstable people distort, as they do the other Scriptures, to their own destruction. (2 Peter 3:15-16)

It's never easy to be confronted by another person. There is a natural tendency to defend our actions with statements like "That was not my intention" or "My desire was to ___." Before we seek to explain our motivations and intentions, we need to carefully listen to what is being expressed and the impact that our actions have had on the other person; we need to listen before we seek to be listened to (James 1:19).

We also must be committed to not dismiss or punish people when they are honest. In many organizations, when brave individuals do speak up, their input is often rebuffed as being overly sensitive, unfair, or not legitimate. They also experience negative consequences for sharing their perspectives (e.g., strained relationships, not being considered for promotions). If there is an environment where constructive input is dismissed or punished, it is very unlikely that the organization will make much progress.

PRACTICAL, TIMELY EXAMPLES FROM TWO THOUSAND YEARS AGO

The early Christians lived in a very different cultural and historical context than we do in the United States today, but we can learn a great deal about effectively addressing racial injustice in our lives, organizations, and society by studying how they dealt with challenges in their communities. Their examples remain relevant because our relationships and group dynamics continue to share many similarities. We can be challenged and helped by their examples. We can also be encouraged by the ways the Holy Spirit led and empowered them to overcome the major spiritual, cultural, historic, and economic challenges that threatened to tear their community apart. We have the same Helper (John 14) and therefore we can also build countercultural communities of justice and unity in our unjust and divided world.

Discussion/Reflection Questions

1. What are some of the reasons prayer is essential for working toward racial justice?

2. If someone experienced prejudice or disadvantages due to their race in your organization, do you think they would speak up? If not, why not? If so, do you think the leadership of your organization would do a good job of listening and addressing the issue? If not, why not?

3. Does cross-racial power sharing take place in your organization? Why or why not? If so, can you give examples?

4. Is social justice prioritized in your organization? Why or why not?

5. Is the leadership of your organization racially diverse? If so, how does that affect your organization in positive and/or negative ways?

6. What are some principles we can learn from the Antioch church's gifts to the Jerusalem church (Acts 11)? How can we apply those principles in our society today?

7. Do you believe that acts of restorative justice or reparations are encouraged in the Bible? Why or why not?

8. What are some ways that Christians can practice restorative justice or reparations in our society today? Are you doing those actions?

9. Does cultural assimilation and code-switching take place in your organization? If so, can you give some examples of how that hinders your organization's efforts?

10. In regard to courageous conversations, is it more difficult for you to speak up like Paul or to listen like Peter? Why?

11. How do you plan to apply the content in this chapter?

Recommended Prayer

Lord, thank you for empowering the early Christians to live lives of justice and unity in their unjust and divided society. Please help us follow their example. Help our actions to be guided by your perfect wisdom rather than our own ingenuity and planning. Help us rely on your inexhaustible strength rather than our own strength. If there is oppression in our communities, please give the oppressed the courage to speak up, and give the oppressors the humility to listen. Help our communities share power in ways that produce justice and loving, unified relationships with one another. Help us put our love into action and be willing to make financial sacrifices for restoration and the benefit of others. Help us have courageous conversations that are filled with grace and truth. Help us to live out your prayer that we would be unified and demonstrate your love to the world (John 17). Thank you for giving us new lives with you and with one another through the cross.

CHAPTER NINE

FAITHFUL ANTIRACISTS
SEEK OUT HELP AND HELP OTHERS

MARTIN NIEMÖLLER (1892–1984) was a German pastor who went through a dramatic transformation. In the 1920s to 1930s, Niemöller supported the rise of Hitler and the Nazis because he believed a strong leader could unite their country and restore national honor after Germany's defeat in the First World War. He was a committed German nationalist who had served as a U-boat commander. Niemöller supported Hitler, in part, because of his early emphasis on the importance of Christianity in Germany's renewal.[1]

As Hitler sought to seize control over the views and actions of Christians in Germany, Niemöller began to question his support. Hitler and the Nazis called for "purging Christianity of all Judaic elements, including removing the Old Testament from the Bible and recasting Jesus as a blond-haired, blue-eyed Aryan."[2] Niemöller condemned the teachings as heresy. He organized a movement of six thousand pastors who attempted to oppose the Nazi's meddling in the affairs of the church. His actions infuriated Hitler and he was placed in a Nazi concentration camp from 1938 to 1945.

During his time in the camp, Niemöller repented for his complicity with nationalism, ethnocentrism, militarism, and hate. During that time, he wrote the following poem:

> First they came for the Communists, and I did not speak out, because I was not a Communist.
>
> Then they came for the Trade Unionists, and I did not speak out, because I was not a Trade Unionist.

Then they came for the Jews, and I did not speak out, because I was not a Jew.

Then they came for me—and there was no one left to speak for me.

Throughout the remainder of his life, Niemöller became a passionate advocate for justice and peace. In October 1945, he partnered with other German Christian leaders to issue a statement.

By us infinite wrong was brought over many peoples and countries . . . we accuse ourselves for not standing to our beliefs more courageously, for not praying more faithfully, for not believing more joyously, and for not loving more ardently.[3]

Niemöller's life is a powerful example of the transformation that can take place when we recognize our views are not in line with God's will and seek out the help and partnership of others.

Structural Change and Relationships

In this chapter, we focus on the importance of building relationships where we can both receive and give help. You may be thinking, *I thought you said in chapter seven that relationships are not a magical solution?* It is true that we do not believe that mentor relationships are a magical solution that will end racism on their own—it is not that simple. But we also recognize that building the right kinds of mentoring relationships can be a very powerful step toward progress and changing structural dynamics. That's what this chapter is all about.

Seeking Out Help

Imagine trying to climb a mountain for the first time without ever learning from an experienced mountain climber; or trying to repair a car without ever learning from a mechanic; or trying to raise children without ever learning from a parent. Most of us know better than to make those mistakes. We realize trying to accomplish complex tasks on our own will likely result in pain, frustration, and failure. However, when it comes to working toward racial justice, we often find Christians trying to make progress with little or no mentoring or ongoing support. Sadly their efforts typically result in frustration and failure. No amount of resources and hard work can fully suffice without the ongoing help and encouragement from brothers and sisters in Christ.

Help from others can come through a variety of relationships. It can be a formal coach or mentor who you meet with regularly in order to study the Bible, discuss questions, or go through a training curriculum. It can be an informal relationship with a knowledgeable friend you meet with to share about your lives or discuss books. It can be a pastor, professor, or diversity professional in your organization. It can be other Christians you serve alongside while volunteering with an organization focused on racial justice. In this chapter, we refer to all of these types of relationships as "mentors."

The Freedom of Grace and Truth

We find that one of the biggest obstacles to individuals and organizations making progress toward racial justice is an unwillingness to acknowledge areas of sin and weakness. Many people want to portray an image of "I'm doing just great in this area" rather than admitting their fears, anger, biases, and failures. The fear of being labeled a "racist White person" or "angry person of color" often prevents people from having honest conversations about the areas where they are struggling.

As followers of Jesus, we can enjoy the freedom of both grace and truth. As the apostle John wrote about Jesus:

> We have seen his glory, the glory of the one and only Son, who came from the Father, full of *grace and truth*.... Out of his fullness we have all received *grace* in place of *grace* already given. For the law was given through Moses; *grace and truth* came through Jesus Christ. (John 1:14-17, emphasis added)

In healthy mentoring relationships, we do not need to act like we have it all together or try to hide the areas where we are struggling. We can be honest about our struggles and areas where we fall short. When necessary, we can be challenged to do better (truth) while also being reminded that all of our sins are forgiven through Christ's sacrifice for us (grace). When our mentoring relationships are full of the grace and truth Jesus provides, they help us to experience healing, joy, and freedom.

A Word of Caution

There are an abundance of "experts" on the topic of racial dynamics. Many people have strong opinions about race relations in the United States, but a much smaller number have the maturity, knowledge, and experience required to provide effective mentoring that is aligned with the teachings in the Bible. As we have seen, a large percentage of Christians have inaccurate and problematic racial views. If we select one of these individuals to be our mentor, it will hurt rather than help our efforts to be faithful antiracists. It is essential to pray for the Lord to lead us to mentors and to be very discerning about who we select.

In this chapter, we are primarily focused on one-on-one mentoring relationships. But there are other ways we can be "mentored" through books, videos, conferences, workshops, and media outlets. It is essential to be discerning about the information we take in from those sources. There are some important questions to ask about potential mentors and resources.

- Do their teachings align with the teachings in the Bible, including the central themes of justice, inclusion, and special care and protections for the vulnerable and oppressed?
- Do they have a structural understanding of racial injustice?
- Is their understanding of racial dynamics based on their opinions and experiences or on accurate data sources, research, and best practices?

Common Questions

Should I look for mentors who are inside or outside of my racial group? We recommend both. It is typically very helpful to have mentors who are outside of our racial group because they can help us have new eyes to understand racial dynamics. But it is also helpful to have mentors who are in our racial group because they can relate to our experiences and questions and share about their own journey.

Should I look for mentors who are inside or outside of my organization? We recommend both. Mentors that are a part of our own organization will have an insider's perspective on the dynamics as well as experience working within the environment. They will also likely be more accessible for dialogue and collaboration. On the other hand, mentors that are not a part of our organization can provide new perspectives and will be less likely to affirm incorrect views perpetuated by groupthink. Outsiders who specialize in racial dynamics can typically provide more tools, knowledge, and experience than insiders who don't.

Should our organization hire a staff member or diversity professional that can provide mentoring? As we explored in chapter seven, organizations often have problematic, unrealistic expectations for "diversity superheroes." However, under the right circumstances and expectations, diversity professionals can play a very helpful role. In most cases, we advise leaders and organizations to first work with mentors before hiring or designating a diversity professional. The mentor can help the organization lay the foundations for a diversity professional (or team) to play an effective role.

Affirmers Versus Challengers

It is easy to make the mistake of only seeking out mentors who affirm our existing views and actions rather than challenge us to make progress. Here is a fictional scenario based on common dynamics.

Glenville Baptist Church is a predominantly White church in a neighborhood with a growing Hispanic/Latino community. Their church decides to hire a Hispanic/Latino pastor to help their congregation be more effective at connecting with their new neighbors. The hiring committee narrows their decision down to two candidates with extensive experience and strong credentials:

Manuel: Most of the Christian organizations he has been a part of have been predominantly White. When the hiring committee interviews him, his perspective on topics like Bible interpretation, leadership styles, racial dynamics, and politics are similar to the typical views in their congregation.

Santiago: Most of the Christian organizations he has been a part of have been predominantly Hispanic/Latino. When the hiring committee interviews him, his perspective on topics like Bible interpretation, leadership styles, racial dynamics, and politics are similar to the typical views of the majority of Hispanic/Latino Americans.

The hiring committee selects Manuel because "he seems like the best fit." They believe Manuel will do a good job of "connecting with the congregation." They are concerned that some members of the congregation may not respond well to Santiago's views and leadership style.

Manuel is an "affirmer." In most situations, he will likely affirm the organization's approach to racial dynamics rather than challenge them. Ironically, adding Manuel may even hinder the racial progress of the organization rather than help it. If concerns are expressed about the racial dynamics in the church, the leadership can point to hiring Manuel as an indication of their progress and to justify not taking additional action.

Santiago is a "challenger." His views are different from the typical views in the church, but that is a good thing. The church will not make progress if they are stuck following the status quo. If the church hired Santiago and empowered him to lead change, he could help the congregation take some important steps.

Seeking out challengers typically requires more time and energy because our relational networks are often filled with people who share our views. It also requires courage. Most of us would prefer to have our perspectives affirmed rather than critiqued. But effective mentorship requires opening our lives up to people who can bring new perspectives with truth and grace. If our mentors simply confirm our existing views, it defeats the purpose of having a mentor relationship.

Intentionally Pursuing Mentors Who Will Challenge Our Thinking (Chad)

As I shared in the introduction, it wasn't until I was in my early twenties that I really began to grow in my understanding of racial dynamics. I am thankful for the many books, training programs, conferences, and videos that helped me on my journey. But nothing has helped me to grow more than the grace and truth I have experienced through relationships with individuals such as Christina Edmondson, Michaela Gregory, Glenn Bracey, Michael Emerson, Brenda Salter McNeil, Viju Deenadayalu, Jay Hayden, Oral Seudath, Nicole Buchanan, Robert Caldwell, Richard Johnson, Alvin Sanders, Joel Perez, Glen Kinoshita, Korie Edwards, Leah Fulton, Jason Cha, as well as many others.

As a White Christian, I could have easily gone through my life without ever having my racial views significantly challenged. I'm thankful the Lord had another plan. Some of the above relationships happened naturally, but the majority of them required some initiative and intentionality. The extra effort was well worth it. Those relationships have been a tremendous source of joy and growth in my life.

You may be thinking, *I would love to have mentors like the ones you described above, but I have no idea where to find them.* Here are a few recommendations if you are in that situation.

1. *Pray.* Ask God to lead you to mentors and then keep your eyes open. It is fun to see how often "unusual" connections take place when we pray.

2. *Contact local or national organizations.* There are many excellent Christian and secular organizations that focus on racial justice activism, training, and dialogue. For example, we recommend Be the Bridge (bethebridge.com). Prayerfully seek out those organizations in your community and ask them for help with finding mentors.

3. *Utilize the RJUC Coaching Network.* It is described below.

RJUC Coaching Network. From 2019 to 2021, our ministry, Renew Partnerships, partnered with many leaders and experts across the United States to launch the *Racial Justice and Unity Center* (RJUC). The RJUC focuses on providing the following resources:

1. *Assessment.* The RJUC provides research-based assessment tools based on the Bible and the input of leading experts. We will explain how the tools can help in the next chapter.

2. *Coaching Network.* The RJUC helps individuals and organizations connect with experienced, knowledgeable coaches that can provide ongoing mentoring and encouragement.

3. *Organizational Change.* The RJUC helps local and national Christian organizations (churches, denominations, schools, colleges, ministries) develop and implement strategies for making progress.

Criteria for becoming an RJUC coach. The individuals in the RJUC Coaching Network meet certain criteria, including:

- They have stated a commitment to base their coaching on the teachings of the Bible.

- They have at least three years of experience mentoring individuals and/or organizations.

- They have the opportunity to receive feedback, mentoring, and training on the coaching they provide through the RJUC.

The RJUC Coaching Network can help you to find a mentor who will provide accurate, helpful coaching that is based on the teachings in the Bible. But it does not eliminate the need for you to be prayerful and discerning regarding any mentors you select, including those found through the RJUC.

How you can start working with a coach. To start working with a coach, visit rjuc.org. On the website you can learn about the available coaches and request an appointment. Or you can schedule a brief conversation with an RJUC staff member who can help you select a coach and schedule an appointment. After the appointment, you can choose if you would like to continue to meet with the coach, connect with another RJUC coach, or seek out other mentoring options.

Entrusting What We Have Learned to Reliable People

You may have seen a pond with a layer of slimy green algae growing on top and thought, *I wouldn't want to set foot in that water!* The pond was probably filled with algae because the water was stagnant. In order for ponds and lakes to stay healthy and full of wildlife, they need to have a steady flow of water entering and exiting. A similar reality is true in our lives. In order to stay healthy, we must have a steady flow in and out of our lives. If our lives are all about receiving help and input from others, we become stagnant, self-focused, and lifeless. If our lives are all about giving help and input to others, we become exhausted, disillusioned, and resentful.

Becoming an effective faithful antiracist requires cultivating a life of receiving help and then passing what we've learned on to others who will also pass what they have learned on to others, and so forth. As Paul wrote to Timothy: "And the things you have heard me say in the presence of many witnesses entrust to reliable people who will also be qualified to teach others" (2 Timothy 2:2).

Notice that Paul did not tell Timothy, "Go find any random person and entrust them with what I've taught you." Paul instructed Timothy to focus his energy on specific types of people. The following are some key things to look for as you prayerfully consider people to invest your life in.

- *Reliable*: Do they act on what they have learned? Do they show up to appointments? Do they follow through with recommendations?

- *Able to teach others*: Do they have the desire, empathy, grace, and discipline required to effectively teach others?

- *Teachable*: When you provide input, are they defensive or open to instruction?

- *Available*: Are they willing to invest the time required for personal growth and helping others?

WHO ARE YOU UNIQUELY EQUIPPED TO HELP?

Take a few moments to think about a season in your life when you grew in your love for God and other people. What caused the transformation? Was it the Holy Spirit? The Bible? Mentors? Christian community? Experiences?

Most likely, your growth was sparked by a combination of all of the above working in partnership. Mentoring is very helpful, but on its own it is rarely enough to produce change. That is one of the reasons why prayer is so essential. Only God can provide all the ingredients required for personal transformation. God knows each of us intimately and what it will take for us to make progress. Only God can providentially orchestrate all of the necessary elements coming together at just the right time in our lives. We must avoid thinking we can "educate" someone into being a faithful antiracist using our own wisdom and strength.

Think back again to your season of growth and the individuals who helped you during that period. How were they helpful? What did they do? How did God prepare them to play that role in your life?

Our mentors shape us, but we are not our mentors. Jesus' disciples were called to follow his example, but they were not Jesus. Peter was still an impulsive fisherman. Matthew was still an ex-tax collector. Simon the Zealot was probably still passionate about releasing the Jews from Roman rule. Regardless of their differences, Jesus commanded each of them to go and make disciples. Peter, Matthew, and Simon had different approaches to helping people to grow because they had different personalities, experiences, gifts, knowledge, and skills. It is also important to recognize that they were not perfect people. The disciples were still "in process" even as they were helping others.

Consider the example of Niemöller at the beginning of this chapter. As a former supporter of Hitler and the Nazis, he was uniquely equipped to help other Christians who had fallen into the trap of nationalism and antisemitism. He knew from personal experiences the spiritual, emotional, and mental wrestling that was required to disentangle their sense of self-identity and purpose from those lies. During the last four decades of his life, he used that knowledge to help bring freedom, healing, and restoration to his fellow German Christians.

It is likely that there are people on this planet that can best learn from your one-of-a-kind blend of personality, experiences, gifts, knowledge, and skills. We encourage you to take a moment to reflect on how God has prepared you to help others and to ask God to give you supernatural connections with individuals whom you are uniquely equipped to help.

EXPECT OPPOSITION

As we seek to grow in our own lives and help others, we should expect opposition. The Bible frequently warns Christians about the forces that attack and hinder personal and systemic change. That opposition includes the world, the flesh, and spiritual forces of evil.

The world. Do not love the world or anything in the world. If anyone loves the world, love for the Father is not in them. For everything in the world—the lust of the flesh, the lust of the eyes, and the pride of life—comes not from the Father but from the world. (1 John 2:15-16)

The flesh. For the flesh desires what is contrary to the Spirit, and the Spirit what is contrary to the flesh. They are in conflict with each other, so that you are not to do whatever you want. But if you are led by the Spirit, you are not under the law. The acts of the flesh are obvious: sexual immorality, impurity and debauchery; idolatry and witchcraft; hatred, discord, jealousy, fits of rage, selfish ambition, dissensions, factions and envy; drunkenness, orgies, and the like. I warn you, as I did before, that those who live like this will not inherit the kingdom of God. (Galatians 5:17-21)

Spiritual forces of evil. Finally, be strong in the Lord and in his mighty power. Put on the full armor of God, so that you can take your stand against the devil's schemes. For our struggle is not against flesh and blood, but against the rulers, against the authorities, against the powers of this dark world and against the spiritual forces of evil in the heavenly realms. (Ephesians 6:10-12)

We must put on the armor of God (Ephesians 6:10-20). We must rely on God's power through prayer, be led by the Holy Spirit, and receive help and encouragement through relationships with other Christians. Otherwise, we will find our human knowledge, skills, and motivation are no match for the formidable obstacles and adversaries we will face.

Two Key Principles (Christina)

The following are two key principles for helping others that I have learned as a counselor and psychologist.

Connection before content. I have learned that the deeper or more challenging the content, the deeper and more trusting the relationship between people must be. Conversations about racial views often spark strong responses. Some people become animated when they talk, raise their voice, or express emotions. Other people become quiet, reserved, and withdraw from the conversation. The topic touches on experiences and deeply held beliefs that are at the core of how we view ourselves and the world around us.

We are best able to hear the hardest truths from those who have shown us the greatest unconditional love. Teaching for love with love creates an educational space and contract that is brave enough to experience the tension and conflict inevitable in antiracist discipleship. We employ methods of truth and grace to show our formal and informal students that we are committed to their growth and seek their release from internalized racial inferiority and superiority. We offer each learner a space that seeks to challenge them but not embarrass their often-insecure state. This insecurity can be easily masked by a puffed-up presentation.

With our work and research, we often find that strong, trusting relationships lay the foundation for personal transformation. In an RRJP focus group we heard of this transformative experience.

> I was in a men's group with a mix of African American brothers and some white guys, and it was for about a year. We were meeting monthly for a couple hours at a time. . . . It was very eye-opening, and I began understanding white privilege, and the obstacles that African Americans were up against that I never had to deal with. And relationships began growing from that. And asking some hard questions, we were able to do that and still be brothers when it was over with. (White/Black, male, 60s)

The best mentors mirror the perfect mentor, Jesus. Jesus modeled connection before content. From the beginning of his short but world-changing ministry, he drew near to others offering hope, grace, truth, healing, and a robust social ethic. Jesus maintained a deep relational connection to his disciples. Their strong connection allowed Jesus to use his own story and experiences to teach for personal, spiritual, and social transformation.

We can learn important principles from Jesus' interactions with those who followed him and those who rejected him. Jesus' teaching was faultless, yet he was rejected and scorned by the hardhearted. This can help us see that even if we teach others with love, God's power, and accurate knowledge, we may still be rejected or scorned. Like Jesus, we are called to share God's grace and truth regardless if it is accepted or rejected. Even when we are working with an individual or group that is hardhearted, there may be a few teachable individuals like Nicodemus (the Pharisee from John 3) who are open to the message.

Repentance, discomfort, and learning. Repentance, discomfort, and learning are more interconnected than we might realize. Common definitions of repentance highlight the necessity of change or a new way. The mental image is someone heading in one direction, then turning to another direction or, rather, person. In Christian repentance we turn to the person of Jesus. In Scripture, the Greek word *metanoia*, pronounced "met-an'-oy-ah" (μετάνοια) is used frequently and it means "changing one's mind."[4] *Metanoia* is the command, calling, and ministry of the Christian and at the same time the work and credit of the Holy Spirit. That's one of the many paradoxes of the Christian faith. We are commanded to do something that the Spirit wills in us. Interestingly, in psychology, the term *metanoia* refers to a process of experiencing a psychotic "breakdown" followed by a positive psychological rebuilding, healing, or transformation.[5]

Can you imagine teaching toward the goal of a contained "psychological crisis" so that the student can be transformed? I can almost hear my workout coach yelling at me, "First, lady, if it doesn't challenge you it won't change you!" The next morning I am reminded through sore muscles that bodily change is taking place. Likewise, when we learn about the pathology, sociology, and theology around racism, white supremacy, and a more accurate story of American history, we feel deep aches, aches that we want to avoid or resist. The discomfort we feel is quickly interpreted as something being wrong, rather than the truth that stretching, challenge, and transformation is nearby. The breakdown of pride, self-delusion, and whitewashed views of America, for example, lead to a crisis of identity and fear of loss that is central to the dismantling of racial idolatry.

In our research we found individuals who recognized that pain and discomfort are barriers that must be overcome in order to see progress.

> There are a lot of wounds in the area of race, and talking about it is painful but if we can keep trying to listen and understand each other's perspectives we will grow into a more respectful, knowledgeable and appreciative university culture. (White, female, 60s)

> I think we are not comfortable with discussing racial differences, and this can hinder class discussions, interpersonal growth and understanding, and addressing the broader social issues surrounding race and diversity. (White, female, 20s) [6]

It is important to help the individuals we work with to expect and deal with the discomfort of change. If they have no tolerance for discomfort, they will abort the necessary breakdown process before transformation can take root. Knowing that discomfort is inevitable and necessary to both learning and repentance prepares the teacher and learner to stay the course.

As we push through the discomfort, we experience true *learning*. Learning is defined by psychologists in many ways, but there is significant agreement on what learning produces—change. Learning is the process of acquiring new, or modifying existing, knowledge, behaviors, or values. The ability to learn is possessed by humans and animals; there is also evidence for learning in certain plants.[7] In other words, life is required for learning. That is true for physical growth and spiritual growth. When we are spiritually alive, our minds are being renewed and we are open to transformational learning (Acts 26:20; Ephesians 5:8-9).

HELPFUL ACTIVITIES

The following are some activities that can be helpful as you work with others.

- *Discuss the Bible:* Read and discuss the many Bible passages we have looked at in this book.

- *Pray together:* Pray for the strength and wisdom to effectively work toward racial justice.

- *Share life:* Spend time together in the normal routines of life.

- *Serve together:* Check with local churches/ministries for projects you can be a part of.

- *Discuss a book or documentary video:* See the notes in this book for recommended resources.

- *Discuss their assessment results:* We will explore this in the next chapter.

DISCUSSION/REFLECTION QUESTIONS

1. What is the relationship between structural changes and relationships? Can you have one without the other?

2. In regard to growing as a faithful antiracist, do you typically seek out help and support or go it alone? Why?

3. Why are grace and truth both essential in effective mentoring relationships?

4. Are you currently being taught about racial dynamics through relationships, books, conferences, media outlets, or other ways? If so, how did you select those individuals or resources? How do you know if the information is biblical and accurate?

5. Are you helping other people to grow in the area of racial justice? If so, are the individuals you are working with reliable and able to teach others (2 Timothy 2:2)?

6. As you think about your life, skills, and personality, what types of individuals are you uniquely equipped to help in the area of racial justice?

7. Have you experienced opposition from the world, the flesh, and the spiritual forces of evil as you have sought to be a faithful antiracist? If so, how have you dealt with the opposition?

8. When seeking to help others, do you tend to lean toward connection or content? What happens if you have one without the other?

9. Have you experienced the connection between repentance, discomfort, and learning in your life? If so, can you give an example?

10. How do you plan to apply the content in this chapter?

RECOMMENDED PRAYER

Lord, thank you that we do not need to go it alone in our efforts to work toward racial justice. Thank you that we can rely on your ongoing power and guidance. Thank you for giving us brothers and sisters in Christ that can help us along on our journey. Please lead us to mentors that are aligned with your will. Help us receive their input with teachability and humility. Please release us from any evil and destructive thoughts and actions that remain in our lives. Help us to use what you have taught us to help others. Help us see the unique ways you have shaped us, and lead us to individuals who we are uniquely equipped to help. Give us the power to overcome the challenges of the world, the flesh, and the spiritual forces of evil. Help us find an effective balance of both connection and content with the individuals we work with. Give us wisdom as we seek to help the people around us grow closer to you and practice your perfect will. Amen.

CHAPTER TEN

FAITHFUL ANTIRACISTS EFFECTIVELY MEASURE PROGRESS

IMAGINE YOU ARE MEETING with your doctor and she explains, "I have some concerns about your health. I think it would be good for you to make some lifestyle changes, or you may be facing some serious health problems down the road." You return a year later and explain that you have made some changes and you're feeling fine. Do you think she would just take your word for it and assume that you are now healthy? No, if she is a good doctor, she would require evidence that your health has improved. She and her staff would listen to your breathing, measure your weight, and check your blood pressure. She will probably order specific types of tests, like an EKG to test for heart issues or blood work to measure your cholesterol levels and white blood cell count. Fortunately, medical experts have developed a number of ways to quickly assess the health of our bodies and identify areas that could be problematic. Doctors know they can't exclusively rely on a patient's opinion that "I'm feeling fine."

Similarly, when it comes to making progress toward racial justice, we cannot be content with a general sense of "We're doing pretty good." When we talk with individuals and organizations about their views and actions related to racial dynamics, we often hear comments like "I know there is room for improvement, but generally speaking, things are going pretty well."

As evidence that things are going well for them personally, they will often share items like:

- I have many cross-racial friendships.

- I attend a multiracial church.

- I have ____ on racial diversity (read books, watched movies, attended conferences, etc.).

As evidence that things are going well for their organization, they will often share items like:

- Our organization has increased the percentage of people of color from 5 percent to 10 percent.

- We have a very welcoming environment where everyone is treated the same.

- We have a new diversity committee.

- We have hired a pastor who is a person of color.

- We have a new training program.

As we saw in previous chapters, the above items are inadequate ways to measure progress. It is possible to do all of the above items and still actively or passively support racial injustice. Our goals and the standards we use to measure progress toward those goals have a major impact on how successful our efforts are. As metrics expert Jerry Muller explains, "[Measurements] can be a good thing. . . . But they can also distort, divert, displace, distract, and discourage. While we are bound to live in an age of measurement, we live in an age of mismeasurement, over-measurement, misleading measurement, and counterproductive measurement."[1]

An Example of the Challenges of Measuring Progress

Here is an example of a problematic *metric* (standards used to measure progress):

Teresa is a pastor in a predominantly White church. Her responsibilities include coordinating the Welcoming Team. She is very motivated to create a racially inclusive environment at their church, so she carefully observes the way that the Welcoming Team members greet people of color that visit. She determines they are doing an effective job because in almost every interaction that she observes, the Welcoming Team members are very warm and welcoming to individuals of color.

Teresa's metric, the warmth of the welcome team: Teresa assumed that the warmth of the welcome team is an indication that their church is creating an inclusive environment. But, "warmth" is subjective and an unreliable indicator of inclusion. Christian leaders often overestimate the significance of their congregation's "warmth" toward people in other racial groups. Sadly, it is possible to be warm toward people in other racial groups while actively or passively supporting racial injustice. Robert Jones, director of the Public Religion Research Institute, did extensive research on the views of White Christians and discovered a "stunning contradiction."

> White evangelical Protestants, for example, report the warmest attitudes toward African Americans (an average score of 71 on a scale of 1 to 100), while simultaneously registering the highest score on the Racism Index (0.78 on a scale of 0 to 1). While this stunning contradiction is most pronounced for white evangelical Protestants, the pattern also exists among white mainline Protestants and white Catholics. . . . White Christians think of themselves as people who hold warm feelings toward African Americans while simultaneously embracing a host of racist and racially resentful attitudes that are inconsistent with that assertion.[2]

In other words, in Teresa's church it is very likely that White Christians have warm feelings and actions toward people of color while at the same time holding to racial views that perpetuate racial injustice both within their organization and within society. Their church needs more effective metrics that measure the underlying views and actions that prevent racial justice.

Teresa's method for measuring the metric, personal observation: Teresa attempted to assess the dynamics in her organization by observing the warmth of the welcome team members toward people of color. Her method of measuring is very limited because it involves only one perspective (hers). She is limited by the fact she can only observe one interaction at a time and by her own cultural perspectives and biases. Furthermore, the welcome team members may know that Teresa is especially concerned that they be welcoming to people of color and therefore make a point of being welcoming whenever Teresa is around. In other words, her presence in the room may affect the "data" she is collecting.

EFFECTIVE METRICS CONNECT TO REAL-LIFE EXPERIENCES

The above example illustrates some common pitfalls involved with developing effective metrics and methods for measuring them. Another common pitfall is developing metrics that are theoretical and disconnected from the real-life experiences of individuals.

The following is an exercise to help you reflect on grounding metrics in real-life experiences. Please read the following book excerpt written by Drew Hart. It provides a candid description of his experience as a Black student on a predominantly White Christian college campus.

When I surveyed the campus at a distance, people seemed very friendly and smiley. But when I walked down the main walkway through campus, many people would move to the edge of the sidewalk and look down or away as they passed by. I saw a pattern in which students primarily did this around me and other people of color. I saw people's posture change in an odd way when I joined in group conversations where everyone present didn't know who I was. To be fair, though, I didn't notice this behavior at first. It is only after you have seen it for the hundredth and thousandth time that its recurrence becomes clear as day. And then there were the comments. . . .

People made horrific comments about black students on campus, including some students who routinely referred to all the black males on campus as "thugs" and "troublemakers." I overheard white students insinuating that being on the basketball team was the only reason that most of the black male students were accepted to the school in the first place. Black female students also experienced constant slights, from cultural ignorance and insensitivity, overt stereotypes, and inappropriate touching. In particular, I remember many of the black women on campus talked about people constantly touching their hair without permission. Also, any sign of confidence and assertiveness was always articulated as being rude, angry, disruptive, and out of place. . . .

The ongoing racial prejudice on campus was more persistent and life-draining than anything I had seen in my life. Nothing, including the black church I had grown up in, had prepared me for white

Christian community. I was becoming cynical and at times very bitter about the church and its racism. I sometimes shared my experiences with white students on campus, but most did not take my words very seriously. I had to deeply recalibrate my social networks based on these experiences just so I could make it through. Each little cut, on its own, was insubstantial. But by the end of my time in college, I found myself with a thousand paper cuts that hurt like hell.[3]

Imagine you are on the leadership team of the campus that Hart described above, and it is your responsibility to develop a process for measuring the university's progress toward creating a more racially inclusive environment. Consider the following questions:

- What are some effective metrics which the campus could use to gauge their progress toward building a racially inclusive campus? Why do you believe they are effective?

- What are some effective methods the campus leaders could use to measure their progress? Why do you believe those methods are effective?

- What if students in different racial groups have different opinions about the dynamics on campus? Should the leadership take one group's perspectives into consideration more than another group's? Why or why not?

Later in this chapter, we will share some examples of metrics we think would be helpful for campuses like the one Hart attended.

UNDERSTANDING DYNAMICS CAN IMPROVE MOTIVATION

We find that two of the most common objections to racial justice efforts are "It is not fair for some racial groups to get special treatment" and "Focusing on the desires of people of color is reverse racism against White people." That type of pushback can be reduced if leaders help their members understand the racial dynamics in their organization.

Let's look at an example from our research. We asked students and employees on Christian college campuses if they agreed with the statement,

"People of color are often put at a social disadvantage on our campus." See the results in figure 10.1. Notice that only 19% of White students, 31% of Hispanic/Latino students, 51% of Black students, and 28% of Asian students agreed. However, we know from other research and conversations with campus leaders that many of the campuses had dynamics that were similar to what Drew Hart described above. For a large percentage of the students, there was a disconnect between their perceptions and the realities on their campus.

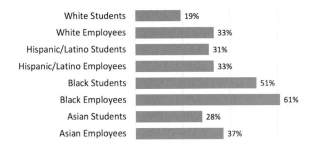

Figure 10.1. Students and employees on Christian college campuses who agreed with the statement "People of color are often put at a social disadvantage on our campus" (RPCCS, 2016-2020, n=13,580)

We also asked the students and employees if they believed there should be more or less of several types of activities that could help improve the racial dynamics on their campus. Figure 10.2 shows responses by White students. The top bar shows the responses by the White students who agreed that people of color were often put at a social disadvantage on their campus (*Believe POC Disadvantaged*). The bottom bar shows the responses by all other White students (*All Others*).

As you can see in figure 10.2, White students who did not believe that people of color were disadvantaged on their campus were less than half as likely to believe there should be more efforts to improve the racial dynamics. This is not surprising—if students don't believe there is a problem, they will not see the need to address it. We hope these findings will motivate leaders to measure the racial dynamics in their organization and then look for effective ways to communicate areas they discover need growth. Helping members to understand the dynamics within their organization can help to increase support for efforts to make progress.

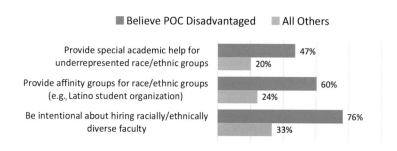

Figure 10.2. White students who indicated their campus should do more of the listed activities (RPCCS, 2016-2020, n=13,580)

ABOUT THE RJUC ASSESSMENTS (CHAD)

In the remainder of this chapter, we share about the RJUC assessment tools and how they can help individuals and organizations. If you choose to use different assessment tools or approaches, that's great. We hope this section will help you think through some areas to take into consideration as you develop and implement other methods for measuring progress.

How the assessments have been (and are being) developed. When we began our 2019–2020 national research (see rrjp.org for details), one of our primary goals was to collect data to use in developing new assessment tools to help Christian individuals and organizations make progress toward racial justice. From 2019 to 2021, our research team and many other experts across the United States (including Christina) spent hundreds of hours developing the assessment questions and reporting systems. In the coming years, we plan to continue to improve the tools as we collect data and receive feedback. Therefore, the versions that are available when you read this book may have some differences from the descriptions in this chapter, but they should be pretty close.

How the assessments are unique. We are not aware of any other assessment tools that focus on measuring racial dynamics based on the Bible, current research, best practices, and a structural understanding of racial injustice. We are also not aware of any assessment tools that have had such a large number of Christian leaders and experts involved in the design process.

Using the personal assessment. To use the RJUC personal assessment, visit rjuc.org. The assessment takes about twenty minutes to complete. After finishing the questions, you will receive a free (lite) report with your scores in approximately eight categories. You will also have the option to schedule an appointment with an RJUC coach to discuss a full version of the report, which includes your scores in approximately thirty categories.

Using the organization assessment. After completing the personal assessment, you can then take the organization assessment. It takes about fifteen minutes to complete. After finishing the questions, you will receive a free (lite) report with your organization's scores in approximately five categories. For a more accurate measure of the dynamics in your organization, the RJUC can collect responses from many individuals in your organization and then provide your leadership with an analysis and summary of the findings. The RJUC can also work with large organizations with many locations, for example a church denomination, and help them develop strategies for measuring racial dynamics throughout their entire organization in an ongoing way.

Scores in the RJUC Personal Assessment Report

The following are the scores that are currently included in the full version of the RJUC Personal Assessment Report along with the types of questions they are designed to answer. You will probably notice many similarities between the content we have covered in this book and the items measured in the assessment.

- **Understanding of past racial realities:** Do you have a general understanding of the history of racial dynamics in the United States?

- **Understanding of current racial realities:** Do you have a general understanding of current racial realities in the United States?

- **Structural explanations for racial disparities:** Do you point to structural causes as the reason for racial disparities?

- **Motivation to work toward racial justice:** Are you motived to work toward racial justice?

- **Willing to apply the Bible:** Are you willing to apply Bible passages with themes and principles related to racial justice?

- **Colorblindness:** Do you believe it is best to try to ignore a person's race/ethnicity or avoid talking about racial issues?

- **Neutrality toward racial dynamics:** Do you tend to be "neutral" on issues related to racial dynamics?

- **Nonstructural explanations for racial disparities:** Do you point to nonstructural causes as the reason for racial disparities?

- **Belief in white superiority:** Do you believe that White people are generally better than, or superior to, people in other racial groups?

- **Belief that White people are disadvantaged:** Do you believe that White people are generally disadvantaged?

- **Unwilling to apply the Bible:** Are you unwilling to apply Bible passages with themes and principles related to racial justice?

- **Willing to act on the Bible:** Are you willing to act on Bible passages with themes and principles related to racial justice?

- **Structural actions:** Are you willing to do structural actions that promote racial justice?

- **Nonstructural actions:** Are you willing to do nonstructural actions that promote racial justice?

- **Action in society:** Are you willing to participate in activities that promote racial justice in society?

- **Action in Christian organizations:** Are you willing to participate in activities that promote racial justice in Christian organizations (church, college, K-12 school, etc.)?

- **Bias against groups:** Do you have negative feelings and/or make negative assumptions about people who are _____ (White, Hispanic/Latino, Black, Asian, Native, multiracial, undocumented immigrants)?

- **Racial identification:** To what degree do you identify with the racial group(s) that you are a part of?

- **Cultural assimilation:** Are you culturally assimilating?

- **Christian nationalism:** Do you support Christian nationalism?

- **Linked future with groups:** Do you believe your future is linked with the future of people who are _____ (White, Hispanic/Latino, Black, Asian, Native, multiracial, undocumented immigrants)?

Scores in the RJUC Organization Assessment Report

The following are the scores that are currently included in the full version of the RJUC Organization Assessment Report.

- **Bible-based approach to making progress:** Does the organization have a Bible-based approach to building healthy racial dynamics?

- **Effective approach to making progress:** Does the organization have an effective approach to building healthy racial dynamics?

- **Motivated to make progress:** Is the organization's leadership motivated to make progress toward racial justice and unity?

- **Taking action to make progress:** Is the organization's leadership taking action to make progress toward racial justice and unity?

- **Healthy systemic dynamics:** Does the organization have healthy systemic dynamics?

- **Productive dialogue:** Is there honest, productive dialogue taking place in the organization?

- **Unhealthy environment:** Are there unhealthy racial dynamics in the organization?

- **Pressure to assimilate:** Do the individuals who are not in the cultural majority feel pressure to change their behavior in order to be accepted or "successful" (e.g., maintain relationships, keep their job, be selected for leadership positions, etc.)?

- **Tokenism:** Are tokenistic, symbolic gestures used to demonstrate "progress" rather than more substantive, systemic, and sacrificial changes?

- **Dynamics favors group:** Do the policies, activities, and climate of the organization favor the views and preferences of people who are _____ (White, Hispanic/Latino, Black, Asian, Native, multiracial, undocumented immigrants)?

- **Leadership selection favors groups:** Are individuals who are _____ (White, Hispanic/Latino, Black, Asian, Native, multiracial, undocumented immigrants) more likely to be given influential leadership roles in the organization?

ONE AND DONE?

When we visit our doctor, they do not say, "We do not need to check your weight, blood pressure, or breathing because we did all of that last year." Doctors repeat the same tests on a regular basis because they know it is essential to track key indicators of our health. In the same way, if we want to make progress toward racial justice we need to track our individual and organizational progress over time. A "one and done" approach to assessment will not be adequate for your personal development or the development of your organization. We recommend using tools to measure your progress a minimum of every one or two years.

PROGRESS REQUIRES SELF-INITIATIVE

In most areas of our lives, progress requires self-initiative. For example, our country is filled with workout facilities and paths for running and biking. It is also filled with people who want to be physically fit, but they lack the self-initiative required to use the resources that are available to them. We have to get out there and into the gym or onto the paths if we want to see results.

In the last two chapters, we shared some recommendations for finding mentors and measuring progress. Equipped individuals and effective tools are available to help you. Now it is up to you to decide if you will take advantage of them. You are the primary person who will decide if you will make progress, and how quickly. We hope and pray you will *get out there* and take the self-initiative to pursue helpful resources and grow in your efforts as a faithful antiracist.

DISCUSSION/REFLECTION QUESTIONS

1. Have you or your organization used ineffective methods to measure your progress toward racial justice? If so, can you give examples?

2. Consider Drew Hart's description of his experience on a Christian college campus. What were some of the "thousand paper cuts" that he experienced?

3. Review the types of scores in the RJUC Personal Assessment Report. Before reading this book, which, if any, of those areas did

you use to measure your personal development in the area of racial dynamics? Why?

4. Review the types of scores on the RJUC Organization Assessment Report. Before reading this book, which, if any, of those areas did you use to measure your organization's development in the area of racial dynamics? Why?

5. Take the RJUC Personal Assessment (rjuc.org). Did it help you to understand your views and actions and determine action steps for progress? If so, how?

6. How do you plan to apply the content in this chapter?

Recommended Prayer

We praise you because your standards for righteousness and justice are always true and accurate. As we read in Isaiah:

> *So this is what the Sovereign* Lord *says:*
> *"See, I lay a stone in Zion, a tested stone,*
> *a precious cornerstone for a sure foundation;*
> *the one who relies on it*
> *will never be stricken with panic.*
> *I will make justice the measuring line*
> *and righteousness the plumb line;*
> *hail will sweep away your refuge, the lie,*
> *and water will overflow your hiding place." (Isaiah 28:16-17)*

As we seek to follow your will, help us to understand your measuring line of justice and your plumb line of righteousness. Help us align our standards for righteousness and justice with yours. As we seek to measure our progress toward those standards, help us to choose methods that are effective and aligned with your will for the church and our society.

CHAPTER ELEVEN

FAITHFUL ANTIRACISTS HELP TO CHANGE OUR SOCIETY

JESUS FREQUENTLY CALLED his followers to be change agents in the world. One of the most well-known examples is found in the Sermon on the Mount.

> You are the salt of the earth. But if the salt loses its saltiness, how can it be made salty again? It is no longer good for anything, except to be thrown out and trampled underfoot. You are the light of the world. A town built on a hill cannot be hidden. Neither do people light a lamp and put it under a bowl. Instead they put it on its stand, and it gives light to everyone in the house. In the same way, let your light shine before others, that they may see your good deeds and glorify your Father in heaven. (Matthew 5:13-16)

Tragically, from the Puritan John Winthrop's famous speech in 1630 until today, a steady stream of religious and political leaders have used Jesus' instructions to be a "city on a hill" to paint a picture of American exceptionalism and motivate American nationalism.[1] Throughout this book, we have seen some of the damage those ideologies have produced.

Jesus was not calling his followers to destructive ideas of false superiority or destructive nationalism. He was calling them to live lives of mercy and peacemaking. Just a few verses before the above passage, Jesus declared: "Blessed are the merciful, for they will be shown mercy" and "Blessed are the peacemakers, for they will be called children of God (Matthew 5:7, 9). And in the verse immediately after the above passage, he declared: "Do not think that I have come to abolish the Law or the Prophets; I have not come to abolish them but to fulfill them" (Matthew 5:17).

In chapter two, we saw that social justice and special kindness and protections for the oppressed were central themes in the Law and the Prophets. In the Sermon on the Mount, Jesus called his followers to live lives of love, mercy, peacemaking, and righteousness. That was the saltiness and light that Jesus called them to share in their society. And that is the saltiness and light that Jesus is still calling us to share in our society.

PRINCIPLES FOR DISRUPTING INJUSTICE FROM A WELL-KNOWN ACTIVIST

Throughout this book, we looked at three powerful forces that have sustained racial injustice throughout US history: religion, economics, and politics. In this chapter we will focus on action steps that can help disrupt these forces and promote racial justice in our society. Focusing on the teaching of our country's most famous Christian activist, Rev. Martin Luther King Jr., we draw from his final book, *Where Do We Go from Here?* (*WDWG*).[2] Published in 1967, just months before he was murdered, King wrote *WDWG* with the input of other civil rights workers who had been serving with him on the frontlines for many years. Sadly, King's words remain relevant today because so few of his recommended action steps have been implemented. In our society, King is frequently quoted and praised, but his specific recommendations are rarely followed.

In *WDWG*, King primarily focuses on systems that disadvantage Black people and advantage White people. Unfortunately, King's focus continues to be very relevant due to the pervasive anti-Black racism that persists in our society. In this book, we have sought to have a broader focus that includes racial injustice of all types. The quotes we share in this chapter from *WDWG* primarily address anti-Black racism, but the principles King shares can easily be applied to anti-Indigenous racism, anti-Hispanic/Latino racism, anti-Asian racism, and other types of racial injustice. The interviews mentioned at the end of chapter three also provide principles and action steps for working to promote justice among other racial groups.

To provide clarification regarding King's terminology in the *WDWG*, please note the following:

- *White liberals*: King uses this term for White individuals who desire racial progress as opposed to *White segregationists* who overtly oppose racial progress.

- *Men*: King uses gender-specific terms like *men* and *man* to refer to all humanity (men and women). We are thankful for the contemporary shift to using more gender-inclusive language.

- *Negroes*: As you are probably aware, *negroes* was commonly used in the 1960s for people of African descent but is currently not a socially acceptable term. Therefore, we have replaced *negro* with [*African American*] in quoted material.

FOLLOWING BLACK LEADERSHIP WHEN SEEKING TO ADDRESS ANTI-BLACK RACISM

This first point builds on what we learned in chapter eight regarding empowering leaders within oppressed communities to lead efforts to correct injustice (Acts 6:1-7). Oftentimes efforts are made to address anti-Black racism in society without incorporating the leadership of Black individuals—this leads to frustration, lack of trust, paternalism, and wasted effort. King explains the need for Black leadership.

> There is another mood, however, which represents a large number of [African Americans]. It is the feeling that . . . [African Americans] must be their own spokesmen, that they must be in the primary leadership of their own organizations. . . . It is the psychological need for those who have had such a crushed and bruised history to feel and know that they are men, that they have the organizational ability to map their own strategy and shape their own programs, that they can develop the programs to shape their own destinies, that they can be their own spokesmen.[3]

In the quote above, King mentioned several reasons why it is important for people of color to lead.

1. It empowers people of color who have too frequently been disempowered.

2. It recognizes that people of color are best equipped to create their own strategies and programs.

3. It allows people of color to be their own spokespersons.

BEING "WILLINGLY OBEDIENT TO UNENFORCEABLE OBLIGATIONS"

Disrupting systems of racial injustice is first and foremost a *heart issue*, King explains.

> The ultimate solution to the race problem lies in the willingness of men to obey the unenforceable. . . . Desegregation will break down the legal barriers and bring men together physically, but something must touch the hearts and souls of men so that they will come together spiritually because it is natural and right. . . . True integration will be achieved by men who are willingly obedient to unenforceable obligations.[4]

The effectiveness of our efforts to promote racial justice often comes down to our level of motivation. No amount of rhetoric, strategies, or laws will bring about racial justice in our society. Ultimately, we must do the work and make the sacrifices. The work and sacrifices that are required cannot be forced on anyone. As King wrote, they are "unenforceable obligations."

But what if we lack the motivation to do the unenforceable obligations? Paul prayed for his fellow Christians, "May the Lord make your love increase and overflow for each other and for everyone else, just as ours does for you" (1 Thessalonians 3:12). Supernatural love for others must be the power that sustains our racial justice efforts. Therefore, our most important action step for promoting racial justice is remaining in Christ and Christian community (John 15–17) and walking in the Spirit (Galatians 5). Only then will we have the "love, joy, peace, forbearance, kindness, goodness, faithfulness, gentleness and self-control" (Galatians 5:22-23) required to be obedient to unenforceable obligations.

If you lack motivation to help people in racial groups who are being oppressed, we encourage you to prayerfully and intentionally seek out environments where you can be in proximity to those who are suffering. If we take the effort to attend a different church, live in a different neighborhood, shop in a different business, workout in a different environment, or eat in different restaurants, then it provides opportunities for us to have contact with people who are experiencing the painful consequences of racial injustice. Of course, being close to other people doesn't automatically produce empathy, but if you go in prayer and with a desire to connect to the lived experiences of others, it is likely that the Lord will use those experiences to grow your passion for racial justice.

Addressing the Roots of Racial Injustice in Our Society

Throughout this book, we have focused on concepts like white dominance and belief in white superiority because they are powerful realities that sustain racial injustice. But oftentimes they are not explicitly talked about with efforts to promote racial justice. It is more common to hear terms like *racial issues*, *racial tensions*, and sometimes even *white privilege*. These terms can be helpful, but it is important to recognize that they describe *results*, they do not describe the *cause* of the results. It is easy to fall into the trap of talking about racial injustice like we talk about the weather—an inevitable part of our lives that we have to deal with. But racial injustice isn't a natural disaster. It is more like atmospheric changes that result from human pollution.

Racial injustice was created through the choices of many people, and it is sustained through the choices of many people. King explains we must be willing to acknowledge that reality and reflect on the reasons why many people have chosen to build and sustain systems for their own benefit that subject other human beings to unjust treatment:

> It would be neither true nor honest to say that the [African American's] status is what it is because he is innately inferior or because he is basically lazy and listless or because he has not sought to lift himself by his own bootstraps. To find the origins of the [African American] problem we must turn to the white man's problem.[5]

We cannot effectively work against racial injustice in our society if we are unwilling to acknowledge and address the white supremacy ideologies, distortions of Scripture, and greed that have created and sustained it. We must be willing to explicitly name those realities and then work to address them with courage and the leading of the Holy Spirit.

Partnering with Others

In the summer of 2020, millions of individuals took to the streets and protested for racial justice in cities all across the country. Protests can be very helpful, but they often do not result in the structural changes that are required to eliminate racial injustice. As one of the most prolific organizers of nonviolent action in US history, King was well aware of the strengths and limitations of protests.

Mass nonviolent action will continue to be one of the most effective tactics of the freedom movement. . . . But mass nonviolent demonstrations will not be enough. They must be supplemented by a continuing job of organization. To produce change, *people must be organized to work together in units of power.* . . . More and more, the civil rights movement will have to engage in the task of organizing people into permanent groups to protect their own interests and produce change in their behalf. This task is tedious, and lacks the drama of demonstrations, but it is necessary for meaningful results. (emphasis added)[6]

The systems that sustain racial injustice are very powerful and deeply rooted in our society. The actions of one individual, no matter how sacrificial, will not bring about change on their own. We must collaborate with other people and organizations to be successful in our efforts. King gave a special challenge to White individuals because of their influence in society.

The fact remains that a sound resolution of the race problem in America will rest with those white men and women who consider themselves as generous and decent human beings. . . . When evil men plot, good men must plan. When evil men burn and bomb, good men must build and bind. When evil men conspire to preserve an unjust status quo, good men must unite to bring about the birth of a society undergirded by justice.[7]

We occasionally have conversations with individuals (especially young adults) recently motivated to engage in racial justice activism who want to start a new organization, club, social media account, event, or conference. Starting new things can be a great idea, but it is essential to partner with experienced activists before trying to start new things. Working in partnership with experienced activists can keep you from wasting a lot of time, energy, and money. Plus, it's more fun and encouraging to do things with other people who are already passionate about racial justice than it is to try to build something from scratch.

You may think, *I don't know of other people and organizations to partner with.* With some intentionality, it is likely you can find them. Millions of people and thousands of organizations across the United States are currently working for racial justice. They include racial justice organizations as well as churches, schools, colleges, and ministries that have a strong racial justice emphasis. There's a good chance there's already at least one organization like this within a few miles of where you live or work. If you are not currently involved with one of those organizations, now is a great time to seek them out.

DISRUPTING RELIGIOUS FORCES THAT PERPETUATE RACIAL INJUSTICE

King's challenge to the church still resonates today.

> The church has a special obligation. It is the voice of moral and spiritual authority on earth. Yet no one observing the history of the church in America can deny the shameful fact that it has been an accomplice in structuring racism into the architecture of American society. The church, by and large, sanctioned slavery and surrounded it with the halo of moral respectability. It also cast the mantle of its sanctity over the system of segregation.[8]

King frequently experienced both the support and opposition of other Christians. If we are working toward racial justice, it is likely that we will experience the same. One of the most complex challenges we face as faithful antiracists is graciously working with our brothers and sisters in Christ who are opposed to racial justice efforts. Sadly, there is an arm of Christianity in the United States that has been uniquely shaped to defend racism and resist repentance from racial injustice. We offer a few recommendations for working with those individuals and organizations.

Pray for grace, humility, patience, and love. It is easy to get frustrated with other Christians who don't "get it." But we must approach every conversation with grace, humility, patience, and love, as Paul writes in Romans 12.

> For by the grace given me I say to every one of you: Do not think of yourself more highly than you ought, but rather think of yourself with sober judgment, in accordance with the faith God has distributed to each of you. (Romans 12:3)

Love must be sincere. Hate what is evil; cling to what is good. Be devoted to one another in love. Honor one another above yourselves. . . . Bless those who persecute you; bless and do not curse. . . . Do not be conceited. Do not repay anyone evil for evil. Be careful to do what is right in the eyes of everyone. If it is possible, as far as it depends on you, live at peace with everyone. (Romans 12:9-18)

Notice that Paul wrote, "Hate what is evil" (v. 9). When we observe the evil of racial injustice in ourselves, others, our organizations, and our society, it is good and appropriate to feel a sense of repulsion and indignation. But we cannot allow our hate for evil to translate into disdain for ourselves or others. We must remain devoted to one another in love (Romans 12:10) while also practicing biblical accountability and reconciliation (Galatians 6:1-10).

Focus on teachings in the Bible. We hope this book has helped you to see the major emphasis that the Bible places on social justice and compassion for the oppressed. These passages are often ignored or downplayed by individuals and organizations that are opposed to racial justice. When we interact with brothers and sisters in Christ who disagree with working toward racial justice, we must be equipped to graciously point them to the teachings in the Bible that motivate our work.

Avoid being a part of religious organizations that support injustice. If you are part of an organization that is actively or passively supporting racial injustice, we encourage you to share your concerns with the leadership. If they insist that racial justice is a distraction from the gospel, unbiblical, or not a high priority, then we encourage you to pray about whether that is the organization that God would have you be a part of. Simply "letting our feet do the talking" is one of the most powerful ways we can disrupt racial injustice. When the membership of a Christian organization declines, it is a powerful message to the leadership.

DISRUPTING ECONOMIC FORCES THAT PERPETUATE RACIAL INJUSTICE

In the quote below, King explains that the people who are suffering from racial injustice are less interested in words of affection or superficial relationships and more interested in tangible efforts to provide them with access to "a good job, a good education, a decent house and a share of power."

The white liberal must see that the [African American] needs not only love but also justice. It is not enough to say, "We love [African Americans], we have many [African American] friends." They must demand justice for [African Americans]. Love that does not satisfy justice is no love at all. . . . The white liberal must affirm that absolute justice for the [African American] simply means . . . that the [African American] must have "his due." There is nothing abstract about this. It is as concrete as having a good job, a good education, a decent house and a share of power. . . . A society that has done something special against the [African American] for hundreds of years must now do something special for him, in order to equip him to compete on a just and equal basis.[9]

Use our purchasing power. One of the most effective ways we can disrupt economic forces is with the dollars we spend on food, clothing, entertainment, and more. The economic boycotts organized by the civil rights movement in the 1960s are a great example. King explains the central role that the boycotts played in bringing about change.

Our dramatic demonstrations tended to obscure the role of the boycott in cities such as Birmingham. It was not the marching alone that brought about integration of public facilities in 1963. The downtown business establishments suffered for weeks under our almost unbelievably effective boycott. The significant percentage of their sales that vanished, the 98 percent of their [African American] customers who stayed home, educated them forcefully to the dignity of the [African American] as a consumer.[10]

When consumers are willing to change their purchasing habits, it can have an enormous impact. We offer a few practical ways you can use your dollars to promote racial justice.

- *Refuse to shop at businesses that support racial injustice.* If you connect with local racial justice activism groups you can learn about boycotts of local businesses that are supporting racial injustice.

- *Refuse to support corporations that support racial injustice.* Unfortunately, corporations often verbalize support for racial justice and make large donations but are unwilling to change their economic practices that perpetuate injustice. We recommend reading Darren Walker's article "9 Ways Corporations Can Actually Address Racial Inequality" for practical steps that we can advocate for corporations to take.[11]

■ *Shop at businesses owned by people of color.* If you don't know which businesses are owned by people of color, we encourage you to reach out to pastors and leaders of color in your community, use a directory service like supportblackowned.com or byblack.us, or search for "Black-owned businesses" on Google Maps.

Disrupt housing and school segregation. For many decades, social scientists and racial justice activists have pointed out the strong link between housing segregation and education disparities. As Anurima Bhargava writes:

> Housing and education in America have long been inextricably and intricately linked. First, due to the nation's history and widespread practice of assigning students to their neighborhood school, where housing is segregated, so are schools. . . . Second, funding for schools is often tied to property taxes; consequently, the funding available for and quality of schooling is closely related to the value of the property within the residential area being served. Not surprisingly, racially segregated schools in areas of concentrated poverty have fewer resources, higher teacher turnover and a lower quality of education. Third, residential insecurity and mobility have an adverse and often significant impact on student engagement and educational attainment.[12]

In other words, segregated neighborhoods produce and perpetuate segregated schools. Segregated schools produce and perpetuate segregated neighborhoods. Schools in wealthy neighborhoods have more money because school funding is tied to property taxes. Children living in poorer neighborhoods often have less secure housing arrangements, which hurts their ability to receive a good education.

Many people are surprised to learn that the US school system is more racially segregated today than it was before school segregation was declared illegal sixty years ago. As Beverly Daniel Tatum points out:

> Some 60 years after *Brown v. Board of Education*, a series of key Supreme Court decisions . . . have eliminated strategies such as

cross-district busing, dismantled local court supervision of desegregation plans, and limited use of race-based admissions to ensure diversity in magnet-school programs. According to an analysis by the UCLA Civil Rights Project, the number of intensely segregated schools with zero to 10 percent white enrollment has more than tripled as these options for desegregation have been curtailed. Students are, once again, predominantly assigned to public schools based on where they live—and to the extent that neighborhoods are segregated, the schools remain so.[13]

King and his civil rights colleagues challenge the underlying ideologies of white supremacy and racism that continue to keep White people from living in neighborhoods with people of color.

To hem a people up in the prison walls of overcrowded ghettos and to confine them in rat-infested slums is to breed crime, whatever the racial group may be. It is a strange and twisted logic to use the tragic results of segregation as an argument for its continuation. . . . However much it is denied, however many excuses are made, the hard cold fact is that many white Americans oppose open housing because they unconsciously, and often consciously, feel that the [African American] is innately inferior, impure, depraved and degenerate. It is a contemporary expression of America's long dalliance with racism and white supremacy.[14]

King and the civil rights movement fought passionately for housing integration for good reason. They recognized that housing and school segregation were powerful tools that perpetuated financial benefits for White people. But as King's earlier words on "unenforceable obligations" stated, true integration in housing and education can only be accomplished through willful decisions. Protests and laws can remove barriers to White neighborhoods, but they cannot force White neighbors to stay in the neighborhood or treat their new neighbors equitably. Protests and laws can integrate schools, but they cannot force White teachers and students to stay in the school and give the new students the same educational experience as White students. Creating integrated neighborhoods and integrated schools requires the type of compassion and love that should characterize our lives as Christians.

The following are some practical ways you can help disrupt housing and school segregation.

- *Buy or rent.* Intentionally choose to live in a racially diverse neighborhood.

- *Welcome.* Welcome people of other races who move into your neighborhood.

- *Address barriers.* Address barriers to integration in your neighborhood, such as police who practice racial profiling and real estate agents who perpetuate housing segregation.

- *Educate.* Educate yourself and your children regarding the causes of housing segregation. Many history books currently provide an incomplete and misleading picture of how housing segregation was created. For example, one of the most commonly used history books says simply, "African Americans found themselves forced into segregated neighborhoods."[15] There is no mention of the over one hundred years of intentional policies by local, state, and national governments that produced the segregation. We recommend watching the five-minute video "Matter Of Place" created by The Fair Housing Justice Center.[16]

- *Support.* Support local, state, and national government initiatives that promote housing integration. Contact your representatives and ask what is currently being done to promote housing integration and what you can do to be supportive.

DISRUPTING POLITICAL FORCES THAT PERPETUATE RACIAL INJUSTICE

Here are six ways we can help disrupt the political forces perpetuating racial injustice.

- *Vote.* Vote for local, state, and national officials who support racial justice.

- *Support voting rights.* Oppose laws and policies that make it more difficult for people in some racial groups to cast their vote.

- *Write.* Write government officials and ask them to advocate for laws and policies that support racial justice.
- *Peacefully protest.* Peacefully protest government policies and actions that sustain racial injustice.
- *Join alliances.* Participate in political alliances focused on racial justice.
- *Speak up.* Be willing to voice your opposition to laws, policies, and candidates that sustain racial injustice.

In December 2019, *Christianity Today* (*CT*) published an article that is a good example of speaking up against the political forces that sustain racial justice. Here is an excerpt:

> To the many evangelicals who continue to support Mr. Trump in spite of his blackened moral record, we might say this: Remember who you are and whom you serve. Consider how your justification of Mr. Trump influences your witness to your Lord and Savior. Consider what an unbelieving world will say if you continue to brush off Mr. Trump's immoral words and behavior in the cause of political expediency. If we don't reverse course now, will anyone take anything we say about justice and righteousness with any seriousness for decades to come? Can we say with a straight face that abortion is a great evil that cannot be tolerated and, with the same straight face, say that the bent and broken character of our nation's leader doesn't really matter in the end?[17]

CT received a strong rebuke by many of its readers and even Trump himself.[18] *CT* then published an excellent response by Timothy Dalrymple, president and CEO.

> Politics matter, but they do not bring the dead back to life. We are far more committed to the glory of God, the witness of the church, and the life of the world than we care about the fortunes of any party. Political parties come and go, but the witness of the church is the hope of the world, and the integrity of that witness is paramount. Out of love for Jesus and his church, not for political partisanship or intellectual elitism, this is why we feel compelled to say that the alliance of American evangelicalism with this presidency has wrought

enormous damage to Christian witness. It has alienated many of our children and grandchildren. It has harmed African American, Hispanic American, and Asian American brothers and sisters. And it has undercut the efforts of countless missionaries who labor in the far fields of the Lord. . . . We are happy to celebrate the positive things the administration has accomplished. The problem is that we as evangelicals are also associated with President Trump's rampant immorality, greed, and corruption; his divisiveness and race-baiting; his cruelty and hostility to immigrants and refugees; and more. In other words, the problem is the wholeheartedness of the embrace. It is one thing to praise his accomplishments; it is another to excuse and deny his obvious misuses of power.[19]

SMALL STEPS THAT CAN PRODUCE BIG CHANGES

In this chapter, we have shared a few of the practical action steps that can help produce racial justice in our society. Of course there are thousands of additional ways that Christians can help. We hope you will choose to get involved, whether you choose some of the action steps we recommend or other options.

In chapter one, we explained that being a faithful antiracist is an art, not a formulaic process. Like painting a picture, building a chair, shaping a dress, or crafting a meal, it requires knowledge, skill, experience, and creativity. Most importantly, it requires the leading of the Holy Spirit. We need a master artist who can guide our hands and help us to create something beautiful. When we rely on the Master Artist, it relieves us from the pressure of feeling like we need to single-handedly fix it all. We cannot and we will not. But if we are willing to submit to God's leading he can use each of our unique gifts and talents in powerful ways. Brick by brick, we can dismantle the giant walls of racial injustice that have been built and sustained for over four hundred years.

DISCUSSION/REFLECTION QUESTIONS

1. Throughout US history, Christians have used Jesus' instruction to be a "city on a hill" (Matthew 5:14-16) to support American exceptionalism and American nationalism. What do you think Jesus would say to those individuals?

2. King mentioned several reasons why it is important to follow the leadership of Black individuals when seeking to address anti-Black racism. Can you think of others?

3. King wrote, "True integration will be achieved by men who are willingly obedient to unenforceable obligations." Why is *willing obedience* essential for true integration?

4. Do you believe it is essential to discuss topics like the belief in white superiority and white dominance in order to be effective faithful antiracists? Why or why not?

5. Are you currently partnering with others to work toward racial justice? If so, how? If not, what are some steps you can take to begin?

6. In your circle of influence, what are some ways that you can help to disrupt religious forces that perpetuate racial injustice? Are you doing those activities? If not, what are some barriers that prevent you from doing them?

7. In your circle of influence, what are some ways you can help to disrupt economic forces that perpetuate racial injustice? Are you doing those activities? If not, what are some barriers that prevent you from doing them?

8. In your circle of influence, what are some ways that you can help to disrupt political forces that perpetuate racial injustice? Are you doing those activities? If not, what are some barriers that prevent you from doing them?

9. How do you plan to apply the content in this chapter?

Recommended Prayer

We praise you, God, because you are a God of righteousness and justice. Please help our individual actions and the actions of your church to promote righteousness and justice in our society. Give us the love required to be willing to obey the unenforceable. Raise up strong leaders who are led by your Spirit and your Word, who can help us navigate through the complexity and challenges. Help us build strong partnerships that can advance your justice in our society. Help our economic systems to be just and to provide special protections and kindness for groups that are oppressed and vulnerable. Help our political leaders to govern with wisdom, righteousness, and justice. Help us to create healthy, integrated housing and schools where people of all races can thrive. Give us wisdom as we seek to use our limited time, resources, and influence to have the greatest impact. Amen.

EPILOGUE

OUR HOPE AND PRAYER IS THAT the information we share in this book motivates and equips you to be a faithful antiracist in your relationships, the organizations you are a part of, and our society. The obstacles to racial justice are daunting, but with God's help we can overcome them when we work together as one (John 17). We wrap up the book with a fictional news segment to provide an inspirational glimpse into what the future could hold if we are willing to work together in Christ's strength and for his glory.

ENCOURAGING NEWS

The following is a transcript of a TV news report that takes place in the not-so-distant future.

Grace: Good evening, I'm Grace Hopewell. Tonight we have a special segment focused on racial inequalities. As you are probably aware, over the last several years the poverty and incarceration rates for Black, Indigenous, and Hispanic Americans have dropped, and educational attainment and income rates have risen. The number of individuals of color in leadership roles in government and corporations has been increasing. These are just a few of the encouraging signs that racial inequalities are decreasing. The changes have been opposed by many people, but according to a recent poll by our network, 62 percent of Americans support them. Tonight, we have a special segment focusing on the key role that Christians and Christian organizations have been playing with the changes. We are going to take a brief look at a few examples across the country. My first guest is Mark who is at Titus High School in Dallas, Texas. Mark, how are Christians helping to close the racial education gap?

Mark: Hi, Grace. At state and national levels, Christians have been advocating for policy changes that would allow schools in low income neighborhoods to receive the same resources as schools in wealthy neighborhoods. And at the local level, many Christian organizations have partnered with public schools in their community. Titus High School is one example. They have partnerships with four local churches to provide childcare for their teachers, tutoring for their students, and even help with maintaining the school facilities so that the school can use their funds in other ways. All of this has contributed to Titus seeing a 36 percent increase in their graduation rate over the last three years.

Grace: That is encouraging to hear, but I understand there is still much work to be done.

Mark: Yes, that is true. School administrators are encouraged by the changes, but are quick to add that we still have a long way to go before we eliminate the significant racial disparities in our education system. They believe community partnerships like the ones at Titus are essential in order for the progress to be sustained.

Grace: Thank you, Mark. Now let's head over to Teressa who is at the headquarters of Techsphere Electronics. Teressa, how have Christians been influencing racial dynamics in the corporate world?

Teressa: For many decades, corporations have communicated support for racial justice programs and donated money, but activists have pointed out that their actions within their own organizations often do not match their rhetoric. For example, after the racial justice protests in 2020, Techsphere made public statements in support of racial equality and gave sixty million dollars toward racial justice programs, but they did little to address the lack of racial diversity in the leadership of their organization. In recent years, Christians have been at the forefront of the movement to encourage corporations to support racial justice within their organizations. For example, Christians played a central role in organizing a national boycott of Techsphere last year. Techsphere acted quickly when they realized they were losing customers. Five years ago, their board of directors was only 5 percent individuals of color. Currently, their board is 35 percent individuals of color. Three years ago, their employees were 13 percent individuals of color. Currently, they are at 37 percent individuals of color. The steps they have taken have done more than just boost their public image, they have helped to boost their bottom line. The Techsphere executives I have spoken with emphasize how increasing the racial diversity in their organization has helped them to be more innovative and responsive to their customers.

Grace: Thank you, Teressa. Our next guest is Governor Rosenthal. Governor Rosenthal, thank you for joining us. How have Christians been promoting racial justice in our political systems?

Governor Rosenthal: When I first became active in politics twenty-three years ago, only 21 percent of Christians in the United States believed that racial injustice should be a high priority. Today, 62 percent believe it should be a high priority. That shift has allowed us to make changes at state and national levels in regard to housing, education, incarceration, and other key areas.

Grace: Why was the support of Christians so important?

Governor Rosenthal: Christians are one of the largest groups in our country. It is very difficult to make changes without their political support. Until recently, one of the quickest ways to lose a large percentage of Christian voters was to emphasize racial justice, but that is no longer the case. Now those of us who want to take a stand for justice are able to without fearing a major backlash from our Christian constituents. It is an exciting time.

Grace: Thank you, Governor Rosenthal. For our final interview, let's head to Pastor Mitchell in Evansville, Indiana. Pastor Mitchell, we have just heard several examples of Christians having a major impact on racial dynamics in our country. What is fueling this new movement?

Pastor Mitchell: Thank you for inviting me. To answer your question, I would first point out that the movement isn't really new. Many Christians have been engaging in racial justice activism in our country for many centuries. Beyond that, Christians around the world have been standing for social justice for thousands of years. But what is new is the fact that a large percentage of Christians in all racial groups are participating in the efforts. That has made a big difference. As far as what is fueling the movement, I believe God is. In Isaiah 61:8 the Bible teaches us that God loves justice. I believe Christians are simply doing what God has called them to do.

Grace: But that verse has always been in the Bible. Why has it taken so long for Christians in our country to act on it?

Pastor Mitchell: That is a great question. There are many reasons that go back hundreds of years to the ways that White Christians merged Christianity with nationalism, slavery, and white supremacy. That history continues to shape the thinking and actions of many people today, but it is encouraging to see that a growing number of Christians are being freed from that destructive legacy.

Grace: Martin Luther King Jr. famously said that the most segregated hour in our country is eleven a.m. on Sunday morning. Are Christian organizations starting to see that change?

Pastor Mitchell: Yes, they are. For example, our church has historically been almost entirely Black. But over the last few years it has become about 20 percent White, Hispanic, and Asian. Many of those individuals are young adults and young families who had not formerly been attending church. I think they are attracted to communities where people are seeking to live out Jesus' command for us to treat others the way we want to be treated.

Grace: Sounds like you are saying that breaking down the racial divisions in the church is not just about people of color attending predominantly White churches.

Pastor Mitchell: That's right. It used to be very rare for White Christians to be a part of churches that were not predominantly White and led by White people, but that is starting to shift.

Grace: Why is that important?

Pastor Mitchell: Racially integrated churches can be a good thing or a bad thing. They are a good thing if the members have a healthy community where everyone is treated with love and justice and there is leadership sharing. They are a bad thing if one group is being catered to and other groups are being neglected. In the past, most multiracial churches primarily catered to the desires of the White members, but we are starting to see that change.

Grace: It sounds like Christians aren't just trying to change society, they are trying to change themselves and their churches as well.

Pastor Mitchell: That's right. We have to take the plank out of our own eye before we can take the speck out of our brother's eye.

Grace: Well, I think that is a good note for us to end on. Thank you, Pastor Mitchell.

ACKNOWLEDGMENTS

Christina Barland Edmondson and Chad Brennan would like to thank:

- Cindy Bunch, Tara Burns, Krista Clayton, Rachel Hastings, Ellen Hsu, Maila Kim, Helen Lee, Ethan McCarthy, and many others on the InterVarsity Press team. Thank you for your patience with us newbie authors and the great work and many, many hours you invested in this book!

- Laurie Brennan, Timothy Cho, Michaela Gregory, Kevin Holland, Tobias Houpe, Mark Krenz, and Leah Touissant. Thank you, manuscript reviewers, for helping to make the book more clear and effective.

- Glenn Bracey and Michael Emerson. Thank you for your generous support, encouragement, and help throughout the data analysis and writing process.

- Ed Gilbreath. Thank you for helping this book to go from an idea to a reality.

- Ray Chang, Mark Charles, Shane Claiborne, Curtiss De Young, Lisa Fields, Ed Gilbreath, Dominique Gilliard, Debbie Gin, Derwin Gray, Katelin Hansen, Daniel Hays, Brooke Hempell, Michelle Higgins, Daniel Hill, Alex Jun, Kathy Khang, Duke Kwon, Helen Lee, Michelle Loyd-Paige, Gerardo Marti, Beth Moore, Lecrae Moore, Rich Nathan, Oneya Okuwobi, Dennae Pierre, Tryce Prince, Brenda Salter McNeil, Alexia Salvatierra, Jemar Tisby, Sandra Maria Van Opstal, Brittany Wade, and Michael Wear. Thank you for taking the time to participate in an interview and/or share your perspectives as we wrote.

- Glenn Bracey, Daniel Copeland, Michael Emerson, Laura Fitzwater Gonzales, Jalia Joseph, Nate Risdon, Aunrika Shabazz, and Brittany Wade. Thank you, Race, Religion, and Justice Project (RRJP) research team members, for your hard work to collect the data that we include in this book.

- Lilly Endowment Inc. Thank you for making the majority of the research described in this book possible.

- Elissa Clouse, Daniel Copeland, Brooke Hempell, David Kinnaman, Alyce Youngblood, and other Barna Group team members. Thank you for your encouragement, partnership, and input.

- RJUC Collaboration Team. Thank you for providing many helpful insights with our research during 2019 and 2020.

CHRISTINA BARLAND EDMONDSON WOULD ALSO LIKE TO THANK:

- Mika. Thanks for your love, laughter, encouragement, wisdom, and an abundance of timely distractions from the realities of racism. Toni Morrison was right. "Racism is a distraction." May we guard our moments as an act of resistance.

- My children. You are my greatest motivators. If I could give you a world that is worthy of your potential and intrinsic beauty, I would. As you know, I am only human. With God, however, I will work to be a faithful antiracist because, my beloved Black girls, you deserve every opportunity the God's world has to offer.

- My parents. To have parents that are able to correct and encourage is a gift from God. Thanks for always offering a "Why not?" to every aspiration, dream, and hope. Also, thanks for preparing me to navigate a racist world and actively resist its lies about myself, culture, and God.

- My teachers. My big sister teaching me through hand-me-down books. My first elementary school teacher, a Black woman committed to making learning vibrant and hospitable. My favorite sociology professor, Dr. Bernadette Holmes, another Black woman who taught me much more than subject material but the art of teaching and advocacy. I am truly indebted.

- My students. The classroom can be a place of discovery, healing, challenge, and creativity. Thank you, students, for pushing me and inspiring me with your thoughtful questions, insightful contributions, and necessary disdain for the evils of racism and unethical leadership. May we lament and dream together.

- My church families. I am grateful to the sweet folks I sat with on church pews across the years who modeled faithful community, openness to correction, and the ministry of tears and encouragement. Even as I tell the whole truth about the conflicts and power dynamics of the church, I am indebted to the church and hopeful for all that it will become. I am even grateful for the not so sweet folks who in some cases personified data and theory on racial injustice. God is not done with any of us just yet.

Chad Brennan would also like to thank:

- Laurie. Thank you for being a faithful ally, friend, and partner through all the adventures that led to this book.

- Aliya, Anya, and Milena. Thank you for your endless laughter and love, and constantly challenging me to work for God's plan for love and justice in our world.

- Kyle and Kelsie. Thank you for helping me to look at the world with wit, creativity, and discernment.

- Mom and Dad Brennan. Thank you for creating a home that is filled with love, a focus on Christ, and care for others.

- D. J. and Kelly, Shawn and Ally, Josh and Savannah. Thank you for being supportive, fun, and loving brothers and sisters.

- Mom Blum. Thank you for modeling strength in adversity, a commitment to God's Word, and love for family.

- Michaela Gregory. Thank you for over twenty years as an insightful and patient friend and coworker.

- Timothy Cho, Korie Edwards, Michael Emerson, Leah Fulton, Michaela Gregory, Stephanie Gregory, Richard Johnson, Glen Kinoshita, John Lieb, Tiffany Moncrief, Joel Perez, Alvin Sanders, Noriyo Shoji-Schaffner,

Jerry Stephens, Tom Williams, and our past and present prayer and financial support team members. Thank you for your encouragement, support, and your participation in our ministry with Renew Partnerships. This book would not have been possible without you.

- Marissa Ahmad, Glenn Bracey, Nicole Buchanan, Robert Caldwell, Jason Cha, Larry and Deb Christensen, Garrison Christian, Tom Cox, Andy Crooks, Larry Davis, Viju Deenadayalu, Edward Dhanpat, Christina Edmondson, Michael Emerson, Korie Edwards, Tyler Flynn, Leah Fulton, Alvim Gimarino, Jay Hayden, Richard Johnson, Joe Karlya, Glen Kinoshita, Glen Kleinknecht, David Leedy, John Lieb, Mike Mattes, Brenda Salter McNeil, Todd Mullholand, Rick Nardo, Jeff Nieman, Joel Perez, Tony Plummer, Alvin Sanders, Jeff Schuster, Oral and Melissa Seudath, and many others. Thank you for patiently, graciously, and lovingly investing in my life and helping me to grow in my Christian faith and the concepts we share in this book.

- Meadow Park Church. Thank you for allowing me to spend many days in your library working on this book and filming interviews.

KEY TERMS

OUR GOAL WITH THE FOLLOWING LIST is not to provide a comprehensive definition for each term. That would require many more pages. We are simply providing a quick, concise definition to interpret what we mean when we use these terms throughout the book.

Asian people: Individuals who are understood to have ancestors from Asia.

Black people: Individuals who are understood to have ancestors from Africa.

Bothsidesing: The argument that two groups or individuals are both imperfect, therefore it doesn't really matter which one you choose.

Code-switching: Individuals who are not in the majority group alternating between the values, behaviors, and beliefs of the majority group and their own cultural/racial group in order to fit in or be successful.

Colorblind ideology: The belief that an effective way to promote racial progress is simply ignoring other people's race or "treating everyone the same."

Confirmation bias: When a person only accepts new information that supports their existing beliefs. This typically takes place without conscious awareness.

Cultural assimilation: Individuals who are not in the majority group taking on the values, behaviors, and beliefs of the majority group in order to fit in or be successful.

Cultural toolkit: In the late 1990s, sociologist Michael Emerson identified three "tools" that many Christians use to accept, reject, or interpret information about racial dynamics: accountable freewill individualism, relationalism, and anti-structuralism. Our 2019–2020 research confirmed that the cultural toolkit is still commonly used by Christians.

Evangelical Christians: For an exploration of what it means to be evangelical in our society today, we recommend the series of articles posted on *Christianity Today*'s website at www.christianitytoday.com/ct/2020/january-web-only/evangelical-distinctives.html. With our RRJP research, we defined this group as respondents who indicated the following: (1) I have made a personal commitment to Jesus Christ that is still important in my life today; (2) I believe the Bible is totally accurate in all of the principles it teaches; (3) I have a personal responsibility to tell other people about my religious beliefs; (4) When I die I will go to heaven because I have confessed my sins and have accepted Jesus Christ as my Savior; (5) I disagree with the statement "If a person is generally good, or does enough good things for others, they can earn a place in heaven"; (6) I disagree with the statement "When he lived on earth, Jesus Christ was human and committed sins, like other people."

Groupthink: When a person tends to have inaccurate views because of the influence of other individuals in their group as well as a lack of access to other perspectives.

Hispanic/Latino people: Individuals who are understood to have ancestors from Cuba, Mexico, Puerto Rico, South or Central America, or another Spanish culture.

Interracial: Involving interactions between people in different racial groups.

Meritocracy: A social system in which people have power, influence, and resources based on their abilities, hard work, morals, etc.

Moral licensing: When people use previous behavior that they believe is good/moral to justify bad/immoral behavior.

Motivated reasoning: The tendency for people to be more inclined to accept new information that supports their existing assumptions and desires.

Multiracial people: Individuals who are a part of two or more racial groups.

Native people: Individuals who are a part of the Indigenous peoples of North America.

People of color: Individuals who are understood to have ancestors *not* only from Europe.

Power dynamics: Ways that leadership or authority is distributed in a group or organization.

Practicing Christians: With our RRJP research, we defined this group as respondents who indicated (1) I am a Christian; (2) My religious faith is very important in my life today; (3) I attend religious services at least monthly.

Racial demographics: The statistical racial diversity within a group or organization.

Racial group: A collection of people who are perceived to share geographical ancestry and biological characteristics such as facial features, skin tone, hair color, etc.

Racial hierarchy: A social system in which individuals in different racial groups typically have more or less power, wealth, and influence.

Racial equity: A condition in which a person's race does not provide them with advantages or disadvantages.

Racial identity: A person's sense of connection to their racial group.

Racial inclusion: A condition in which individuals in all racial groups are an integral part of a group, community, or nation.

Racial justice: A condition in which people in all racial groups receive equitable (fair) opportunities and outcomes.

Racism: Race-based discrimination and social hierarchies where individuals receive advantages or disadvantages because of perceived racial differences.

Reparations: Seeking to correct the damages caused by the history of racism in the United States.

Structural racism: When people in some racial groups are given advantages or disadvantages through social systems, e.g., economic systems, political systems, educational systems, criminal justice systems, etc.

Tokenism: Symbolic gestures used to demonstrate progress. They typically hinder more substantive, systemic, and sacrificial changes.

Undocumented immigrants: Individuals born outside of the United States who are living in the United States without receiving permission (documentation) by the government.

White dominance: A group or society where White people control the policies, activities, and dynamics in ways that primarily benefit White people.

White people: Individuals who are understood to have ancestors *only* from Europe.

White normativity: Beliefs or practices that centralize the views and preferences of White people. The views and practices of people in other racial groups are viewed as "special," unusual, or dangerous.

White transparency: A group or society where white dominance and white normativity influence dynamics but their impact remains invisible or unacknowledged.

White superiority (or white supremacy): The belief that White people have better morals, cleanliness, work ethic, intelligence, etc., than people in other racial groups. Therefore, it is good and natural for them to be at the top of the social hierarchy.

APPENDIX B

INTERVIEWEES AND INTERVIEW THEMES

Visit faithfulantiracism.com to watch excerpts from the following interviews.

GLENN BRACEY

Assistant professor of sociology and criminology, Villanova University
Power sharing, measuring progress, white dominance, inclusion, politics, self-care for people of color, controversial terminology, history

RAY CHANG

President and cofounder, Asian American Christian Collaborative
Asian Christians, justice activism, partnerships, impacts of racism, interracial dynamics, anti-Asian prejudice, assimilation

MARK CHARLES

Speaker, writer, consultant
Doctrine of Discovery, empire and Christianity, lament, healing, progress, generational change, correcting injustice, reparations

SHANE CLAIBORNE

Director, Red Letter Christians
Self-work, racial identity, community activism, living in proximity, political activism, partnerships, following the leadership of people of color

CURTISS DE YOUNG

CEO, Minnesota Council of Churches
Activism, partnerships, power sharing, building diverse leadership teams, finding mentors, structural change, politics

MICHAEL EMERSON

Professor and chair of the Department of Sociology, University of Illinois Chicago
Organizational change, social science, power dynamics, controversial terminology, white dominance, signs of progress

LISA FIELDS

Founding director, Jude 3 Project
Apologetics, justice, gospel witness, people leaving the church, listening, political engagement, cross-racial friendships, partnerships

DOMINIQUE GILLIARD

Director of racial righteousness and reconciliation, Evangelical Covenant Church
Lament, confession, remembrance, discipleship experiences, criminal justice data and reform, history, financial activism, partnerships

DERWIN GRAY

Lead pastor, Transformation Church
Multiracial organizations, Christian activism, power sharing, dealing with pushback, training/dialogue, relying on the Holy Spirit

KATELIN HANSEN

Director of operations, Community Development for All People
Pros/cons of multiracial churches, White Christian activists, serving the poor, partnerships, dealing with pushback, self-care

DANIEL HAYS

Dean of Christian Studies and professor of Old Testament, Ouachita Baptist University
Biblical justice, race/ethnicity in the Bible, racial diversity in Christian higher education, being a change agent

MICHELLE HIGGINS

Director of worship and outreach, South City Church
History, heritage, spiritual strongholds, confession, honesty, Christian activism, local/national partnerships, self-work, worship as activism

DANIEL HILL

Pastor, River City Church
Spiritual strongholds, white superiority, deception/misinformation, structural change, repentance, community, power sharing, activism

KATHY KHANG

Speaker, writer, consultant
Humility, curiosity, practical steps, community engagement, family engagement, difficult conversations, national activism

DUKE KWON
Lead pastor, Grace Meridian Hill
Posture of submission and humility, partnerships, historical perspective, reparations in the Bible/today, restitution, Latino/Black Christians

HELEN LEE
Associate director, strategic partnerships and initiatives, InterVarsity Press
Christian publishing, white dominance, leadership sharing, organizational change, barriers to progress, writing on racial justice

MICHELLE LOYD-PAIGE
Executive associate to the president for Diversity & Inclusion,
Calvin University
Self-work, Christian higher education, organizational mission/doctrines, racial climate, student/employee care, self-awareness

GERARDO MARTÍ
Professor of sociology, Davidson College
Historical perspective, social science, leading change, teachability, humility, worship styles, racial climate, power sharing, Latino Christians

BETH MOORE
Founder, Living Proof Ministries
Growing in racial understanding, transparency, spiritual strongholds, justice versus diversity activism, dealing with pushback, barriers to progress

LECRAE MOORE
Rapper, songwriter, record producer
Music, art and justice activism, addressing pain and anger, politics, dealing with pushback, tokenism, overcoming barriers, racial trauma

RICH NATHAN
Senior pastor, Vineyard Columbus
Organizational change, community outreach, immigration, power sharing, leading change, helping congregants, experiencing pushback

ONEYA OKUWOBI
Sociologist and PhD candidate, The Ohio State University
Social science, racial climate, multiracial organizations, power dynamics, self-care for people of color, seminaries led by people of color

DENNAE PIERRE
Executive director, The Surge Network
Relationships, experiential learning, empathy, immigration reform, helping refugees, local/national activism, partnerships

BRENDA SALTER MCNEIL
Associate professor of reconciliation studies, Seattle Pacific University
Organizational change, measuring progress, commitment, being a change agent, power dynamics, societal change, teachability, solidarity

ALEXIA SALVATIERRA
Assistant professor of mission and global transformation,
Fuller Theological Seminary
Changing hearts, relationships before ideas, partnerships, experiential learning, immigration reform, politics, biblical justice and unity

JEMAR TISBY
President, The Witness: A Black Christian Collective
Historical perspective, organizational history, Black-led leadership, pros/cons of multiracial organizations, power sharing, dealing with pushback

SANDRA MARIA VAN OPSTAL
Pastor, Grace and Peace Community
White dominance, self-care for people of color, dealing with disillusionment, Black/Brown Christians, multiracial organizations

BRITTANY WADE
Founder, Wildfire Research
Pros/cons of racial unity/diversity training programs for organizations, measuring progress, barriers, power sharing, racial climate

MICHAEL WEAR
Founder of Public Square Strategies
Political activism, justice, abortion, power dynamics, local and national activism, relationships, systemic change, Christian ethics

NOTES

Introduction

[1]The content in this book was cowritten by the authors. Sections that were written by one author are designated by the author's name in parentheses after the section title.

[2]Christopher Brinson and The Ensemble, "What If God," *What If God Is Unhappy* (Jackson, MS: Malaco Music Group, 1997).

[3]My cousins who live in Hawaii and southern California say I'm so White that I'm "green."

[4]The country where I lived was, and continues to be, approximately 99.8 percent Muslim.

[5]Michael O. Emerson and Christian Smith, *Divided by Faith: Evangelical Religion and the Problem of Race in America* (New York: Oxford University Press, 2000).

[6]Howard Thurman, *The Inward Journey* (New York: Harper Row, 1961), 104.

1 Faithful Antiracists Have Wisdom

[1]BibleProject, *Proverbs*, Wisdom Series video, accessed June 22, 2021, https://bible project.com/explore/video/wisdom-proverbs/.

[2]Individuals like me have the freedom to decide if we want to accept and engage with the realities of racial injustice or try to deny or avoid them. Many of us can disengage from the topic whenever we like and attempt to live as if racial injustice doesn't exist. It is typically much more difficult, or even impossible, for people of color who are suffering under racial injustice to deny or minimize racial injustice. They don't have that option.

[3]James Baldwin, *Notes of a Native Son* (Boston: Beacon Press, 2012), 10.

[4]When we list data for racial groups, we only include individuals who selected one racial group. In other words, the racial groups we use refer to "exclusive" groupings. There is some debate among experts as to whether Hispanic/Latinos should be considered a racial group. The US Census Bureau defines Hispanic/Latino as a person of Cuban, Mexican, Puerto Rican, South or Central American, or other Spanish culture or origin regardless of race; see www.census.gov/topics/population /hispanic-origin/about.html. For the purposes of this book, we refer to Hispanic/ Latinos along with racial groups because Hispanic/Latinos are treated in a racialized way, regardless if they are technically a racial group or not. When we provide data regarding Hispanic/Latinos from our research, we are referring to individuals who only selected "Hispanic or Latino" as their racial or ethnic identity.

[5]Based on 2020 US Census data www.census.gov/quickfacts/fact/table/US/POP 010220#POP010220.

[6]Richard Twiss, *Rescuing the Gospel from the Cowboys: A Native American Expression of the Jesus Way* (Downers Grove, IL: InterVarsity Press, 2015).

[7]For example, we recommend *Divided by Faith* by Michael Emerson and Christian Smith, *White Evangelical Racism* by Anthea Butler, and *White Too Long* by Robert Jones.

[8]In the graphs, "Christians" refers to individuals who identified themselves as a Christian on the survey.

[9]Brown University. "Colonial Enslavement of Native Americans Included Those Who Surrendered, Too," accessed April 24, 2020, www.brown.edu/news/2017 -02-15/enslavement.

[10]Donald L. Fixico, "When Native Americans Were Slaughtered in the Name of 'Civilization,'" History, October 26, 2020, www.history.com/news/native-americans -genocide-united-states.

[11]Henry Louis Gates, "How Many Slaves Landed in the U.S.?" *The African Americans: Many Rivers to Cross* (blog), January 2, 2013 www.pbs.org/wnet/african-americans -many-rivers-to-cross/history/how-many-slaves-landed-in-the-us/.

[12]*USA Today*, "Slavery's History in America," accessed July 2, 2021, www.usatoday .com/pages/interactives/1619-african-slavery-history-maps-routes-interactive -graphic/.

[13]"The Brutal History of Anti-Latino Discrimination in America," History, August 29, 2018, www.history.com/news/the-brutal-history-of-anti-latino-discrimination -in-america.

[14]The responses between the two groups was within the margin of error for the study.

[15]Lincoln Quillian, Devah Pager, Arnfinn H. Midtbøen, and Ole Hexel, "Hiring Discrimination Against Black Americans Hasn't Declined in 25 Years," *Harvard Business Review*, October 11, 2017, https://hbr.org/2017/10/hiring-discrimination -against-black-americans-hasnt-declined-in-25-years.

[16]J. E. Shelton and M. O. Emerson, *Blacks and Whites in Christian America: How Racial Discrimination Shapes Religious Convictions* (New York: New York University Press, 2012).

[17]Race, Religion, and Justice Project (2019–2020) survey respondents who indicated (1) *I am a Christian*; (2) *My religious faith is very important in my life today*; (3) *I attend religious services at least monthly*.

[18]Race, Religion, and Justice Project (2019–2020) survey respondents who indicated the following: (1) *I have made a personal commitment to Jesus Christ that is still important in my life today*; (2) *I believe the Bible is totally accurate in all of the principles it teaches*; (3) *I have a personal responsibility to tell other people about my religious beliefs*; (4) *When I die I will go to heaven because I have confessed my sins and have accepted Jesus Christ as my Savior*; (5) *I disagree with the statement, "If a person is generally good, or does enough good things for others, they can earn a place in heaven"*; (6) *I disagree with the statement, "When he lived on earth, Jesus Christ was human and committed sins, like other people."*

[19]Mark Charles and Soong-Chan Rah, *Unsettling Truths* (Downers Grove, IL: InterVarsity Press, 2019), Kindle, 73.

[20]"Motivated Reasoning," *Psychology*, January 6, 2016, http://psychology.iresearch net.com/social-psychology/attitudes/motivated-reasoning/.

[21]"Motivated Reasoning," *Psychology Today*, www.psychologytoday.com/us/basics /motivated-reasoning, accessed June 22, 2021.

[22]Michael O. Emerson and Christian Smith, *Divided by Faith: Evangelical Religion and the Problem of Race in America* (New York: Oxford University Press, 2000), 76-77.

[23]Emerson and Smith, *Divided by Faith*, 89.

[24]Daniel Cox, Juhem Navarro-Rivera, and Robert Jones, "Race, Religion, and Political Affiliation of Americans' Core Social Networks," PRRI, August 3, 2016, www .prri.org/research/poll-race-religion-politics-americans-social-networks/.

[25]The average household income is based on 2017 US Census data, census.gov /content/dam/Census/library/visualizations/2018/demo/p60-263/figure1.pdf, accessed June 22, 2021. The average wealth and assets is based on 2016 US Census data, census.gov/topics/income-poverty/wealth/data/tables.html, accessed June 22, 2021. The percent living in poverty is based on 2018 US Census data, census .gov/data/tables/time-series/demo/income-poverty/historical-poverty-people .html, accessed June 22, 2021. The rate of incarceration is based on 2014 US Bureau of Justice statistics sources, sentencingproject.org/publications/color-of-justice -racial-and-ethnic-disparity-in-state-prisons, accessed June 22, 2021. Unfortunately, the Bureau of Justice does not currently measure incarceration rates for Asian Americans. The data in the graph is an estimate of the percentage based on the report www.ssc.wisc.edu/soc/racepoliticsjustice/2017/07/07/white-rural -imprisonment-rates, accessed June 22, 2021.

[26]"Breakdown of US Millionaires by Race," Statista, accessed June 22, 2021, www .statista.com/statistics/300528/us-millionaires-race-ethnicity/.

[27]The Reflective Democracy Campaign, "2019 Elected Officials - Summary" accessed June 22, 2021, https://wholeads.us/wp-content/uploads/2019/06/2019-Elected -Officials-Reflective-Democracy-Campaign-Summary.xlsx.zip.

[28]"The 2018 Board Diversity Census of Women and Minorities on Fortune 500 Boards," January 16, 2019, www2.deloitte.com/content/dam/Deloitte/us/Documents /center-for-board-effectiveness/us-cbe-missing-pieces-report-2018-board-diversity -census.pdf.

[29]A stereotype is "A widely held but fixed and oversimplified image or idea of a particular type of person or thing." See Lexico Dictionaries, "Meaning of Stereotype in English," Lexico.com, accessed February 8, 2021, www.lexico.com/definition/stereotype.

[30]Jennifer Cheeseman Day, "Black High School Attainment Nearly on Par With National Average," The United States Census Bureau, June 10, 2020, www.census .gov/library/stories/2020/06/black-high-school-attainment-nearly-on-par-with -national-average.html.

[31]Renee Stepler, "Hispanic, Black Parents See College Degree as Key for Children's Success," Pew Research Center, February 24, 2016, www.pewresearch.org/fact-tank/2016 /02/24/hispanic-black-parents-see-college-degree-as-key-for-childrens-success/.

[32]Liz Sablich, "7 Findings That Illustrate Racial Disparities in Education," Brookings, June 6, 2016, www.brookings.edu/blog/brown-center-chalkboard/2016/06/06 /7-findings-that-illustrate-racial-disparities-in-education/.

[33]act.tv, "Systemic Racism Explained," www.youtube.com/watch?v=YrHIQIO_bdQ, accessed June 22, 2021.

[34]Phil Vischer, "Holy Post - Race in America," www.youtube.com/watch?v=AGUwcs 9qJXY, accessed June 22, 2021.

[35]Renew Partnerships Campus Climate Survey, 2016–2020, rjuc.org/campus-survey.

[36]William Darity Jr., Darrick Hamilton, Mark Paul, Alan Aja, Anne Price, Antonio Moore, and Caterina Chiopris, "What We Get Wrong About Closing the Racial Wealth Gap," Samuel DuBois Cook Center on Social Equity, April 2018, https:// socialequity.duke.edu/wp-content/uploads/2020/01/what-we-get-wrong.pdf.

[37]Diana Farrell, Chris Wheat, and Chi Mac, "Small Business Owner Race, Liquidity, and Survival," 2020, JPMorgan Chase Institute, www.jpmorganchase.com/corporate /institute/small-business/small-business-owner-race-liquidity-and-survival.

[38]See "Examining the Black-White Wealth Gap," Brookings, February 27, 2020, www .brookings.edu/blog/up-front/2020/02/27/examining-the-black-white-wealth-gap/.

[39]See "Black College Graduates and the Student Debt Gap," n.d., https://sites.ed.gov /whieeaa/files/2016/11/Black-College-Graduates-and-the-Student-Debt-Gap.pdf.

[40]Junia Howell and Elizabeth Korver-Glenn, "Race Determines Home Values More Today than It Did in 1980," The Kinder Institute for Urban Research, September 24, 2020, https://kinder.rice.edu/urbanedge/2020/09/24/housing-racial-disparities -race-still-determines-home-values-America.

[41]Farrell, Wheat, and Mac, "Small Business Owner Race, Liquidity, and Survival."

[42]Andre M. Perry, Jonathan Rothwell, and David Harshbarger, "The Devaluation of Assets in Black Neighborhoods," Brookings, November 27, 2018, www.brookings .edu/research/devaluation-of-assets-in-black-neighborhoods/.

[43]Rohit Arora, "Why Black-Owned Businesses Struggle to Get Small Business Loans," *Forbes*, November 24, 2020, www.forbes.com/sites/rohitarora/2020/11/24 /why-black-owned-businesses-struggle-to-get-small-business-loans/.

[44]Jonelle Marte, "Gap in US Black and White Unemployment Rates Is Widest in Five Years," Reuters, July 2, 2020, www.reuters.com/article/us-usa-economy-unemploy ment-race-idUSKBN2431X7.

[45]Radley Balko, "There's Overwhelming Evidence That the Criminal Justice System Is Racist. Here's the Proof," *Washington Post*, June 10, 2020, www.washingtonpost.com /graphics/2020/opinions/systemic-racism-police-evidence-criminal-justice-system/.

[46]"Meritocracy," *Merriam-Webster's Unabridged Dictionary,* accessed February 10, 2021, www.merriam-webster.com/dictionary/meritocracy.

[47]Comments from Renew Partnerships Campus Climate Survey, 2016–2020, rjuc .org/campus-survey.

[48]Gates, "How Many Slaves Landed in the U.S.?"

[49]Chris Eyre, Ric Burns, Stanley Nelson Jr., Dustinn Craig, and Sarah Colt, *We Shall*

Remain, American Experience, 2009, www.pbs.org/wgbh/americanexperience /films/weshallremain.

[50]Comments from Renew Partnerships Campus Climate Survey, 2016–2020, rjuc .org/campus-survey.

[51]Jenny Gathright, "Forget Wealth And Neighborhood. The Racial Income Gap Persists," NPR.org, March 19, 2018, www.npr.org/sections/codeswitch/2018/03/19 /594993620/forget-wealth-and-neighborhood-the-racial-income-gap-persists.

[52]Matt Barnum, "Race, Not Just Poverty, Shapes Who Graduates in America—and Other Education Lessons from a Big New Study," Chalkbeat, March 23, 2018, www .chalkbeat.org/2018/3/23/21104601/race-not-just-poverty-shapes-who-graduates -in-america-and-other-education-lessons-from-a-big-new-stu.

[53]Soong-Chan Rah, *Prophetic Lament: A Call for Justice in Troubled Times* (Downers Grove, IL: InterVarsity Press, 2015).

2 Faithful Antiracists Apply the Bible

[1]Brigit Katz, "Heavily Abridged 'Slave Bible' Removed Passages That Might Encourage Uprisings," *Smithsonian Magazine*, January 4, 2019, www.smithsonianmag .com/smart-news/heavily-abridged-slave-bible-removed-passages-might -encourage-uprisings-180970989/.

[2]"Enslaved People's Lives—The Saint Lauretia Project," accessed May 26, 2020, https://runaways.gla.ac.uk/minecraft/index.php/slaves-lives/.

[3]Comments from Christian College Racial Climate (RPCCS) survey (2016-2020).

[4]"Justice," BibleProject, bibleproject.com/explore/justice.

[5]Christopher J. H. Wright, *The Mission of God's People: A Biblical Theology of the Church's Mission* (Grand Rapids, MI: Zondervan Academic, 2010), 96.

[6]Comments from Christian College Racial Climate (RPCCS) survey (2016–2020).

[7]Christopher J. H. Wright, "Learning to Love Leviticus," ChristianityToday.com, July 22, 2013, www.christianitytoday.com/ct/2013/july-august/learning-to-love -leviticus.html.

[8]C. Marvin Pate, J. Scott Duvall, J. Daniel Hays, E. Randolph Richards, Preben Vang, and W. Dennis Tucker Jr., *The Story of Israel: A Biblical Theology* (Downers Grove, IL: InterVarsity Press, 2004), 93.

[9]For this question, we randomly alternated the terms *foreigners* and *immigrants*. We did not see a significant difference in the responses, regardless of which term was used.

[10]Comments from Race, Religion, and Justice Project (2019–2020), rrjp.org.

[11]US Department of Homeland Security, budgets for fiscal years 2003–2019, www .dhs.gov/dhs-budget. See tables 1 and 2.

[12]Daniel Costa, "Employers Exploit Unauthorized Immigrants to Keep Wages Low," *New York Times*, September 3, 2015, www.nytimes.com/roomfordebate/2015/09/03 /is-immigration-really-a-problem-in-the-us/employers-exploit-unauthorized -immigrants-to-keep-wages-low.

3 Faithful Antiracists Stand for Justice

[1]Timothy Isaiah Cho, "#LeaveLoud from White Horse Inn," Medium, March 23, 2021. https://timothyisaiahcho.medium.com/leaveloud-from-white-horse-inn -d9ca006165be.

[2]Cho, "#LeaveLoud from White Horse Inn."

[3]Comments from Renew Partnerships Campus Climate Survey, 2016–2020, rjuc .org/campus-survey.

[4]Comments from Race, Religion, and Justice Project (2019–2020), rrjp.org.

[5]Eric W. Gritsch, "Was Luther Anti-Semitic?," accessed October 16, 2020, www .christianitytoday.com/history/issues/issue-39/was-luther-anti-semitic.html.

[6]"Calvin's Institutes," accessed October 16, 2020, www.vor.org/rbdisk/html /institutes/index.html.

[7]D. Stephen Long, *Divine Economy: Theology and the Market* (London: Psychology Press, 2000).

[8]David Wayne Jones, *Reforming the Morality of Usury: A Study of Differences That Separated the Protestant Reformers* (Lanham, Maryland: University Press of America, 2004).

[9]"Westminster Confession of Faith, Longer Catechism," accessed October 16, 2020, https://opc.org/lc.html.

[10]Pamela Crosby, "Part of History, African-American Spirituals Still Heal," The United Methodist Church, February 4, 2014, www.umc.org/en/content/part-of -history-african-american-spirituals-still-heal.

[11]Crosby, "Part of History, African-American Spirituals Still Heal."

[12]"Down by the Riverside," origin unknown; first recorded by Fisk University Jubilee Singers, Nashville, TN (Columbia, 1922).

[13]His comments have been simplified and updated to modern English. For the original wording of his sermon, see Jonathan Edwards, *The Works of Jonathan Edwards*, vol. 19, *Sermons and Discourses, 1734–1738*, ed. M. X. Lesser (New Haven, CT: Yale University Press, 2001).

[14]John Piper and Justin Taylor, *A God Entranced Vision of All Things: The Legacy of Jonathan Edwards* (Wheaton, IL: Crossway Books, 2004), Kindle, 149.

[15]Jonathan Edwards, "Draft Letter on Slavery" in *The Works of Jonathan Edwards*, vol. 16, *Letters and Personal Writings*, ed. George S. Claghorn (New Haven, CT: Yale University Press, 1998), 71-76.

[16]Piper and Taylor, *A God Entranced Vision of All Things*, 156.

[17]Bob Stewart, *Banneker: An American Story* (Bloomington, IN: AuthorHouse, 2015).

[18]"To Thomas Jefferson from Benjamin Banneker, 19 August 1791," Founders Online, accessed April 26, 2020, http://founders.archives.gov/documents/Jefferson /01-22-02-0049.

[19]R. Isabela Morales, "Jonathan Edwards Jr.," accessed April 25, 2020, https://slavery .princeton.edu/stories/jonathan-edwards-jr.

4 FAITHFUL ANTIRACISTS UNDERSTAND OUR PAST

[1]Mark Charles and Soong-Chan Rah, *Unsettling Truths: The Ongoing, Dehumanizing Legacy of the Doctrine of Discovery* (Downers Grove, IL: InterVarsity Press, 2019), Kindle, 204.

[2]Adrian Jacobs, "A History of Slaughter: Embracing Our Martyrdom at the Margins of Encounter," *Journal of the North American Institute for Indigenous Theological Studies* 4 (2006): 123-25.

[3]For a much more detailed historical overview we recommend the books *The Color of Compromise* by Jemar Tisby and *Unsettling Truths* by Charles and Rah.

[4]Comments from Renew Partnerships Campus Climate Survey, 2016–2020, rjuc .org/campus-survey.

[5]Charles and Rah, *Unsettling Truths*, Kindle, 96.

[6]Howard Zinn, *A People's History of the United States* (New York: HarperCollins, 1990), 18.

[7]Bartolome Las Casas, *A Short Account of the Destruction of the Indies* (London: Penguin, 2004), 14. Las Casas describes atrocities that are far worse than what we have included in this book.

[8]Governor John Winthrop, "A Model of Christian Charity," *Collections of the Massachusetts Historical Society*, third series (Boston, 1828), 7:31-48.

[9]Richard S. Dunn, "John Winthrop: American Colonial Governor," *Britannica*, accessed April 25, 2020, www.britannica.com/biography/John-Winthrop-American -colonial-governor.

[10]Kevin McBride, "Pequot War," *Britannica*, accessed April 24, 2020, www.britannica .com/topic/Pequot-War.

[11]David R. Roediger, *How Race Survived US History: From Settlement and Slavery to the Eclipse of Post-Racialism* (New York: Verso Books, 2019), Kindle, 225.

[12]"Anglicans/Episcopalians in Virginia," accessed April 25, 2020, www.virginia places.org/religion/anglicans.html.

[13]Coleman Andrews, "These are the 56 People Who Signed the Declaration of Independence," *USA Today*, July 3, 2019, www.usatoday.com/story/money/2019/07/03 /july-4th-the-56-people-who-signed-the-declaration-of-independence/39636971/.

[14]Roediger, *How Race Survived US History*.

[15]David L. Holmes, "The Founding Fathers, Deism, and Christianity." *Britannica*, accessed June 24, 2021, www.britannica.com/topic/The-Founding-Fathers-Deism -and-Christianity-1272214.

[16]Jemar Tisby, *The Color of Compromise: The Truth about the American Church's Complicity in Racism* (Grand Rapids, MI: Zondervan, 2019).

[17]Tisby, *Color of Compromise*.

[18]Henry Louis Gates, "The Truth Behind '40 Acres and a Mule,'" PBS, January 6, 2013, www.pbs.org/wnet/african-americans-many-rivers-to-cross/history/the -truth-behind-40-acres-and-a-mule/.

[19]Robert Jones, *White Too Long: The Legacy of White Supremacy in American Christianity* (New York: Simon and Schuster, 2020), 28.

[20]"Equal Justice Initiative's Report," Equal Justice Initiative's report, accessed April 27, 2020, https://lynchinginamerica.eji.org/report/.

[21]Native American Rights Fund, "Let All That Is Indian Within You Die!" *Legal Review* 38, no. 2 (Summer/Fall 2013), https://narf.org/nill/documents/nlr/nlr38-2.pdf.

[22]"Boarding School—Native Words Native Warriors," accessed April 27, 2020, https://americanindian.si.edu/education/codetalkers/html/chapter3.html.

[23]"US Immigration Before 1965," History, April 20, 2021, www.history.com/topics/immigration/u-s-immigration-before-1965.

[24]"Chinese Exclusion Act," History, August 24, 2018, www.history.com/topics/immigration/chinese-exclusion-act-1882.

[25]Ken Wytsma, *The Myth of Equality: Uncovering the Roots of Injustice and Privilege* (Downers Grove, IL: InterVarsity Press), Kindle, 103-4.

[26]Mark Labberton, ed., *Still Evangelical?: Insiders Reconsider Political, Social, and Theological Meaning* (Downers Grove, IL: InterVarsity Press, 2018).

[27]Becky Little, "How a New Deal Housing Program Enforced Segregation," History, updated June 1, 2021, original October 20, 2021, www.history.com/news/housing-segregation-new-deal-program.

[28]Erin Blakemore, "How the GI Bill's Promise Was Denied to a Million Black WWII Veterans," History, updated April 20, 2021, original June 21, 2019, www.history.com/news/gi-bill-black-wwii-veterans-benefits.

[29]United States Congress, Congressional Record: 82nd Congress, Volume 98, Part 4, U.S. Government Printing Office, 1952, 4320.

[30]"Letter to Martin Luther King," Teaching American History, accessed April 27, 2020, https://teachingamericanhistory.org/library/document/letter-to-martin-luther-king/.

[31]Martin Luther King Jr., "Letter from Birmingham Jail," The Martin Luther King, Jr., Research and Education Institute, April 16, 1963, https://kinginstitute.stanford.edu/sites/mlk/files/letterfrombirmingham_wwcw_0.pdf.

[32]Martin Luther King Jr., Vincent Harding, and Coretta Scott King, *Where Do We Go from Here: Chaos or Community?* (Boston: Beacon Press, 2010), 86.

[33]Eduardo Bonilla-Silva, *Racism Without Racists: Color-Blind Racism and the Persistence of Racial Inequality in America*, 3rd ed.(Lanham, MD: Rowman & Littlefield Publishers, 2009).

[34]Washington Post Live, "Race in America: Fighting for Justice with Bryan Stevenson," *Washington Post*, October 14, 2020, www.washingtonpost.com/washington-post-live/2020/10/14/transcript-race-america-fighting-justice-with-bryan-stevenson/.

[35]"Wallace Quotes," American Experience, PBS, accessed April 14, 2021, www.pbs.org/wgbh/americanexperience/features/wallace-quotes/.

[36]See Korie L. Edwards, *The Elusive Dream: The Power of Race in Interracial Churches* (Oxford: Oxford University Press, 2008).

[37]Edwards, *The Elusive Dream*.

5 FAITHFUL ANTIRACISTS UNDERSTAND OUR PRESENT

[1]"This Little Light of Mine," unknown origin; the version used in the civil rights movement is generally credited to civil rights activist and musician Zilphia Horton.

[2]"Fannie Lou Hamer," American Experience, PBS, accessed April 13, 2021, www.pbs .org/wgbh/americanexperience/features/freedomsummer-hamer/. You can listen to a recording of Fannie Lou Hamer and other Christians singing "This Little Light of Mine" on YouTube, www.youtube.com/watch?v=xhiV6DB_h_8.

[3]"Fannie Lou Hamer," American Experience.

[4]Kay Marshall Strom, *Once Blind: The Life of John Newton* (Downers Grove, IL: InterVarsity Press, 2008), 238.

[5]Timothy Keller, "How Do Christians Fit Into the Two-Party System? They Don't," *New York Times*, September 29, 2018, www.nytimes.com/2018/09/29/opinion /sunday/christians-politics-belief.html.

[6]Laurie Goodstein, "Rev. Dr. Carl F. H. Henry, 90, Brain of Evangelical Movement," *New York Times*, December 13, 2003, www.nytimes.com/2003/12/13/us/rev-dr -carl-f-h-henry-90-brain-of-evangelical-movement.html.

[7]Peter Goodwin Heltzel, *Jesus and Justice: Evangelicals, Race, and American Politics* (New Haven, CT: Yale University Press, 2009), 71

[8]Some historians argue that his approach to racial justice was limited to addressing individual hearts and relationships rather than systemic injustice. That is problematic for the reasons we have explored in this book. See Heltzel, *Jesus and Justice.*

[9]Carl F. H. Henry, *The Uneasy Conscience of Modern Fundamentalism* (Grand Rapids, MI: Eerdmans, 2003), 4.

[10]John Compton, "How the Decline of Religious Institutions Fueled the Rise of the Trump-Evangelical Coalition," Religion in Public, December 9, 2019, https://religion inpublic.blog/2019/12/09/how-the-decline-of-religious-institutions-fueled-the-rise -of-the-trump-evangelical-coalition/.

[11]Carl F. H. Henry, *God, Revelation and Authority* (Wheaton, IL: Crossway, 1999).

[12]Michael O. Emerson and Christian Smith, *Divided by Faith: Evangelical Religion and the Problem of Race in America* (Oxford: Oxford University Press, 2000).

[13]Kirstin Butler, "A Tale of Two Preachers," American Experience, PBS, May 12, 2021, www.pbs.org/wgbh/americanexperience/features/billy-graham-tale-two-preachers.

[14]William C. Martin, *A Prophet with Honor: The Billy Graham Story*, updated ed. (Grand Rapids, MI: Zondervan, 2018).

[15]"*Parade Magazine*, February 1, 1981, Page 115," Newspapers.com, accessed June 29, 2020, www.newspapers.com/image/?clipping_id=9034449.

[16]Sarah Pulliam Bailey, "Q & A: Billy Graham on Aging, Regrets, and Evangelicals," *Christianity Today*, January 21, 2011, www.christianitytoday.com/ct/2011/january web-only/qabillygraham.html.

[17]Randall J. Stephens, "Evangelicals and Trump—Lessons from the Nixon Era," The Conversation, June 15, 2018, http://theconversation.com/evangelicals-and-trump -lessons-from-the-nixon-era-97974.

[18]Alex Lockie, "Top Nixon Adviser Reveals the Racist Reason He Started the 'War on Drugs' Decades Ago," *Business Insider*, July 31, 2019, www.businessinsider.com /nixon-adviser-ehrlichman-anti-left-anti-black-war-on-drugs-2019-7.

[19]Brian J. O'Connor and Lori Perkins, *Everything You Always Wanted to Know about Watergate: But Were Afraid to Ask* (New York: Riverdale Avenue Books, 2017).

[20]Jemar Tisby, *The Color of Compromise: The Truth about the American Church's Complicity in Racism* (Grand Rapids, MI: Zondervan, 2019).

[21]Rick Perlstein, "Lee Atwater's Infamous 1981 Interview on the Southern Strategy," *The Nation*, November 13, 2012, www.thenation.com/article/archive/exclusive-lee -atwaters-infamous-1981-interview-southern-strategy/. The quoted excerpt starts at 16:38 in the recording.

[22]"'Welfare Queen' Becomes Issue in Reagan Campaign," *New York Times*, February 15, 1976, www.nytimes.com/1976/02/15/archives/welfare-queen-becomes-issue-in -reagan-campaign-hitting-a-nerve-now.html.

[23]"'Welfare Queen' Becomes Issue in Reagan Campaign."

[24]Tisby, *Color of Compromise*.

[25]For a thorough analysis of the impact of the war on drugs on Black communities see Michelle Alexander, *The New Jim Crow: Mass Incarceration in the Age of Colorblindness* (New York: The New Press, 2012).

[26]Alexander, *New Jim Crow*.

[27]Alexander, *New Jim Crow*.

[28]Alexander, *New Jim Crow*.

[29]"FOX News Channel Earns Highest-Rated Primetime Monthly Average in the History of Cable Led by Tucker Carlson Tonight," October 27, 2020, www.business wire.com/news/home/20201027006119/en/FOX-News-Channel-Earns-Highest -Rated-Primetime-Monthly-Average-in-the-History-of-Cable-Led-by-Tucker -Carlson-Tonight.

[30]"NYC Pastor's 'White Privilege' Prayer," Eric Metaxas on Tucker Carlson, September 2, 2020, www.youtube.com/watch?v=abGYojSWXyM.

[31]"Believe Black people are treated less fairly" is based on the percent of respondents who selected "Black people are treated less fairly than White people" in regard to hiring, pay, and promotions. "Believe disparities are caused by past discrimination" is based on the percent of respondents who selected "Because many Black people were discriminated against in the past" as a cause for current racial disparities. "Are very motivated to address racial injustice" is based on the percent of respondents who selected "Strongly agree" for "How motivated are you to address racial injustice in our society?"

[32]Alana Abramson, "How Donald Trump Perpetuated the 'Birther' Movement for Years," ABC News, September 16, 2016, https://abcnews.go.com/Politics/donald -trump-perpetuated-birther-movement-years/story?id=42138176.

[33]Suzanne Gamboa, "Donald Trump Announces Presidential Bid by Trashing Mexico, Mexicans," NBC News, June 16, 2015, www.nbcnews.com/news/latino /donald-trump-announces-presidential-bid-trashing-mexico-mexicans-n376521.

[34]Tisby, *Color of Compromise.*

[35]"Trump: I 'felt Ashamed' after 'Disgraceful' NFL Protests," NBC News, accessed November 9, 2020, www.nbcnews.com/politics/donald-trump/trump-i-felt -ashamed-after-disgraceful-nfl-protests-n804901.

[36]"Photo of Trump Remarks Shows 'corona' Crossed out and Replaced with 'Chinese' Virus," NBC News, accessed June 17, 2020, www.nbcnews.com/politics/donald -trump/photo-trump-remarks-shows-corona-crossed-out-replaced-chinese -virus-n1164111 and "Trump Refers to 'Kung Flu,' West Point Ramp and 'Sleepy Joe Biden' as He Returns to Campaign at Tulsa Rally," ABC News, accessed June 22, 2020, https://abcnews.go.com/Politics/trump-heads-tulsa-return-rally-amid-pandemic -mounting/story?id=71307799.

[37]"Trump to Mobilize Federal Resources to Stop Violence, Restore Security," ABC News, accessed October 29, 2020, https://abcnews.go.com/Politics/transcript -trump-mobilize-federal-resources-stop-violence-restore/story?id=71008802.

[38]"Why the Trump Administration Is Slashing Anti-Discrimination Training," NBC News, accessed January 15, 2021, www.nbcnews.com/news/nbcblk/why-trump -administration-slashing-anti-discrimination-training-n1239903.

[39]"How the Faithful Voted: A Preliminary 2016 Analysis," Pew Research Center, accessed June 8, 2020, www.pewresearch.org/fact-tank/2016/11/09/how-the-faithful -voted-a-preliminary-2016-analysis/.

[40]"Religious Group Voting and the 2020 Election." Gallup.com, November 13, 2020. https://news.gallup.com/opinion/polling-matters/324410/religious-group-voting -2020-election.aspx.

[41]Renew Partnerships Campus Climate Survey, 2016-2020, rjuc.org/campus-survey.

[42]"Tracking All of President Trump's False or Misleading Claims," *Washington Post*, January 20, 2021, www.washingtonpost.com/graphics/politics/trump-claims-database/.

[43]Karen Swallow Prior, "Karen Swallow Prior: Voting for Neither," The Exchange, October 28, 2020, www.christianitytoday.com/edstetzer/2020/october/karen -swallow-prior-voting-for-neither.html.

[44]Eugene Scott, "'I Don't Feel That at All': Trump Scoffs at White Privilege in Woodward Book," *Washington Post*, September 11, 2020, www.washingtonpost.com/politics/2020/09/11 /i-dont-feel-that-all-trump-scoffs-white-privilege-woodward-book/.

[45]Isable V. Sawhill and Eleanor Krause, "Gauging the Role of Fox News in Our Electoral Divide," *Brookings*, September 20, 2017, www.brookings.edu/opinions/gauging-the -role-of-fox-news-in-our-electoral-divide/.

[46]Jeffrey Gottfried, Michael Barthel, and Amy Mitchell, "Trump, Clinton Voters Divided in Their Main Source for Election News," Pew Research Center's Journalism Project, January 18, 2017, www.journalism.org/2017/01/18/trump-clinton -voters-divided-in-their-main-source-for-election-news/.

[47]"Biden Defends about Face on Crime Law He Helped Create," ABC News, July 25, 2019, https://abcnews.go.com/Politics/bidens-policy-proposal-face-crime-law-helped -create/story?id=64497898.

[48]"Biden Repudiates White Supremacy, Calls for Racial Justice," January 20, 2021, https://apnews.com/article/biden-inauguration-joe-biden-capitol-siege-donald -trump-race-and-ethnicity-b30876a77ebece44b2c2381571fb6915.

[49]Claire Hansen, "Biden's Order Aiming to End Use of Private Prisons Excludes Immigrant Detention Facilities," *US News & World Report*, January 26, 2021, www .usnews.com/news/national-news/articles/2021-01-26/bidens-order-aiming-to -end-use-of-private-prisons-excludes-immigrant-detention-facilities.

[50]The Leadership Conference on Civil and Human Rights, "39 Human and Civil Rights Leaders Tell President Biden: 'Your Administration Stands at a Precipice,'" September 22, 2021, https://civilrights.org/2021/09/22/39-human-and-civil-rights -leaders-tell-president-biden-your-administration-stands-at-a-precipice/.

[51]"How Americans' Politics Drives Their Religious Views," Niskanen Center, November 8, 2018, www.niskanencenter.org/how-americans-politics-drives-their-religious-views/.

[52]Paul D. Miller, "What Is Christian Nationalism?" *Christianity Today*, February 3, 2021, www.christianitytoday.com/ct/2021/february-web-only/what-is-christian -nationalism.html.

[53]Andrew L. Whitehead and Samuel L. Perry, *Taking America Back for God* (Oxford: Oxford University Press), Kindle, 42.

6 Faithful Antiracists Understand Racial Trauma

[1]Substance Abuse and Mental Health Services Administration, *SAMHSA's Concept of Trauma and Guidance for a Trauma-Informed Approach*, HHS Publication No. (SMA) 14-4884 (Rockville, MD: Substance Abuse and Mental Health Services Administration, 2014).

[2]Jeffrey C. Alexander, Ron Eyerman, Bernhard Giesen, Neil J.Smelzer, and Piotr Sztompka, *Cultural Trauma and Collective Identity* (Berkeley: University of California Press, 2004), www.jstor.org/stable/10.1525/j.ctt1pp9nb.

[3]Thema Bryant-Davis and Carlota Ocampo, "Racist Incident–Based Trauma" *The Counseling Psychologist* 33, no. 4 (2005), 479-500, https://journals.sagepub.com /doi/10.1177/0011000005276465.

[4]"10 Common Reactions to Trauma," In *Concurrent Treatment of PTSD and Substance Use Disorders Using Prolonged Exposure (COPE): Patient Workbook* (New York: Oxford University Press, 2014), 10, www.oxfordclinicalpsych.com/view/10.1093/med: psych/9780199334513.001.0001/med-9780199334513-appendix-9.

[5]Monica T. Williams, Isha W. Metzger, Chris Leins, and Celenia DeLapp, "Assessing Racial Trauma within a DSM–5 Framework: The UConn Racial/Ethnic Stress & Trauma Survey," *Practice Innovations* 3, no 4 (2018), 242-60, https://doi.org/10.1037 /pri0000076.

[6]Nathaniel Vincent Mohatt, Azure B. Thompson, Nghi D. Thai, and Jacob Kraemer Tebesa, "Historical Trauma as Public Narrative: A Conceptual Review of How History Impacts Present-Day Health," *Social Science & Medicine (1982)* 106 (2014), 128-36, https://pubmed.ncbi.nlm.nih.gov/24561774.

[7]Allison Keyes, "A Long-Lost Manuscript Contains a Searing Eyewitness Account of the Tulsa Race Massacre of 1921: An Oklahoma Lawyer Details the Attack by Hundreds of White People on the Thriving Black Neighborhood Where Hundreds Died 95 Years Ago," Smithsonianmag.com, May 27, 2016, www.smithsonianmag .com/smithsonian-institution/long-lost-manuscript-contains-searing-eyewitness -account-tulsa-race-massacre-1921-180959251/

[8]Akilah Dulin-Keita, Lonnie Hannon, Jose R. Fernandez, and William C. Cockerham, "The Defining Moment: Children's Conceptualization of Race and Experiences with Racial Discrimination" *Ethnic and Racial Studies* 34, no. 4 (2011): 662-82, www.tandfonline.com/doi/abs/10.1080/01419870.2011.535906.

[9]Comments from Renew Partnerships Campus Climate Survey, 2016-2020, rjuc .org/campus-survey.

[10]Catherine Wang and Mohammed Rafiq, (2009), "Organizational Diversity and Shared Vision: Resolving the Paradox of Exploratory and Exploitative Learning," *European Journal of Innovation Management*, 12 (1). 12. 10.1108/14601060910928184.

[11]Shannon Sullivan, *Good White People: The Problem with Middle-Class White Anti-Racism*, SUNY series, Philosophy and Race (Albany, NY: State University of New York Press, 2014), Kindle, 71.

[12]Sheila Wise Rowe, *Healing Racial Trauma: The Road to Resilience* (Downers Grove, IL: InterVarsity Press, 2020).

7 Faithful Antiracists Do Not Rely on Magic

[1]Lindsay Dodgson, "Here's What 'Moral Licensing' Means—Business Insider," accessed November 10, 2020, www.businessinsider.com/what-moral-licensing-means-2017-11.

[2]Comments from Renew Partnerships Campus Climate Survey, 2016-2020, rjuc.org /campus-survey.

[3]Daniel Hill, *White Lies* (Grand Rapids, MI: Zondervan), 24-25, Kindle.

[4]Hill, *White Lies*.

[5]David R. Roediger, *How Race Survived US History: From Settlement and Slavery to the Eclipse of Post-Racialism* (New York: Verso Books, 2019), 46.

[6]Kali N. Gross, *Colored Amazons: Crime, Violence, and Black Women in the City of Brotherly Love, 1880–1910* (Durham, NC: Duke University Press, 2006), 66.

[7]M. Krysan and S. Moberg, "Tracking Trends in Racial Attitudes," April 2021, Institute of Government and Public Affairs, University of Illinois System, retrieved from https://igpa.uillinois.edu/programs/racial-attitudes-2021.

[8]Candis Watts Smith and Christopher DeSante, "The Racial Views of White Americans —Including Millennials—Depend on the Questions Asked," Scholars Strategy Network, January 12, 2018, https://scholars.org/contribution/racial-views-white -americans-including-millennials-depend-questions-asked.

[9]Lindsay Dodgson, "People Can Seem More Racist as They Get Older, but It's Not Simply a Case of 'Being from a Different Time,'" Business Insider, July 4, 2018, www.businessinsider.com/why-are-older-people-racist-2018-7.

[10]Korie L. Edwards, *The Elusive Dream: The Power of Race in Interracial Churches* (Oxford: Oxford University Press, 2008), 82.

[11]Jin Cho, "The Elephant and the Giraffe: Becoming Hospitable to Diversity." Churches for the Sake of Others: C4SO (blog), September 1, 2020, https://c4so.org /the-elephant-and-the-giraffe-becoming-hospitable-to-diversity.

[12]Cho, "Elephant and the Giraffe."

[13]Michael O. Emerson, *People of the Dream: Multiracial Congregations in the United States* (Princeton, NJ: Princeton University Press, 2008).

[14]Michael Emerson, personal correspondence with authors, November 5, 2019.

[15]Ryon J. Cobb, Samuel L. Perry, and Kevin D. Dougherty, "United by Faith? Race /Ethnicity, Congregational Diversity, and Explanations of Racial Inequality," *Sociology of Religion* 76, no. 2 (June 1, 2015): 177–98, https://doi.org/10.1093/socrel /sru067.

[16]We're happy to say that many improvements have been made in the church's training program since our interview with Brittany. With the help of research we conducted in their organization, the leadership has taken steps to understand and address the problematic dynamics we describe in this book. Their training program is now playing a more effective role in helping their church to make progress toward racial justice and unity.

8 FAITHFUL ANTIRACISTS FOLLOW THE EXAMPLE OF THE EARLY CHRISTIANS

[1]For more details or to join with their efforts see www.asianamericanchristian collaborative.com.

[2]Kathy Khang, *Raise Your Voice: Why We Stay Silent and How to Speak Up* (Downers Grove, IL: InterVarsity Press, 2018), 83.

[3]Jessica Nicholas, *God Loves Justice: A User-Friendly Guide to Biblical Justice and Righteousness* (Los Angeles: S&E Educational Press, 2017), Kindle, loc 1652.

[4]Drew G. I. Hart, *Who Will Be A Witness?* (Harrisonburg, VA: MennoMedia, 2020), Kindle, 206.

[5]Korie L. Edwards, *The Elusive Dream: The Power of Race in Interracial Churches* (Oxford: Oxford University Press, 2008), Kindle, loc 91-96.

[6]Dan Steel, "What the Diverse Church in Antioch Can Teach Us Today," The Gospel Coalition, July 24, 2018, www.thegospelcoalition.org/article/diverse-church -antioch-teach-today/.

[7]"What Does 'Christian' Mean (Acts 11:26)?" Biblical Hermeneutics Stack Exchange, accessed January 20, 2021, https://hermeneutics.stackexchange.com/questions/21020 /what-does-christian-mean-acts-1126.

[8]Jemar Tisby, *How to Fight Racism* (Grand Rapids, MI: Zondervan, 2021), Kindle, 92.

[9]Duke L. Kwon and Gregory Thompson, *Reparations: A Christian Call for Repentance and Repair* (Grand Rapids, MI: Brazos, 2021).

[10]Kwon and Thompson, *Reparations*, 196.

[11]Courtney L. McCluney, Kathrina Robotham, Serenity Lee, Richard Smith, and Myles Durkee, "The Costs of Code-Switching," *Harvard Business Review*, November 15, 2019, https://hbr.org/2019/11/the-costs-of-codeswitching.

[12]Warren W. Wiersbe, *The Bible Exposition Commentary*, vol. 1 (Wheaton, IL: Victor Books, 1996), 464.

[13]Patrick M. Lencioni, *The Five Dysfunctions of a Team: A Leadership Fable* (Hoboken, NJ: John Wiley & Sons, 2010), 202.

9 Faithful Antiracists Seek Out Help and Help Others

[1]James Strasburg, "Martin Niemöller: Confessing Pastor and Repentant Nationalist," *Christianity Today*, May 17, 2019, www.christianitytoday.com/history/people/pastors andpreachers/martin-niemoller-confessing-pastor-repentant-nationalist.html.

[2]Strasburg, "Martin Niemoller."

[3]"The Stuttgart Declaration of Guilt," accessed February 1, 2021, http://marcuse .faculty.history.ucsb.edu/projects/niem/StuttgartDeclaration.htm.

[4]Thayer and Smith, Greek Lexicon entry for "Metanoia," The NAS New Testament Greek Lexicon, 1999.

[5]Petrushka Clarkson, *On Psychotherapy* (Hoboken, NJ: John Wiley and Sons Ltd., 1993).

[6]Comments from Renew Partnerships Campus Climate Survey, 2016-2020, rjuc .org/campus-survey.

[7]Monica Gagliano, Vladyslav V. Vyazovskiy, Alexander A. Borbély, Mavra Grimonprez, and Martial Depczynski, "Learning by Association in Plants," *Sci Rep* 6, 38427 (2016).

10 Faithful Antiracists Effectively Measure Progress

[1]Jerry Z. Muller, *The Tyranny of Metrics* (Princeton, NJ: Princeton University Press, 2018), Kindle, 4.

[2]Robert Jones, *White Too Long: The Legacy of White Supremacy in American Christianity* (New York: Simon & Schuster, 2021), Kindle, 171.

[3]Drew G. I. Hart, *Trouble I've Seen: Changing the Way the Church Views Racism* (Harrisonburg, VA: Herald Press, 2016), 40.

11 Faithful Antiracists Help to Change Our Society

[1]"John Winthrop Dreams of a City on a Hill, 1630," The American Yawp Reader, accessed June 26, 2021, www.americanyawp.com/reader/colliding-cultures/john -winthrop-dreams-of-a-city-on-a-hill-1630.

[2]Martin Luther King Jr., Vincent Harding, and Coretta Scott King, *Where Do We Go from Here: Chaos or Community?* (Boston: Beacon Press, 2010).

[3]King Jr., Harding, and Scott King, *Where Do We Go from Here?*, 99.

[4]King Jr., Harding, and Scott King, *Where Do We Go from Here?*, 105.

[5]King Jr., Harding, and Scott King, *Where Do We Go from Here?*, 71.

[6]King Jr., Harding, and Scott King, *Where Do We Go from Here?*, 139.

[7]King Jr., Harding, and Scott King, *Where Do We Go from Here?*, 93.

[8]King Jr., Harding, and Scott King, *Where Do We Go from Here?*, 101.

[9]King Jr., Harding, and Scott King, *Where Do We Go from Here?*, 95.

[10]King Jr., Harding, and Scott King, *Where Do We Go from Here?*, 151.

[11]Darren Walker, "9 Ways Corporations Can Actually Address Racial Inequality," *Time*, August 4, 2009, https://time.com/5875304/racial-inequality-corporations.

[12]Anurima Bhargava, "The Interdependence of Housing and School Segregation," n.d., accessed June 26, 2021, www.jchs.harvard.edu/sites/default/files/A_Shared _Future_Chapter_24_Interdependence_of_Housing_and_School_Segregation.pdf.

[13]Beverly Daniel Tatum, "Segregation Worse in Schools 60 Years after Brown v. Board of Education," *Seattle Times*, September 14, 2017, www.seattletimes.com/opinion /segregation-worse-in-schools-60-years-after-brown-v-board-of-education/.

[14] King Jr., Harding, and Scott King, *Where Do We Go from Here?*, 127.

[15]Richard Rothstein, *The Color of Law: A Forgotten History of How Our Government Segregated America* (New York: Liveright, 2017), Kindle, 199.

[16]Erase Racism, *Matter Of Place by The Fair Housing Justice Center*, accessed June 26, 2021, *www.youtube.com/watch?v=WkYfa5lX-nU*.

[17]Mark Galli, "Trump Should Be Removed from Office," *Christianity Today*, December 19, 2019, www.christianitytoday.com/ct/2019/december-web-only/trump-should-be -removed-from-office.html.

[18]Allan Smith, "Trump Blasts Evangelical Magazine after It Calls Him 'Profoundly Immoral,' Seeks His Removal," NBC News, December 20, 2019, www.nbcnews.com /politics/trump-impeachment-inquiry/trump-blasts-evangelical-magazine-after -it-calls-him-profoundly-immoral-n1105621.

[19]Timothy Dalrymple, "The Flag in the Whirlwind: An Update from CT's President," *Christianity Today*, December 22, 2019, www.christianitytoday.com/ct/2019/december -web-only/trump-evangelicals-editorial-christianity-today-president.html.